Before America

Don Sharkey
Sister Margaret, S.N.D. de Namur
Most Reverend Philip J. Furlong

Social Studies Consultants

Walter L. Willigan, Ph.D.
   Professor of History
   St. John's University
   Jamaica, New York

John J. Mulloy, M.A.
   History Department
   Central High School
   Philadelphia, Pa.

Sister M. Paschal, C.S.J.
   St. Joseph Motherhouse
   Tipton, Indiana
   Teacher Editions

W. H. Sadlier, Inc.
NEW YORK, CHICAGO

ST. PETERS SCHOOL
HURON, OHIO

TO THE PUPIL

Many people think that history is a dead subject. If you know what happened, all the excitement and mystery is gone. And what is the use of reading and studying about people and things that have nothing to do with the people and things around us today?

Well, as you read this book, you will discover how wrong many people can be. History is not "dead." History is what *has* happened, plus what is happening *now*. What the people of the past did has had an effect on you, your family, and all the people around you. What you and the people of your times do will affect the people who come long after.

From the earliest dawn of history, the principal needs of men have been food, clothing, and shelter. When he had found ways to take care of these needs, man found time to devote to arts, crafts, and education. But he still had to gain a victory over wild animals and savage invaders. Through this struggle he developed a "culture." Culture means anything and everything that man makes, does, and thinks. The culture of men changes with time and place. There have been many different cultures through the ages. The influence of each age upon the one that follows is the subject of this book.

You will have an opportunity to learn to locate countries on a map. You will see where man lived, from the earliest days to our own times. You will follow him step by step as he built his different cultures—the glorious Grecian culture and the mighty one of Alexander the Great are just two examples. You will see that no matter how many cultures he built, or where he built them, his principal needs were always the same—food, clothing and shelter. We are filling the same needs today. It will be interesting to report on and discuss the way men of different ages in different places filled these needs, and to compare how they did it with the way we are doing it today.

Copyright © 1965, 1966
by William H. Sadlier, Inc.
Manufactured in the United States of America

CA 2—3–66 C

MARCH PRINTING 1966

Contents

INTRODUCTION
Looking at the Past, page 1

ONE
The People of Earliest Times

1 Learning about the Past, 4
   The Study of History, 4
   Learning How People Lived, 9
   The People Who Lived
     Before History Was Written, 16
2 The People of the Nile, 20
   Early Egyptian Civilization, 20
   Egyptians Develop Many Skills, 22
3 Early Civilization in Southwest Asia, 28
   The Valley of the Two Rivers, 28
   The Lydians and the Persians, 33
   A Nation of Traders, 34
   God's Chosen People, 36
4 The People of Ancient India and China, 39
   Early Indian Civilization, 39
   Ancient China, 44

TWO
Civilization Comes to Europe

5 The People of Ancient Greece, 50
   Aegean Civilization, 50
   Early Greece, 53
   How People Lived in Sparta, 55
   How People Lived in Athens, 57
   The Greeks Defeat Mighty Persia, 59
   Great Artists, Thinkers,
     and Writers of Ancient Greece, 61
   Greek Ideas Spread Far, 66
6 The People of Ancient Rome, 70
   Early Rome, 70
   Rome Conquers the World, 74
   Romans Lose Their Self-Government, 78

THREE
The Roman Empire

7 A New Government for Rome, 84
   The Beginnings of the Roman Empire, 84
   Achievements of the Romans, 88
   The Jews in the Roman Empire, 92

8 Christianity in the Roman Empire, 97
　The Rise of Christianity, 97
　The Roman Empire Becomes Weaker, 100
　The Church After Persecution, 105
　The Fall of the Western Empire, 108

FOUR
The Middle Ages (500-1500)

9 Western Europe Rebuilds, 114
　The Byzantine Empire, 114
　Europe Faces New Problems, 118
　Europe Becomes
　　a Christian Continent, 120
　The Moslems Threaten
　　Christian Europe, 124
　The Pope's Kingdom, 128
　The Emperor Charlemagne, 129
10 How People Lived in Feudal Times, 133
　The Growth of Feudalism, 133
　Lords and Knights, 136
　The Church and Knighthood, 140
　The Common People, 141
11 The Crusades Change Europe, 145
　The Crusades, 145
　Trade and New Towns
　　Weaken Feudalism, 152
12 Thirteenth Century Europe, 157
　How People Lived in the Towns, 157
　The Craftsmen and Their Guilds, 162
　Great Churches and Cathedrals, 165
　Schools, Scholars, and Teachers, 168
　Great Artists and Writers, 171
　The People of Europe Learn More
　　About the Far East, 172

FIVE
The Rise of Nations in Europe

13 The Story of England, 176
　Early England, 176
　The Beginning of Modern England, 182
　The People of England Receive
　　More Rights and Liberties, 186
14 How Some Modern Nations Developed, 195
　The King of France Becomes
　　More Powerful, 195
　Feudalism Comes to an End, 196
　Spain and Portugal Become
　　Strong Nations, 200
　Germany and Italy Fail to Unite, 202
　Russia in the Middle Ages, 205

SIX
Western Civilization Expands

15 New Ideas Change the World, 210
　People of Europe Become Interested
　　in Ancient Greece and Rome, 210
　Architects and Sculptors
　　of the Renaissance, 214
　Some Painters of the Renaissance, 217
　Books Come Into Wide Use, 220
　New Discoveries in Science, 221
16 Revolt, Reform, Rivalry, 224
　Background of Religious Revolt, 224
　The Protestant Revolt
　　Begins in Germany, 225
　The Revolt Spreads, 228
　The Revolt in England, 229
　The Catholic Reformation, 231
　Rivalry for Trade, Treasure,
　　and New Lands, 232
17 Europe Finds a New World, 236
　Europeans Learn More About the World, 236
　The Way Is Opened, 242
　The Nations of the Western Hemisphere, 245

Yesterday, Today, and Tomorrow

　Art and Architecture, 257
　Crafts and Manufacturing, 258
　Language and Literature, 260
　Science, Invention, Discoveries, 262
　Education, 264
　Growth of National Spirit, 265
　Law and Government, 267
　Religion, 270

List of Maps

Early Civilizations, 10-11
The Valley of the Nile, 20
The Fertile Crescent, 29
The Persian Empire, 34

India, 39
The Land of Chou, 46
Ancient Greece, 52
Alexander's March, 68
Italy, 74
The Vast Roman Empire, 86-87
Palestine, 93
The Divided Roman Empire, 104
German Invasions in the Western Empire, 110
The Byzantine Empire, 115
The Moslem Empire, 124
Empire of Charlemagne, 131
The Crusades, 149
England from the Time of Alfred the Great to William the Conqueror, 178
Western Europe, 194
The Iberian Peninsula, 200
The Holy Roman Empire, 203
Russia, 206
Renaissance Europe, 211
Routes to the Orient, 236-237
Route of Bartholomeu Dias, 240
The Spirit of Discovery, 244-245
Explorations in the New World and the Papal Line of Demarcation, 246
North America Before and After the French and Indian War, 250
Territorial Possessions in the New World, 252

List of Features

The Stream of History, 2-3
How We Know About the Past, 6-7
How Events in History Are Dated, 8
The March of Man, 14-15
Early People, 16-17
Discoveries of Ancient Man, 18
The Key to a Puzzle, 25
The Law of Hammurabi, 31
Gifts of Greece, 66
The Gordian Knot, 67
Roman Government, 71
Cincinnatus, 72
The Gifts of Rome, 88-89
Roman Persecutions, 98-99
Emperors of Rome, 101
Knighthood, 138-139
Guilds, 162-163
The Great Cathedrals, 166-167
St. Augustine, 179
Normans Come to England, 182-183

On Trial, 186
The Great Charter, 190-191
The Art of the Renaissance, 218-219
Discoveries in Science, 222
The Spirit of Discovery, 244-245
The Spanish and the Portuguese in the New World, 248-249
The French in the New World, 251
The English in America, 253
A Nation of Many People, 254-255

CREDITS

The full color global relief photographs reproduced on the pages listed below were photographed for the exclusive use of William H. Sadlier, Inc., in their textbooks and related publications. The photographs are of the six-foot geophysical relief globe, photographed by special arrangement with Rand McNally & Company, copyright 1963, New York. The global photography was done by Caru Studios.

Global relief photographs: 10-11, 39, 46, 86-87, 115, 194, 203, 206, 211

The maps reproduced on the pages listed were made by Caru Studios: 14-15, 20, 29 (top), 34, 52, 68 (top), 74, 93, 104, 110, 124, 131, 149, 178, 200, 236-237, 240, 244-245, 246, 250, 252

The illustrations reproduced on the pages listed were made by the following artists: Art Staff Inc., 6-7, 18, 161, 165, 176-177; Caru Studios, 23, 35, 38, 58, 63 (bottom), 118, 150-151 (top), 154 (bottom), 179, 202; Danska, 216, 217; Nicholas Eggenhofer, 146-147; Helen K. Fulkerson, 2-3, 31 (top), 66, 71, 138-139, 250-251, 254-255; Don Lambo, 30, 50, 51, 55, 67 (bottom), 247; Nathaniel Pousette-Dart Associates, 108, 109, 121, 133, 144, 148, 172-173, 180, 181, 184, 185, 201, 220; Jim Weathers, 1, 5, 25, 72, 98-99, 101, 162-163, 179, 186, 190-191, 231; John C. Wonsetler, 12, 13, 21, 22, 24, 26, 29 (bottom), 31 (bottom), 32, 33, 36, 37, 40, 41, 42, 45, 47, 48, 53, 54-55 (top), 56-57, 60, 62-63 (top), 64-65, 67 (top), 68 (bottom), 70, 73, 75, 77, 78-79, 80, 82, 85, 88-89, 90, 94, 95, 97, 102, 106, 107, 111, 116, 117, 119, 120, 122, 123, 125, 126, 127, 128, 129, 130, 134-135, 136-137, 141, 142-143, 151 (bottom), 153, 154 (top), 155, 156, 158-159, 160, 168-169, 170, 171, 182-183, 187, 188-189, 192, 196, 197, 198-199, 204, 205, 207, 208, 212-213, 215, 222, 225, 226, 227, 228, 229, 231, 233, 235, 238, 239, 241, 242, 243

The photographs reproduced on the pages listed were obtained from the following sources: Charles Phelps Cushing, 258, 261, 266, 267, 268; F. Sadlier Dinger, 43; European Art Color Slide Co., N.Y.—Peter Adelberg, 218, 219, front cover (top left); Courtesy of Ford Motor Co., 1 and 16 (N.Y. World's Fair Pavilion), 259; Ewing Galloway, 9, 17 (bottom), 116, 167; Courtesy of Museum of Natural History, 17 (top); Religious News Service Photo, 271; Stevens Institute of Technology, 264; Wide World Photo, 263.

INTRODUCTION
Looking at the Past

Bill and Kathy would never forget their visit to the World's Fair in New York. One of the most exciting exhibits they had seen there was the "Magic Skyway." They were telling some friends back home about it one day.

"You ride through the whole show in a new Ford convertible," Bill was saying.

"Oh, you can't imagine how thrilling it was!" exclaimed Kathy. "Everything was so real and lifelike. The figures all moved. I was scared when we rode by the giant dinosaurs that once roamed the earth."

"The exhibit told the story of our earliest ancestors," Bill explained. "They lived in caves, dressed in animal skins, and hunted wild beasts for their food."

"Another part showed the first dwellings built by man," continued Kathy. "They were crude compared to houses today."

"Don't forget that the tools used by the cavemen were made out of stone," Bill said. "That was before man invented the wheel."

Visitors to the World's Fair ride through a world of dinosaurs created by Walt Disney for the Ford "Magic Skyway" exhibit.

1

"Just think of it," Kathy said. "These cavemen were our ancestors."

"We are going to study about our ancestors in school this year," Bill remarked. "I'm glad I saw 'Magic Skyway' at the Fair. It will help us understand how much we owe to our ancestors."

Your history classes this year will be about people who lived long before there was a United States of America. You will learn about many things that all of us owe to the people who lived in the past. You will see that God has given mankind the gift of being able to use his mind and his hands to provide for himself and his family, and to build a civilization in which his race will be able to grow.

The Indians were the first inhabitants of North and South America. They probably came from Asia by way of Alaska. Most likely they were looking for a better place in which to live. They used their gifts to adjust and adapt to the new land and climate.

Hundreds and hundreds of years after the Indians had come, people from Europe discovered America. Our country was built by people from many other countries. Most of the people who settled in what is now the United States came from England. That is why you speak the English language. But people also came here from other parts of the world. All these people were your ancestors.

Among your friends and classmates you will find boys and girls whose ancestors brought many gifts to America. They helped develop our civilization and make a new nation under God.

The Stream of History

One of the best ways to learn history is to keep in mind the time and the place of great historical events and developments. To help you do this, a time line has been placed at the beginning of each unit. The time line will indicate the main events covered in the unit and will show the span of history in each era as it is studied.

Far back in time, history rises to form a stream. This stream of history is the story of man's life and of the millions of years before man existed on the earth. On these two pages we have pictured "The Stream of History" from the beginnings of marine life to the creation of man, and through the Stone Age to the time civilization first begins.

Note the enormous expanse of time between the beginning of life on the earth and the first valley civilizations in Egypt and Sumeria. The stream of history continues through the ancient Chinese and Indian civilizations to the Golden Age of Greece, a high point in history. The Roman Empire flows on

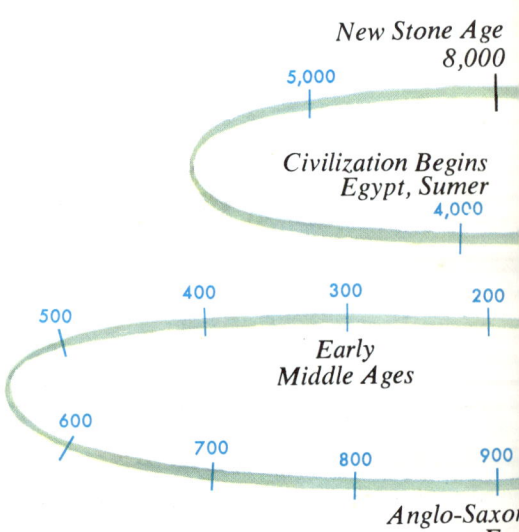

into the early Middle Ages. This is followed by the Renaissance period, one of the greatest eras in human history. Modern times gives rise to an age of exploration and discovery, an age of revolution and unity among nations, and finally, to the present time, an age of challenge.

The stream of history shows the story of man's progress in time. It pictures the rise and fall of nations and empires, and also how one civilization merges with another. Note how little time man has actually lived on earth. How fortunate is modern man who can benefit from the rich heritage of the past!

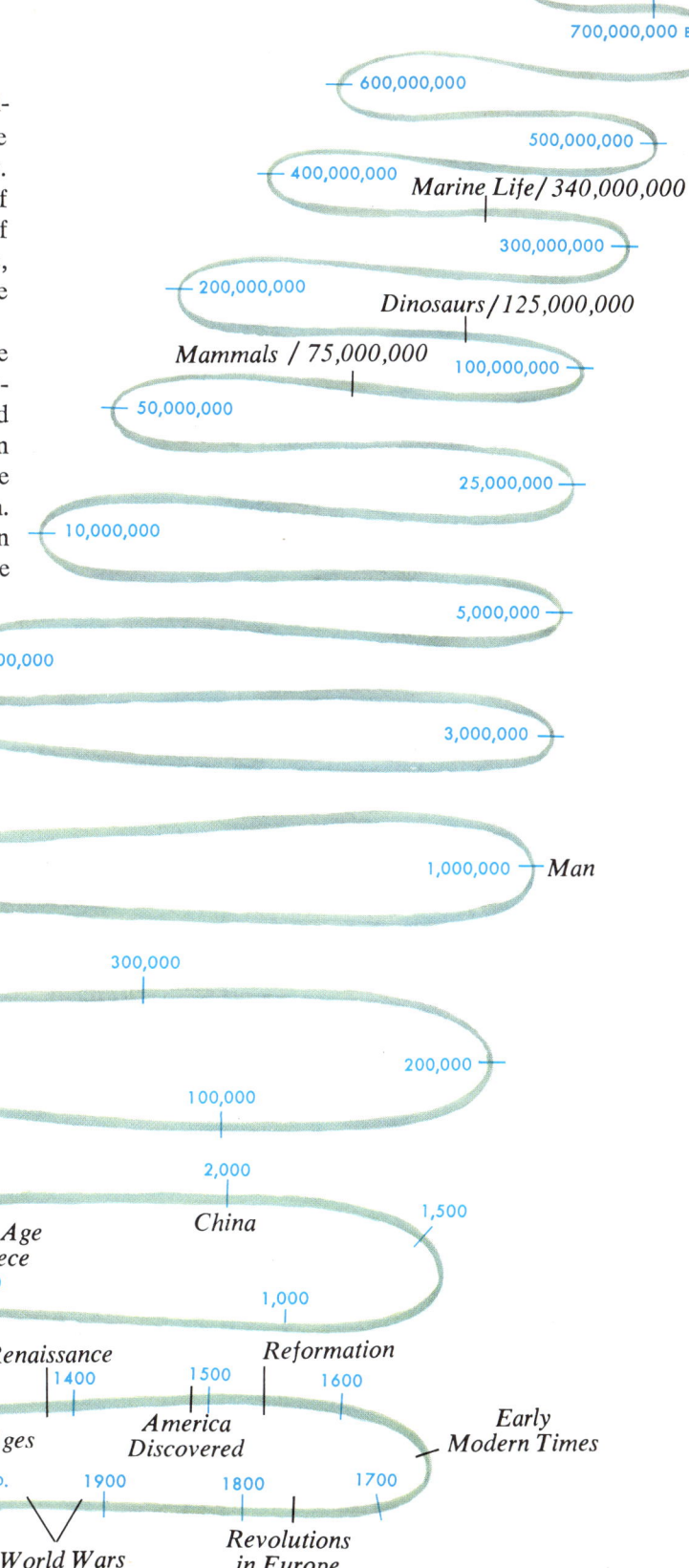

ONE The People of Earliest Times

Chapter 1
Learning about the Past

Men have been on earth for over a million years, but they have been able to write for only a few thousand years. We do not have written records for most of the story of man's life on earth.

Even though we have no written records, scientists and historians have gathered clues about the way people lived before history was written. We shall read about what they discovered from these clues left so long ago.

1 1
The Study of History

We Owe Everything to People Who Have Lived in the Past. Have you ever stopped to think that we owe almost everything we have to people who lived in the past? Right now you are reading this book. The book is printed in the English language. At one time there was no English language. How was the language formed? That is one of the things you will find out later in the year.

If you stop to think about the matter, you will realize that it is a wonderful thing to be able to read at all. It is also wonderful to be able to write. For thousands of years, men were not able to read or write. Even today, there are many people in the world who cannot read or write. Think of what they are missing! We owe a great debt to the people who figured out a system of reading and writing.

Every word in this book is formed from an alphabet of twenty-six letters. With these same twenty-six letters thousands and thousands of words can be formed. The Chinese language does not have letters. Each word has its own mark, or character. A boy or girl in China must learn hundreds of characters before being able to read or write. Where did we get our alphabet? From people who lived several thousand years ago. You will also read about this later in the year.

Within just a few minutes you could think of many other things we owe to people of the past. Here are a few examples: the way we build our houses, the way we make our clothes, the way we produce our food.

How We Learn About the Past. When something important happens in our day,

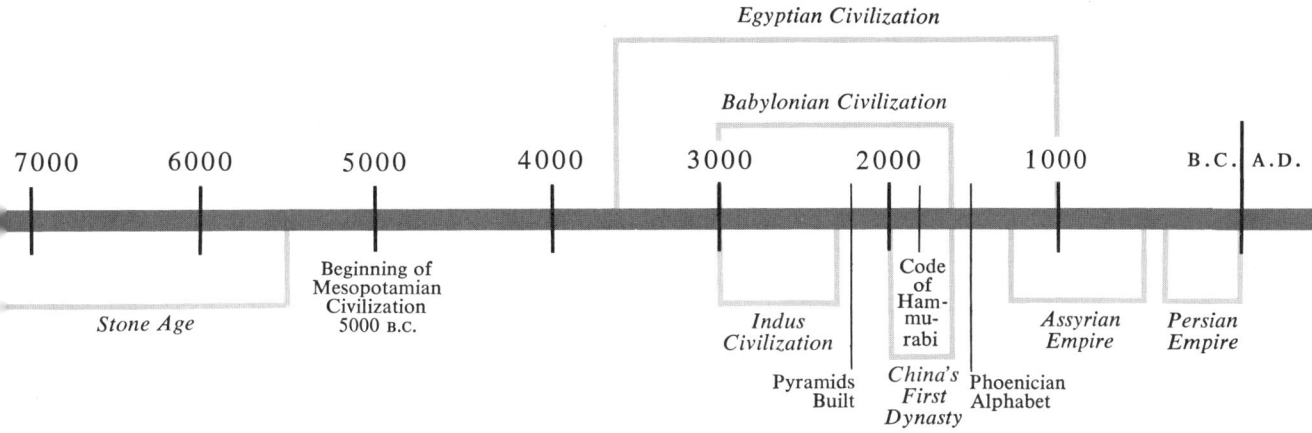

reporters and cameramen rush to the scene. Soon we are reading about the event and seeing pictures of it in our newspapers. We may also see movies of it, both on television and in the theaters. Later, we may read magazine articles about it. Still later, we may read books about it.

Years from now, when a man wants to write a history of our times, he will have many records to study. He will look at old newspapers, magazines, books, and films. These will tell him not only what happened but will also tell him how we dressed, what kind of houses we lived in, how we traveled, and how we did many other things.

Reporters and photographers record the events of today which will become part of the history of our times.

5

But how do we learn about the people who lived before there were newspapers, magazines, books, and cameras? That is the work of men called *archaeologists*. These men are something like detectives. They search the world for clues that will tell them how people lived in the past.

Some ancient peoples, such as the Egyptians, had a form of writing. Archaeologists have discovered many of these writings. Other men have learned how to read them. These writings tell us much about how the people lived.

Archaeologists have also learned much by studying ancient buildings. By studying temples, for example, they have learned about the religious beliefs of people who lived long ago.

But many people did not know how to write, and many people did not erect buildings that have lasted. Archaeologists have learned something about these people from the tools they left and the pictures they drew. In Spain and France there are pictures on the walls and ceilings of many caves. Archaeologists tell us that these pictures are at least 15,000 years old and perhaps much older.

Many secrets of the past lie buried beneath the earth's surface. Many centuries ago the city of Pompeii, in Italy, was buried by the lava from a volcano. Archaeologists have dug deep into the earth and have found this city. Most of the buildings are still standing. This gives us a good idea of how the people of ancient Pompeii lived.

How We Know About the Past

Archeologists are investigating the past. They have constructed a picture of early man from paintings, bones, tools, and monuments.

2 From Under the Sea

4 From Monuments

1 From Caves

3 From Under the Earth

5 From the Jungle

6 By the Careful Work of Scientists

How Events in History Are Dated

Christianity. Most nations date all events from before and after the birth of Christ. Actually, Christ was born a few years before the date we now use.

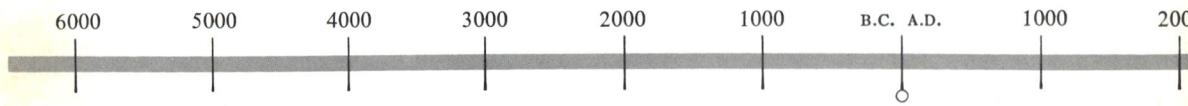

The Jewish Year. The Jewish Year begins with the Creation. Instead of A.D. and B.C. the Jewish calendar uses A.M. (Anno Mundi—the year of light). Their first year began in 3761 (B.C.), and you can see what year it will be in our year 2000 A.D.

The Chinese Calendar. The Chinese people use 60 to divide their calendar year, much as we use 7 to determine our year. Their first cycle of 60 began in the year 2277 B.C., and you can see what year the Chinese will celebrate in 2000 A.D.

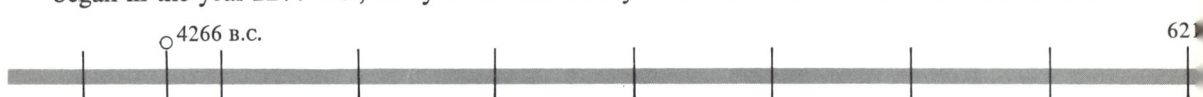

The years before Our Lord was born are called B.C. These letters mean "before Christ." When we say something happened in 3000 B.C., we mean that it happened three thousands years before Our Lord was born.

The years after the birth of Our Lord are called A.D. These letters stand for the Latin words *anno Domini* which mean "in the year of Our Lord." Because of the meaning of the words, the A.D. is sometimes put before the number. When we read "A.D. 205," we know that this means "in the year of Our Lord 205." Usually, the letters are put after the number: "205 A.D." Either way, they mean the same thing. We do not use the letters A.D. at all unless they are necessary. We do not say that Columbus discovered America in 1492 A.D. because everyone knows that America was discovered after the birth of Our Lord. We simply say 1492. For the years before Christ we use B.C.

The years before the birth of Christ are numbered backward. As time goes on the numbers become smaller instead of larger. A man born in 100 B.C. might learn to walk in 99 B.C., learn to talk in 98 B.C., get married in 75 B.C., and die in 20 B.C. This is the opposite of the way the A.D. years are numbered.

We should remember that the people who lived before the birth of Christ did not call the years B.C. A man would not say, "I was born in 256 B.C.", because he had no way of knowing when Christ would be born. The people of that time had other ways of numbering the years.

If you were born in 210 B.C., in what year would you have celebrated your 70th birthday?

1 2
Learning How People Lived

A Word We Should Know. As you read this book, you will often see the word "culture." In fact, that is what this book is about: the cultures of different people who have lived in the past. It is important, therefore, to understand what the word means.

You will hear different meanings for the word, but we wish to know what it means to archaeologists and historians. To these students of history, the word culture means anything and everything that man makes and does and thinks.

All groups of men have a culture of some kind. Members of a savage tribe, deep in the jungle, have a certain kind of tool, a certain kind of house, certain religious beliefs. These are parts of their culture.

Many parts of our culture change frequently. At the beginning of our own century few Americans had ever seen an automobile. No Americans had ever seen airplanes, television, or electric refrigerators. Yet, think how common these things are today! And they are all part of today's American culture.

We Americans are part of Western culture. This culture includes most of the people of Europe, North and South America, and Australia. Western culture is different from the Oriental (Eastern) culture found

The pictures (right) show how people live today—worshipping, working, going to school, and relaxing together at home.

Early Civilizations

The early civilizations arose along the banks of great rivers. The ancient splendor of the realm of the pharaohs of Egypt was set in the valley of the Nile. The fertile valley of the two rivers, Tigris and Euphrates, was the cradle of the wonders of Babylon and other kingdoms named in the Bible. Farther east, where flows the Indus River, ruins of a third ancient civilization lie buried. At the far eastern ends of the earth, the fabled glory of Cathay had its beginnings in the lands drained by the Hwang Ho River.

in China, Japan, and other nations of the Far East. But different cultures influence each other. We of the West have borrowed many ideas from the Orient. The Orient, in turn, has borrowed many ideas from us. The Japanese, for example, have paved roads, automobiles, jet planes, television, and many other things that came from the West.

Uncivilized people live in simple huts and caves. They gather their own food and make their living by hunting and fishing.

We who are a part of Western culture have certain things in common. Most of us are Christians, and almost all of us believe in God. We use the same alphabet. We live in the same kinds of houses and wear the same kinds of clothes. Most of us believe in freedom and democracy, although not all have been able to achieve these things.

Within the large cultures, such as Western and Oriental, there are many divisions. Japan and China are both part of Oriental culture, but the Japanese and Chinese do not live in exactly the same way. The United States and Mexico are both part of Western culture, and they are neighboring countries. But they are different in many ways. We can speak of an American culture and of a Mexican culture.

Another Important Word: Civilization. You probably already have some idea of what the word "civilization" means. When a man goes deep into the jungle or far out on a desert, you say " he has left civilization behind." This man may meet some people living in the jungle or crossing the desert, but people do not always mean civilization.

People who live in a civilization are called civilized people. People who have no civilization are usually called uncivilized people, or savages.

How do we tell whether people are civilized?

Civilized people usually have a written language, while uncivilized people do not. Civilized people have gained a certain amount of control over the forces of nature. They cut down the forests and use the land for planting crops and for raising cattle and other animals. They put the rivers to work

Civilized people use modern methods of farming. They make their living by planting crops and by raising cattle.

to produce power. They dig minerals out of the earth to produce heat and tools. Uncivilized people live with nature but do not control it. They make their living by hunting and fishing or gathering wild berries and fruit. They do not try to cut down the forests or tame the rivers or make the earth bring forth crops.

Civilized people depend upon each other for almost everything in life. The farmers produce more than enough food for themselves, and they sell what is left over to others. Other people work in factories and mines, practice law or medicine, or work as carpenters or plumbers. An uncivilized family must gather its own food, make its own house and its own clothes, and do almost everything else for itself.

Civilized people have well-organized governments. Uncivilized people have very simple governments, and sometimes they have almost no government at all.

Civilized people have well-built houses. They have towns and cities connected with each other by good roads and highways. Uncivilized people live in simple huts or caves. They often live in villages but not in anything that could be called a town or city. They sometimes have simple trails but no roads.

Sometimes it is hard to tell whether a group of people is civilized. They may have some marks of civilization but not all. People who are somewhere between being savages and being civilized are usually called barbarians.

As you can see, the words "culture" and "civilization" are related. Both refer to the way people live, but they do not mean exactly the same. All people have a culture, but not all people have a civilization.

The March of Western Civilization. As far as we can tell, civilization began in northeast Africa and in western Asia. From there, it spread both east and west. The civilization that spread to the west became Western Civilization. We Americans are interested in this because we are part of Western Civilization. In this book we shall read about the spread of Western Civilization.

Civilization spreads in various ways. Sometimes savages learn the ways of civilization from their more civilized neighbors. Sailors and traders and missionaries teach the ways of civilization to the people they meet. Armies sometimes bring civilization to the people they conquer. This works the other way, too. Barbarian armies have adopted the civilization of the people they conquered. Then they have taken that civilization back to their homelands.

In these and other ways civilization spread from Africa and Asia to the islands of the Aegean Sea and then to Greece. From Greece, civilization spread across Europe. The Romans, who borrowed their civilization from the Greeks, became powerful and ruled a vast empire. It was while Rome ruled the world that Our Lord was born. In the centuries after the birth of Christ, almost all the people of Western Europe became Christians. Thus, Western Civilization became a Christian civilization. After 1492 people from Europe carried this Christian civilization to the New World.

That is the story we shall be reading this year: the spread of Western Civilization.

Look up the word "culture" in a dictionary. What meanings do you find besides the one given in this lesson?

The March of Man

1 The pinpoint on the globe shows man's earliest home. From here he inhabited the whole earth.

3 Greek colonies in southern Italy, Africa, and Asia also helped spread Greek civilization to other parts of the world.

5 In time, Roman power was crushed. The Church saved what was best in Roman civilization. New nations arose in Europe and helped to spread Christian civilization beyond the seas to the New World.

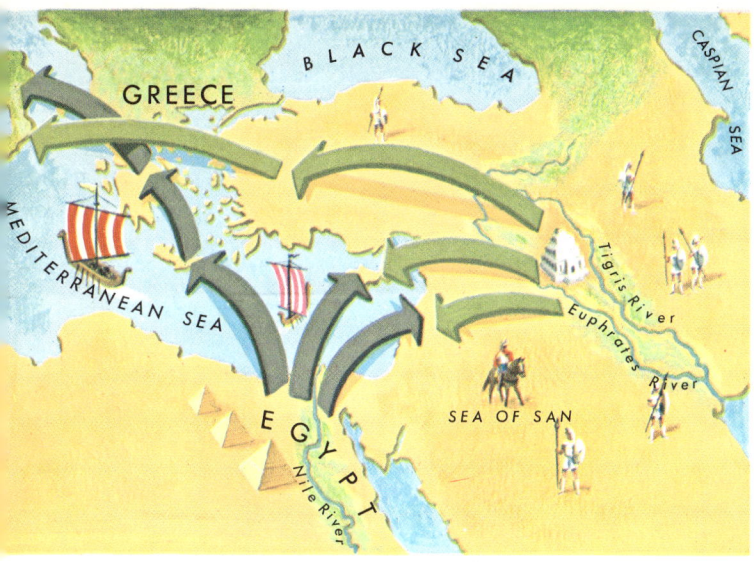

2 Civilization took root in the Valley of the Tigris and Euphrates rivers in Asia and along the Nile River in northeast Africa. From these two centers sailors, traders, and soldiers carried the knowledge of civilized man to other regions. Civilization reached Greece by means of island stepping-stones in the Mediterranean Sea.

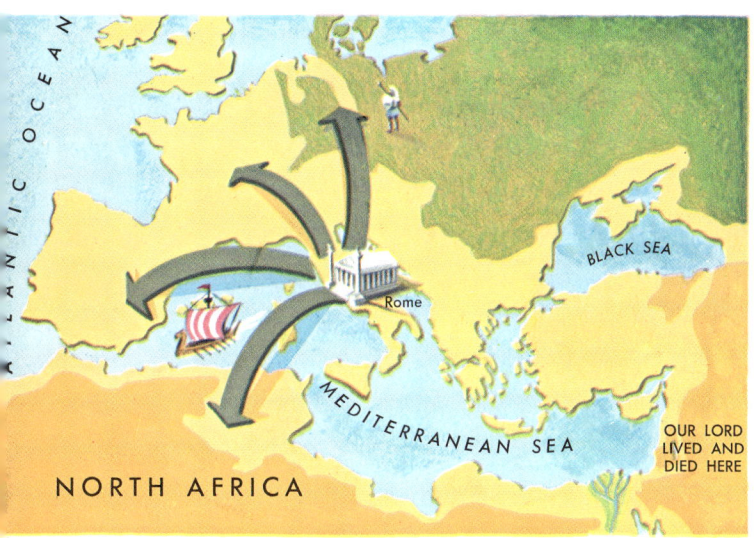

4 The Romans learned the ways of civilized man from the Greeks who lived in southern Italy. In time the Romans came to rule all of the then-known world. Our Lord was born while Rome ruled the world. The Apostles and early missionaries helped to make Christian what had been a pagan civilization.

6 From the time Columbus discovered America millions of people from Europe came to the Western Hemisphere. They founded the United States, Canada, and Latin America.

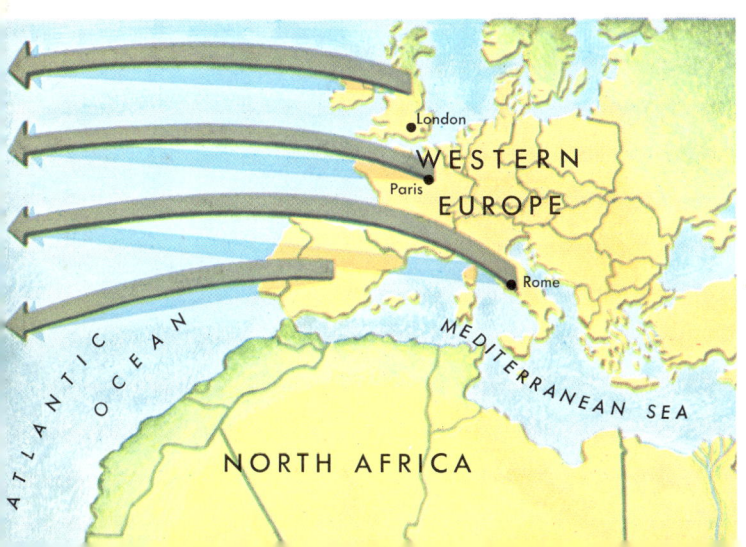

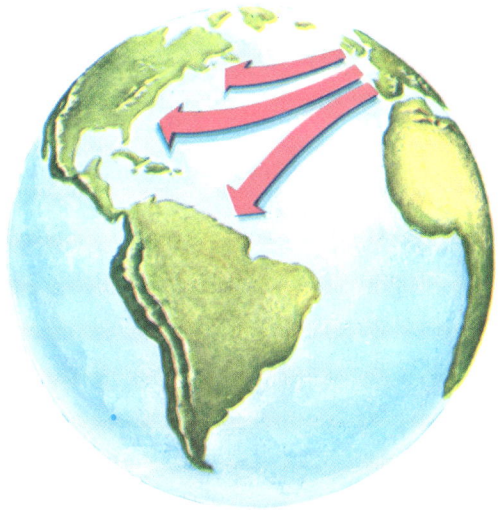

1 3
The People Who Lived Before History Was Written

Man Is a Newcomer on Earth. Archaeologists and other scientists tell us that man has been living on this Earth for more than a million years. To us, that seems a very long time. But our Earth is probably 4½ billion years old. This means that man is a newcomer on our planet.

If we could compare all of Earth's history to one year, then each month would be 375 million years. Each day would be about 12 million years, and each hour would be about half of a million years. In that case, man has been on Earth about two hours. He appeared around ten o'clock on the night of December 31.

Before Man Learned to Write. For most of the million years that men have been on Earth they have not been able to write. They could not leave a record of the things they did. The oldest written records that we have are from about 3500 years before the birth of Christ. That was about 5500 years ago.

We say that people who lived before there were written records lived in prehistoric times. *Pre* means "before." *Prehistoric* means "before history was written."

As we read earlier in this chapter, archaeologists have studied certain clues from prehistoric times and can tell us a little about the people who lived then. The archaeologists tell us that there was an Old Stone Age when man made his tools and weapons by chipping stones. Later, man learned to polish stones and thus make better tools and weapons. This was in the New Stone Age. Next he learned to mix tin with copper, and the result was bronze. This was the beginning of the Bronze Age. Next came the Iron Age. We might say that we are still in the Iron Age. We use steel in almost everything we build today, and steel is made from iron.

You may have noticed as you read the paragraph above that no dates were given for the various ages. That is because these ages came at different times in various parts of the world. In some places men entered the Iron Age over a thousand years before the birth of Christ. But many of the American Indians were still in the Stone Age when

Early People

1 The story of early man has been pieced together from bits of his bones, tools, and weapons scattered from different caves. Early man had the ability to speak, to use fire, and to make tools.

Columbus discovered America. Today, in a few parts of the world, there are people who are still in the Stone Age.

So, there are some things that we know about our prehistoric ancestors. But there are many more things that we don't know. The people of those times left no written records, and so we have no way of knowing what they thought. We know little or nothing about their religious beliefs. We do know that all men believed in a god.

Early Discoveries and Inventions. Nobody knows how man discovered fire. Perhaps he did it when he struck two pieces of flint together and produced a spark. Or perhaps he found it when lightning set a tree afire. Perhaps he obtained fire from a flaming volcano. It is possible that different people found fire in different ways. But fire was a big help to early man, just as it is a big help to us today. With fire, man could keep away dangerous animals, could cook his food, and could keep warm. Man could not have discovered the uses of copper, tin, and iron without fire because fire was used to smelt these metals.

Man learned to roll things on logs. From this he developed the wheel. This was one of the greatest inventions of all time. With the wheel man could haul much heavier loads and do many new kinds of work. Wheels were also used to polish stone weapons and tools. Thus the wheel played a big part in the start of the New Stone Age.

2 Tools made it easier for early man to kill game, catch fish, and dig for roots and other food. The first tools consisted of shaped stones, sticks, or bones.

3 Early man was the creator of the paintings found in many caves by archeologists. Drawn with great skill, the cave paintings glow vividly, even after thousands of years, and tell the story of early man.

4 Massive blocks at Stonehenge, England, are relics of the New Stone Age. They are believed to have been the center of tribal ceremonials, and possibly the burial place of chieftains.

Discoveries of Ancient Man

Man's first and greatest discovery was fire. With fire, man could warm his cave, cook his food, and smoke his meat to preserve it. A fire in the mouth of the cave also kept the wild animals away at night.

Man used fire to make other useful objects. He could burn out the inside of a log, and then chip away the charred wood to form a boat. Man found he could make pottery by heating clay jars until the clay was hard.

Early man moved heavy objects by rolling them over logs or by dragging them on wooden runners. The invention of the wheel combined the ideas of rolling and dragging.

Early man's tools were made of chipped flint stone. The tools of the Stone Age were replaced by metal ones when man learned to mine copper ore and to melt it. The Egyptians mined copper as early as 4000 B.C.

Man later discovered that by adding tin to copper he could produce a harder metal called bronze. This metal was used in Egypt by 3000 B.C. Iron, which is more difficult to mine than copper or tin, was little used in Egypt before 1500 B.C.

Fire

Wheel

Clay

Copper   Bronze   Iron

Prehistoric man also learned to make jars by molding clay and baking it until it was hard. This enabled him to keep water in his cave or hut. He also used the jars for storing certain kinds of food. After the invention of the wheel, man was able to mold clay with a potter's wheel. In this way, he made better jars in a shorter time.

Man Becomes a Food Producer. The earliest people were food gatherers. This means that they did not produce their own food. They gathered wild berries and fruit. They took shell fish from the shallow parts of lakes and streams. They killed animals. At first they probably dug pits with their hands and drove the animals into the pits. Later they had stone axes. When men discovered the bow and arrow, their hunting became a little easier.

About the beginning of the New Stone Age some people found that they could produce food. They learned that they could plant crops and raise certain kinds of grain. They found that they could raise certain kinds of animals which could be used as food. This was the beginning of farming.

The change from food gathering to food producing was one of the turning points of history. Men who had farms settled down and lived in one place. They no longer wandered from place to place in search of food. Farmers built their houses close together in little villages. Each village had to form some sort of government. Food producers had a little more time than food gatherers, so they learned to weave cloth and to make better tools and to build sturdier houses.

We cannot say that the first food producers had a civilization. But they had settled down to live in one place, they had sturdy houses, and they had simple forms of government. These were important steps on the road to civilization.

> Why is writing a chief mark of a civilized people?

Chapter 1. REVIEW

Learning to Use New Words
Use each of the following terms in an original sentence, expressing something you have learned in Chapter 1:

archaeologist   oriental   civilization
culture   prehistoric

Knowing the Important Facts
1. Mention two ways civilization has moved from one area to another.
2. List three sources of information by which people in the future can learn about our times. How are scientists today able to find out how men lived thousands of years ago?
3. Explain what is meant by A.D. and B.C.
4. Describe five marks of a civilized people.
5. Name the five ages of man from prehistoric times to the present.

Thinking Through the Facts
1. Can you explain why one culture in the world often adopts the ideas of another culture?
2. Explain why civilized people are dependent upon others for the most things in life.
3. Why do we in the United States have a western culture or civilization?
4. Why was the wheel one of man's greatest inventions?

Developing a Time Sense
Arrange the following events in the proper time order:
1. Old Stone Age
2. Birth of Christ
3. Man learns to mix copper and tin
4. Pre-historic man learns to use fire
5. Beginning of recorded history

Chapter 2 The People of the Nile

More than twelve thousand years ago, a group of people who were looking for a home came upon the valley of the Nile River in northeast Africa. These people had probably been traveling across miles and miles of North African desert. They must have been delighted when they saw the river and the green plants growing on both sides of it. They settled along the banks of the river. In time, the descendants of these people built the country of Egypt, which had one of the earliest civilizations.

2·1 Early Egyptian Civilization

Egypt Is the Gift of the Nile. In many ways, Egypt was an ideal place to live. For centuries, it was not conquered by any other people because it was protected by the desert and by the sea.

The climate was warm and dry. The people did not have to worry about rain or about cold weather. Grain for food was growing wild.

But the best thing about Egypt was the Nile River. In July of each year, rains and melting snows in the faraway mountains caused the Nile to overflow its banks. The river washed down rich soil from the mountains. When the river went back into its banks, it left a rich deposit of soil, called silt.

The early Egyptians found that it was easy to raise crops in this silt. They did not even have to plow the ground. All they had to do was scatter the seeds and then cover them over by dragging a branch of a tree over them.

The crops needed water, however, and this was a problem. The banks of the river were high because of the silt that had been left there year after year. How could water be raised from the river to the fields? To do this, the Egyptians invented the shadoof. This was a long pole on which a skin bucket was hung by a rope. The other end of the pole was weighted with a ball of hardened mud. The worker pulled on the empty bucket and dipped it into the river. When it was full, he raised it and swung it around. Then he emptied it into a ditch which carried the water to the fields.

In time, the Egyptians farmed not only in the silt left by the river but also in land which had been desert. This land was watered by ditches or canals. On this former desert land, the Egyptians used plows.

Making desert land fertile by bringing water to it is called irrigation. We don't know whether the Egyptians or the people of the Valley of the Two Rivers in Asia were the first to use irrigation, but both of them were using it many centuries before the birth of Christ. Today, irrigation is used in many dry lands, especially in the southwestern part of the United States.

We can see that without the Nile River there would not have been a country of Egypt. For that reason Egypt is called the "gift of the Nile."

Egypt Becomes a Kingdom. For hundreds of years the Egyptians lived in little scattered villages along the banks of the Nile. Each village was ruled by a chief, and the

Here is how Egyptians, by a series of ditches, brought water from the Nile to their fields.

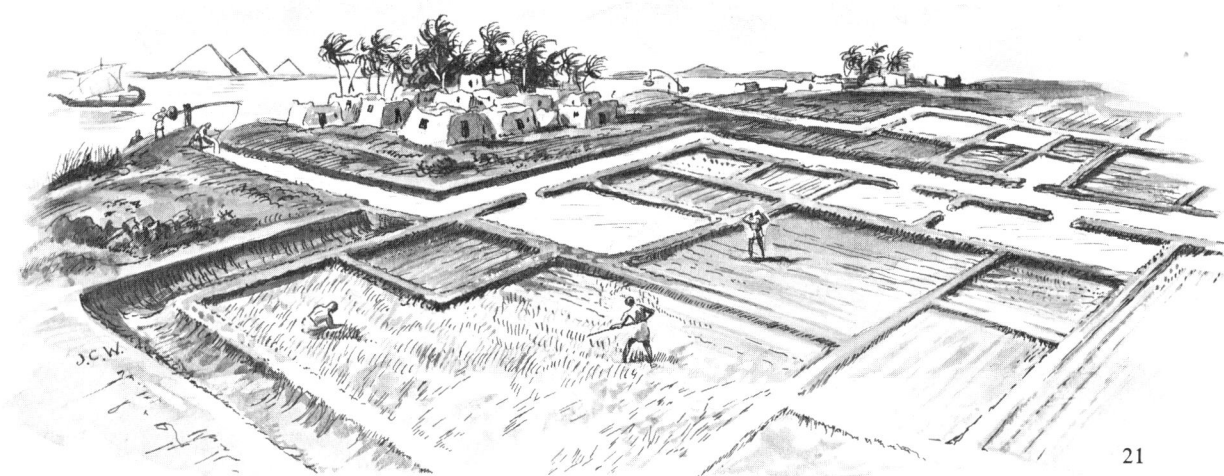

Egyptians Develop Many Skills

Many Egyptians Became Craftsmen. Because the soil yielded such big crops, not all Egyptians had to be farmers. Some became craftsmen.

Potters made jars and vases from clay. Some men made bricks from the clay mixed with straw. Others made houses with the bricks.

The art of making glass was probably first discovered by the Egyptians. They found that they could make glass by melting sand and other substances. This produced a thick liquid. Before the liquid had a chance to cool and harden, a glass blower would put some of it on the end of the tube in his mouth and blow. The hot glass would swell up into a hollow sphere. Then the glass blower would mold it into a vase or some other object.

Flax grows well in Egypt, and the Egyptians learned to make thread from it. They also learned how to weave the thread into beautiful linen.

There were many other kinds of craftsmen in Egypt, including goldsmiths, woodworkers, leatherworkers, metalworkers, blacksmiths, and tailors.

The Egyptians Were Traders. The Nile River was the highway of Egypt. All the towns and villages were close to it, so it was natural that the Egyptians would build boats to go from one part of the country to another. After they learned to make river boats, they made ships which would travel

The busy city of Memphis was the capital of Upper and Lower Egypt. Look closely and you will see the pyramids in the background.

chief had no one over him. The villages were completely independent of each other. Later, the settled land was organized into two kingdoms: Upper Egypt and Lower Egypt. About 3200 B.C. a strong leader, Menes, gained control of both kingdoms. Menes built the city of Memphis near the mouth of the Nile, and he made it the capital of his kingdom. Under Menes and his successors Egypt became a rich and powerful nation.

The king of Egypt became known as the Pharaoh. All the land in the kingdom was his property. The people considered their ruler a god. They had so much reverence for him that they did not even pronounce his name.

Briefly describe the Egyptian method of irrigation.

on the sea. The ships carried corn, cloth, jewels, leather goods, and other things that were produced in Egypt. The ships brought back wood, gold, copper, ivory and spices.

The men who sailed to other countries learned about the cultures of these countries, and they taught other peoples something about the ways in which Egyptians lived and worked.

The Egyptians Were Builders. You have probably seen pictures of the Egyptian pyramids. These pyramids were built several thousand years ago, and about seventy of them are still standing. The pyramids were tombs for the Pharaohs.

The highest of the pyramids was built at Giza for the Pharaoh, Cheops. It covers thirteen acres and is 481 feet high, the height of a fifty-story building. This pyramid is one of the Seven Wonders of the Ancient World. It was built about 3000 years before the birth of Christ.

It took thousands of men many years to build this pyramid. Each stone had to be cut from a great mountain of rock. Then it had to be moved many miles to the site of the pyramid. Finally, it had to be taken to the top of the stones which formed the base of the pyramid, and put in its proper place. As the pyramid rose higher, each stone had to be lifted that much higher. The Egyptians at that time had no horses nor mules to do their hauling. All their labor had to be done by human strength.

The Egyptians built other things besides pyramids. They erected huge temples to their gods and goddesses. Their temples had many giant-size statues.

The Sphinx, which is also at Giza, is a statue which has the body and claws of a lion and the head of a man. The body is

River water goes from the shadoof to canals to fields. Civilizations begin when man starts to grow food.

A boundary dispute. Egyptians learned to settle quarrels over property lines by having their lots surveyed.

172 feet long, and the statue is 66 feet high. It was carved from solid rock about 5000 years ago.

Other Accomplishments of the Egyptians. When the Nile overflowed its banks each year, it often washed away the boundaries between the fields that belonged to one man

An artist puts the finishing touches on his work. He is painting a portrait of the pharaoh on the walls of a tomb.

and the fields that belonged to his neighbor. Although all land was considered to belong to the Pharaoh, in everyday practice it belonged to the man who farmed it.

It was necessary to find a way to measure land so that each person could tell what belonged to him. The Egyptians figured out a way to measure land by using straight lines and angles. This is called surveying. The Egyptians were the first people to survey their lands. Today, surveyors have modern instruments to help them, but they still use the principles discovered by the ancient Egyptians. In order to do their surveying, the Egyptians had to have some knowledge of mathematics, especially geometry.

The early Egyptians also knew much about chemistry, and they made medicine from herbs. They worked out a calendar of twelve months of thirty days each. This, of course, was shorter than the actual year. Later, this was corrected, and the Egyptians had a calendar of 365 days.

The Egyptians divided the time between one sunset and the next into twenty-four hours. At first they guessed the hour by looking at the sun to see how high it was in the sky. This was not very satisfactory. They noticed that a tree casts a long shadow at sunrise. The shadow gets shorter and shorter till noon, when it is shortest of all. Then in the afternoon it grows longer and longer. Using this idea, Egyptians built a shadow clock. This was a long piece of wood with a crosspiece at one end. The wood was marked off into hours. In the morning the crosspiece was set toward the east, and its shadow fell along the piece that was marked. The place of the shadow showed the hours till noon. Then the crosspiece was set toward the west, and the hours of the afternoon were marked by the lengthening shadow.

Picture Writing. For a long time the people of Egypt did not know how to write. They began writing by making little pictures. When they wanted to write about a man, for example, they drew a crude picture of a man. When they wanted to write about the sun, they drew a circle. In time, they simplified this writing by making just a few lines instead of drawing a complete picture. Instead of drawing a man, they might just draw two lines to represent the legs of a man walking.

The written language came to have hundreds of characters, each representing a word or a syllable. This form of Egyptian figure writing is called hieroglyphics.

A plant called papyrus grew in the swamps near the Nile. The Egyptians found a way to make a crude paper from this papyrus. The sheets of papyrus were joined together in long rolls. At each end, there was a stick. A person read this roll, or scroll as it was called, by unrolling the papyrus a little at a time and rolling it onto the other stick. The Egyptians never had the kind of books we have, but the scrolls served the same purpose as our books.

A sort of ink was made from water, vegetable gum, and soot. A pointed reed was used as a pen.

Not many Egyptians could read. There were people called scribes who were specially trained to read and write for others. The scribes were very important and were highly respected.

The Key to a Puzzle

1 A famous stone with writing on it was found in 1799 at the mouth of the Nile River by a French officer. No one was able to decipher it for more than fifty years.

2 There were three kinds of writing on the Rosetta Stone. One was picture writing, another was an unknown Egyptian writing, and the third was written in Greek. Actually, the same message was contained in each form.

3 When scholars finally found the meaning of the writing, a great puzzle was solved. Now they were able to learn how the Egyptians lived, worked, and what they believed.

Through the looking glass. A wealthy Egyptian woman admires herself in a mirror. Her servants are attending to her comfort.

The People Belonged to Various Classes. The nobles and wealthy people of ancient Egypt lived pleasant lives. Their houses were made of wooden frames plastered over with sun-dried clay. The houses were surrounded by large gardens with fishponds and palm trees and high walls. There were many servants to care for the spacious homes and gardens.

The middle class lived in the better sections of the towns. They led comfortable lives. This class included merchants, shopkeepers, physicians, lawyers, builders, and craftsmen.

The great majority of the people were in the lowest class. These included the workers and the farmers. They lived in the poorer sections of the towns. Farmers did not live in the country. Many of them lived in one room mud huts. Farmers and workers toiled from dawn to dusk and received very little in return. The workers were little better than slaves. It was they who did the backbreaking work of building the pyramids.

The Egyptians Believed in Life After Death. The Egyptians saw the work of the gods in everything about them. The two most important things in their lives were the sun and the Nile River. The sun gave them heat and light, and it made their crops grow. The Nile River gave them silt, fish, a water highway, and—most important of all—the water without which they could not live. It was natural then that the two most important gods would be the sun god, Re, and the god of the Nile, Osiris. There were also many other gods.

The Egyptians believed firmly in a life after death. They believed that at some time the spirit might wish to go back into the body. Rich people took great pains to preserve the bodies of their dead. The Egyptians became experts at preserving bodies. Many of these bodies, called mummies, are still in existence.

We have already seen that the pyramids were built as tombs for the Pharaohs. They show how important the body was considered. The pyramids and other tombs contained many treasures for the buried person to use in the next life.

The poor people complained that they would not have a very good chance in the next life because they could not afford fancy tombs and could not afford to have their bodies preserved. Some of the later Pharaohs listened to these complaints and made it possible for the poor people to do more for their dead.

We have learned much about the civilization of the ancient Egyptians from the pyramids and other tombs.

A Long History. The Egyptians lived in their Nile Valley for many centuries and built a strong country. Later Pharaohs formed armies and conquered other nations. Egypt became a great empire and reached the height of her power by 1500 B.C.

Little by little Egypt became weaker. The Egyptians lost their empire. Then Egypt itself was invaded by people from other countries, and it lost its independence. The things that Egyptians had learned and the discoveries that they had made were not lost to the world, however. They were passed on to the people who came after them, and we are still benefiting from the discoveries made by the ancient Egyptians.

1. Why was the method of burying the dead of such importance to the ancient Egyptian?
2. What have we learned from the tombs of the ancient Egyptians?

Chapter 2. REVIEW

Learning to Use New Words

Use each of the following terms in an original sentence, expressing something you have learned in Chapter 2.

shadoof   mummy
Rosetta Stone   pyramid
hieroglyphics   Pharaoh
papyrus   craftsman
scribe

Knowing the Important Facts

1. Who was the leader who unified Egypt into one powerful nation?
2. Make a list of several occupations, other than farming, found in Egypt.
3. Describe the three classes of people in Egypt.
4. What system was used to keep a record of events in Egypt?

Thinking Through the Facts

1. Why has Egypt been called the "Gift of the Nile"?
2. Why do Americans fear floods? Why were floods helpful in Egypt?
3. In what section of our country is crop irrigation used on a large scale? Compare modern methods of irrigation with those used by the Egyptians.
4. Why were scribes needed in Egypt? Would they be useful in the United States today? Give reasons for your answer.

Developing a Time Sense

Arrange the following events in the proper time order:
1. Egypt reaches the height of power
2. Cheops builds his pyramid
3. Menes unites Upper and Lower Egypt
4. The Rosetta Stone is found

Chapter 3
Early Civilization in Southwest Asia

About the same time the Egyptians were settling the area around the Nile, another civilization arose in the southwest corner of Asia. This is the region that is close to Europe and to Africa. It touches the Caspian Sea, the Persian Gulf, the Arabian Sea, the Red Sea, and the eastern end of the Mediterranean Sea. Today, this region is often in the news. A few of the countries it contains are Iran, Iraq, Jordan, Syria, and Israel. We often see these names in today's headlines. Most of the names were not known, however, in the period covered by this chapter.

The whole continent of Asia is called the East, and Southwest Asia is the part of the East that is closest to us. For that reason, we usually call this region the Near East. We have already studied about one of the countries of the Near East, Egypt. Although Egypt is an African country, its development has been so closely connected with the countries of Southwest Asia, that they are grouped together.

3 1
The Valley of the Two Rivers

The Valley of the Two Rivers Is a Fertile Land. Much of the land in the Near East gets little rain. As a result, there are vast stretches of desert which are of no use for raising crops or animals. We would not expect a civilization to rise in a desert.

There are regions in the Near East, however, that receive water and are good for raising crops and animals even though they get little rain. One of these regions is the Valley of the Two Rivers.

Two great rivers, the Tigris and the Euphrates, receive their water from the melting snow in the mountains. They flow, almost side by side, southeast through a broad level plain. Both empty into the Persian Gulf. The land between the two rivers and bordering them is often called the Valley of the Two Rivers.

Each year these rivers swell into a great flood. They bring tons of rich soil down from the mountains. When the flood is over and the rivers are back in their banks, the soil has been left along both sides of the two rivers. People who lived near the rivers found that they could raise crops if they drained the swamps and dug canals to carry river water to the rainless desert. It took the work of many people to do these tasks. This is one of the marks of civilization: people working together for a common cause.

The farms produced such large crops that not everyone had to be a farmer. Some became potters, weavers, and traders. This is another sign of civilization: people performing various tasks for each other.

Sumerian Civilization. The land at the mouths of the Tigris and Euphrates was called Sumer. The people who lived there were called Sumerians. They may have come from the highlands, east of the Tigris. With them, they probably brought the knowledge of how to make copper tools and weapons. They found no copper in the Valley of the Two Rivers. After they had started their farms, they traded food to other peoples for copper.

The Sumerians discovered the use of the wheel, and so they were able to build carts and carriages and wagons.

The Sumerians also worked out a way of writing. They wrote on wet clay tablets which were dried in the sun. They made wedge-shaped characters, each of which stood for a word or a syllable. This is called *cuneiform* writing. The word "cuneiform" means "wedge-shaped."

The temple and its priests played an important role in Sumer. In each village or city the people built a temple to the local god. All the farm land in that area belonged to the temple. When the farmers gathered their crops, they took them to the temple to be stored.

We see that the Sumerians had almost all the marks of civilization that were named in an earlier chapter. These included the use of writing.

Therefore, we can say that Sumer, in the

Sumerians built cities of colorful enameled brick. Palaces and temples were well constructed and splendidly decorated.

Everyone took part in the life of the Fertile Valley. Some grew food, others built great temples and palaces.

lower part of the Valley of the Two Rivers, had one of the earliest civilization of which we have any record. This civilization began sometime around 3500 B.C.

The Sumerians seldom had a central government for their entire region. Instead they had city-states. Each city had its own independent government. At times the ruler of one city-state would gain control over other cities, but this never lasted very long. When the Sumerians were finally united, it was by conquerors from other places.

The Babylonians Become the Rulers of the Valley. North of Sumer, but in the Valley of the Two Rivers, was the city of Babylon. Hammurabi, King of Babylon, conquered Sumer about 1900 B.C. and became ruler of the entire southern part of the valley.

The Babylonians knew how to write. They had learned this from the Sumerians. The Babylonians were skilled builders. They made bricks from clay and built temples and other large buildings. They also knew a great deal about arithmetic and about the stars and planets. They divided the week into seven days of twenty-four hours each, and they divided the hour into sixty minutes.

The Law of King Hammurabi

Hammurabi was a great and wise king of Babylon. When he came to the throne, there were so many different laws that people did not know which ones to follow. King Hammurabi made a code of important laws so that all would know them throughout the land.

Some of the laws were just, but many were severe and unjust. Here are a few of them: *1.* If a son strikes his father, his fingers shall be cut off. *2.* If a person puts out the eye of a rich man, his own eye shall be put out; if it is the eye of a poor man, he shall pay a fine. *3.* If a builder builds a house which falls down, the builder shall be put to death.

We probably got our way of measuring time from the Babylonians.

The sun dial was invented by the Babylonians. The shadow which the sun cast on the dial told what hour of the day it was.

Some of the Babylonians became merchants and traders. They sold to their own people, and they sold to other countries.

The Assyrians Were a Nation of Warriors. To the north of Babylon was Assyria, a land of fierce warriors. The Assyrians were one of the first people to use horses. Their soldiers charged into battle in war chariots drawn by swift steeds. This struck terror into the hearts of the enemy. This is one reason why they won so many battles.

The Assyrians became the masters of the Valley of the Two Rivers. They destroyed the city of Babylon and made their own city of Nineveh the capital. It became one of the most beautiful cities of the time.

The Assyrians conquered one land after another. In 672 B.C., they conquered Egypt.

The Chaldeans Establish the Second Babylonian Empire. The Assyrians fought so many wars that they gradually became weak. A group of people called the Chaldeans revolted against them. The Chaldeans became masters of the valley. They destroyed the city of Nineveh.

In fearful war chariots the Assyrians rode roughshod to smashing victory over their enemies.

The Hanging Gardens were on a great platform, covered with earth, supported by columns that were seventy-five feet high.

The ruler of the new empire was a Chaldean named Nebuchadnezzar. He ordered the city of Babylon rebuilt, and it became the capital once more. It was surrounded by strong walls to protect it. The walls were so thick that a chariot with four horses could turn around on top of them. The walls had a hundred gates of glittering brass plates, hammered in beautiful designs.

To please his wife, King Nebuchadnezzar built the famous Hanging Gardens of Babylon. They were one of the Seven Wonders of the Ancient World.

The Chaldeans borrowed from the cultures of the people they had conquered, and they also made important discoveries of their own. They worked out tables of the movements of the sun, moon, and planets. They did this without the aid of telescopes and other important instruments that we have today. One astronomer figured the length of the year to within twenty-six minutes.

The Chaldeans also figured out a system of arithmetic which was later adopted by the Greeks and handed down through the centuries.

After Nebuchadnezzar the second Babylonian Empire became weaker. In 538 the Valley of the Two Rivers was conquered by the Persians. It became part of the great Persian Empire.

All the other people who had ruled the Valley of the Two Rivers had lived in the valley. The Persians, however, came from outside the valley. For many centuries after that the Valley of the Two Rivers was to be ruled by conquerors from the outside.

1. Who were the earliest settlers in the Valley of the Two Rivers?
2. Mention three groups of invaders who conquered the Valley.

The Lydians and the Persians

The Lydians Invent Coins. In other parts of the Near East, two new nations were rising. They were Lydia and Persia.

Lydia was in Asia Minor, in what is today the country of Turkey. The Lydians found much gold in their streams, and the civilized people of the world had already recognized that gold was a valuable metal. The Lydians also carried on much trade with other peoples. As a result, Lydia became a very wealthy country. Perhaps you have heard the expression "rich as Croesus." This expression began because Croesus was the King of Lydia and probably the wealthiest man in the world at that time.

About 650 B.C. King Croesus had his picture and name stamped on pieces of silver. He also ordered that the weight of the piece of silver be stamped on it. In this way people knew exactly what each piece of silver was worth. They were the world's first coins.

The first trade had been by barter. This means exchanging one kind of goods for another, just as you might trade a coke for a candy bar. Sumerians, as we have seen, traded food for copper. This was a very difficult way of doing business.

Later, silver rings and bars were used for money. They made trading much easier, but the rings and bars were seldom the same weight and size. They had to be weighed each time they were traded.

The Lydians made trade much easier when they invented coins.

"Sixpence to spend and sixpence to lend." Lydians simplified trading by making popular the use of coins.

The Persians Build a Great Empire. Tribes known as the Medes and Persians lived east of the Valley of the Two Rivers. These tribes united into a strong nation which was called Persia. The land the Persians lived in is today called Iran.

The Persians conquered other peoples of the Near East. A few years after 600 B.C. King Croesus of Lydia surrendered to them. Next, they defeated Babylon and became masters of the Valley of the Two Rivers. Egypt also fell to them.

When a king rules other countries besides his own, we call him an emperor. The land he rules is called an empire. We have already read about the Assyrian Empire and the two Babylonian Empires. The Persian Empire was far larger than these. It was the largest empire the world had known till that time.

The Persians built roads throughout their empire. The chief road, from Susa to Sardis, was fifteen hundred miles long. There were many inns along this road. Here messengers could change horses, and travelers could spend the night.

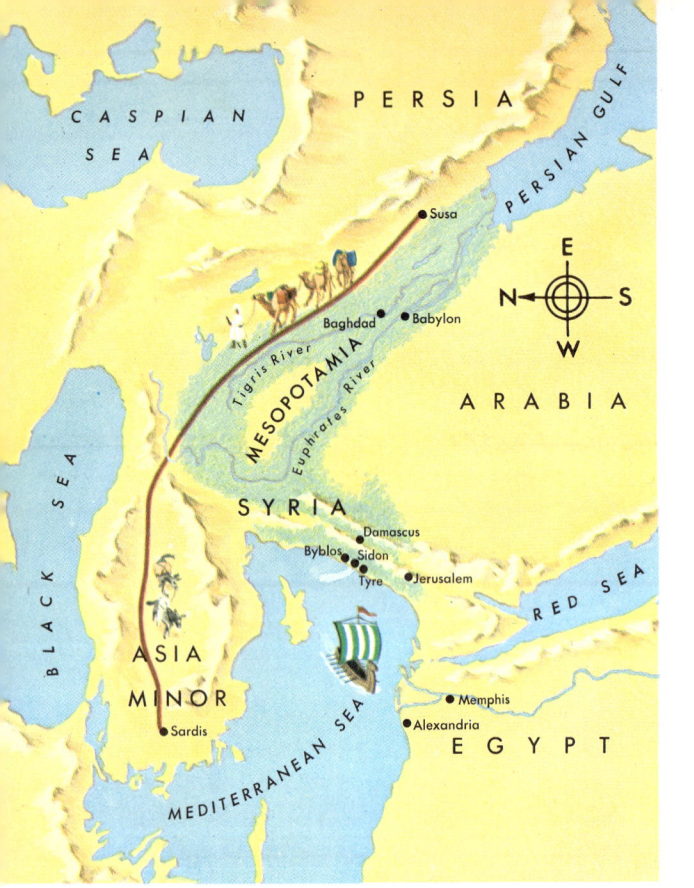

The roads helped tie the empire together and enabled the people of one region to borrow from the cultures of people who lived in other regions.

From the Lydians, the Persians learned the use of coins. The same coins were used throughout the vast empire, and they made trade much easier.

The Persians conquered almost all the people they knew. There was one people, however, whom the Persians could not conquer. These were the Greeks.

How did the rise of the Persian Empire help spread civilization?

3 3

A Nation of Traders

The Phoenicians Were a Seafaring People. Along the eastern shore of the Mediterranean Sea is a narrow strip of fertile land. On the northern part of the fertile section lived the Phoenicians. On the southern part lived the Hebrews.

The land in which the Phoenicians lived was 200 miles long and about twenty miles wide. It was a land of pastures, orchards, and vineyards. There was not enough land for all the Phoenicians to be farmers, so many of them looked for other ways to make a living. Because they lived along the shore of the Mediterranean, many of them turned to the sea for a living. From the Egyptians, the Phoenicians learned how to build and operate ships. Many Phoenicians became sailors, fishermen, and traders. Because of the ships, traders were able to go to other parts of the world where they bought and sold goods. Some Phoenicians also became manufacturers and sold their manufactured goods to the traders. Among the goods which the Phoenicians manufactured were purple dye, glass, woven fabrics, and fine metalwork.

The Phoenicians learned about ships from the Egyptians, but they became better shipbuilders and sailors than their teachers. Some of the Phoenician ships were small and were rowed by men sitting on one level. Other ships were rowed from two or three levels. The ships also had sails. The Phoenicians sailed from their end of the Mediterranean to the other, and they did not stop there. They sailed through the Strait of Gibraltar out onto the Atlantic Ocean. This was a very daring thing to do in those days. They sailed to England where they bought tin. They sailed down the west coast of Africa where they bought ivory.

The Phoenicians established trading posts in various parts of the world. One of these posts on the northern coast of Africa grew into the city of Carthage.

The Phoenicians have been called "carriers of civilization." Less civilized people learned from them how things were done in civilized countries. The Phoenicians taught these people how to build houses, how to raise crops, how to use coins, and how to do many other things that the civilized people did.

The Phoenicians and the Alphabet. At first, the Phoenicians used the Egyptian form of picture writing. Later the Phoenicians used an alphabet of twenty-two consonants. Later still, the Greeks added the vowels. We do not know whether the Phoenicians de-

The Phoenicians were students who improved what they learned. They taught people better ways of living and doing things.

veloped this alphabet themselves or whether they borrowed it from some other people. We do know that the Phoenicians spread the use of the alphabet to the people they visited. In the centuries to come the use of the alphabet would spread across Europe, and the people of Europe would bring it to the New World. There have been some changes, but our alphabet of twenty-six letters grew from the one the Phoenicians used 3000 years ago.

As we read, Chinese boys and girls must learn hundreds of characters before they can learn to read and write. The same is true in other countries. You have to learn only twenty-six letters. For this you can thank the Phoenicians.

1. What encouraged the Phoenicians to become traders?
2. Where was the land of the Phoenicians located? What were the advantages and disadvantages of this location?

3 4 God's Chosen People

The Hebrews Believed in God. The Hebrews, or Jews, were the neighbors of the Phoenicians on the narrow strip of fertile land at the east end of the Mediterranean Sea. The Hebrews did not give us such gifts as the alphabet, the wheel, coins, or a system of measuring time. They did not establish a huge empire. They did not take ships to far parts of the world. But they performed a service for us that is greater than any performed by other peoples. They kept alive the belief in the one true God.

All the peoples that have been mentioned in this chapter had a religion of some kind. They knew that some power greater than themselves had created the world and the sun and the moon and the stars. They had no way of knowing about the true God, so they "invented" gods of their own. In some cases each little village had its own god. In other cases a whole country would worship the same gods. Sometimes the power of the king impressed the people so much that they came to believe the king was a god. Some of the false gods were believed to demand human sacrifices, and many people were killed in the temples in order to please these gods.

The Hebrews believed in the one God. They were surrounded by people who worshipped false gods. Often they were tempted to worship these gods themselves, and many of them did for a time. But they never completely forsook their God. They could not have held to their belief if they had not been given help by God Himself. The Hebrews were God's chosen people. They had a special mission in the world: to keep alive the belief in God and to prepare the way for the Redeemer.

The Hebrews have given us the forty-five books of the Old Testament, which is part of the Bible. The Bible is the most important book in the world. It is the inspired word of God. In part, the Old Testament is a history of the Jewish people. But it is more than that. It contains the words of God's prophets, the promises God made to His people, and the rules by which God wishes us to live. The Bible has beautiful

Man has believed in God always and everywhere, and some have worshipped Him in very strange and mysterious ways.

poetry, and it has thrilling stories. You learned much about the Bible when you studied Bible History.

The Hebrews Reach the Promised Land. Abraham, the father of the Hebrew race, lived near the city of Ur in the Valley of the Two Rivers. He left there about the time that Hammurabi ruled the valley.

The Old Testament tells us that Jacob, who was Abraham's grandson, had twelve sons. The eleventh son was named Joseph. Joseph's brothers sold him into slavery, and he was taken to Egypt. The Pharaoh, as the ruler of Egypt was called, admired Joseph and gave him a high position in the government. Joseph invited his family to come to Egypt to live. About seventy-five people came. They settled in Goshen.

At first the Pharaohs were happy to have the Hebrews in Egypt. Later, as the number of Hebrews increased, the Pharaohs became afraid of them. One Pharaoh ordered that boy Hebrews be killed as soon as they were born.

God raised up a leader named Moses who was to take the Hebrews from Egypt into the Promised Land. While the Hebrews were making the journey, God gave Moses the Ten Commandments. The Hebrews wandered in the desert for years. Finally, they reached Palestine, which was the Promised Land. Moses died just before his people reached Palestine.

King Solomon Builds a Temple. There were twelve tribes of Hebrews, each descended from one of the sons of Jacob. At first they were not united under one government. The first king of the whole Hebrew nation was Saul.

God told Moses that he would see the Promised Land, but because Moses had disobeyed Him, he would not enter it.

Saul was followed by David, a great warrior and a writer of beautiful songs. These songs are called the Psalms, and they are used in many ceremonies of the Church.

The next king was Solomon, David's son. The Hebrew kingdom reached its greatest height under Solomon. In Jerusalem, the capital of the Hebrew nation, Solomon built a great temple in which the Hebrews could worship God. He hired Phoenician workmen to help build the temple. Phoenician ships brought beautiful objects from many parts of the world for the temple.

The Hebrews Are Taken to Babylonia. After the rule of King Solomon the Hebrew nation divided into two parts. The ten northern tribes formed the Kingdom of Israel. The two southern tribes formed the Kingdom of Judah with Jerusalem as the capital.

The people of Israel were conquered by the Assyrians in 722 B.C. They were taken away, and they mixed with other peoples.

Solomon ordered a great temple built on land that David had bought. A copy of the law of God was kept in it.

They disappeared from history. Today, we call them the Ten Lost Tribes of Israel.

This left only the two tribes of Judah to keep alive the belief in one God. About 586 B.C. Judah was conquered by Nebuchadnezzar, King of Babylon. He destroyed the city of Jerusalem with its beautiful temple. He took the Hebrews to Babylonia. This period of Hebrew history is called the Babylonian Captivity. In captivity, the Hebrews clung to their religion.

When King Cyrus of Persia conquered Babylonia, he permitted the Hebrews to go back to Palestine. He even helped them rebuild their temple.

1. Who was the first king of the Hebrew People?
2. Mention three reasons why it would be valuable to read the Old Testament.

Chapter 3. REVIEW

Learning to Use New Words

Use each of the folowing terms in an original sentence, expressing something you have learned in Chapter 3:

fertile sacrifices
cuneiform prophets
emperor Near East

Knowing the Important Facts

1. What two rivers were of great importance to the Near East?
2. Who was the Babylonian ruler who ordered one set of laws for his entire kingdom?
3. Make a chart showing three contributions to civilization made by the Babylonians, Chaldeans, and the Phoenicians.
4. What great gift was given to us by the Hebrews?
5. What did King Croesus do of benefit to mankind?

Thinking Through the Facts

1. Why did the Phoenicians become traders, and how did they spread their civilization?
2. How were the Persian kings able to control and develop their vast empire?
3. Why were the world's first coins issued? Why does the government regulate the minting of coins in America today?
4. What were the roles played in the history of the Hebrews, by each of the folowing: Abraham, Joseph, Moses, David, and Solomon?
5. Why was the Valley of the Two Rivers the scene of the fall of one civilization after another?

Developing a Time Sense

Arrange the following events in the proper time order:

1. The Babylonian captivity of the Hebrews
2. Cuneiform writing is developed by the Sumerians
3. King Croesus of Lydia mints the first coins
4. Hammurabi makes one set of laws for Babylonia

Chapter 4

The People of Ancient India and China

While civilizations were developing in the Near East, civilizations were also growing up in India and China. First, we shall take a brief look at life in Ancient India.

When people speak of Ancient India, they mean the entire Indian peninsula, not just the country of India as it exists today. The peninsula is vast. It is larger than Western Europe. It is roughly the shape of a triangle with the ocean on two sides and the highest mountains in the world on the other side. India is on the continent of Asia, but is often called a subcontinent in itself.

4·1

Early Indian Civilization

Life along the Indus. The climate of India is warm. The soil is fertile and makes fine farmland. In most years there is heavy rain in the summer months, and this makes the crops grow. The civilizations we have already read about were in lands that were warm and had good soil and plenty of water. It is not surprising, therefore, to learn that there was an early civilization in India.

We know very little about the early history of India. We do know that there was a civilization along the Indus River by 2200 B.C. The remains of two ancient cities, 350 miles apart, have been found on the banks of this river. In addition to the cities, there were probably many farms and villages. It is believed that this Indus Civilization extended from the mountains in the north to the ocean in the south. This is a distance of 950 miles.

The cities had straight streets and drainage systems. The houses were well built and had their own wells and baths. In order to do so much building, the people must have had some knowledge of surveying and geometry.

We do not know as much as we would like to know about the people who built these cities. We do know that they had dark skins, because their conquerors have left this description of them. The people had a form of writing, and some of their writings have been found, but nobody knows how to read them.

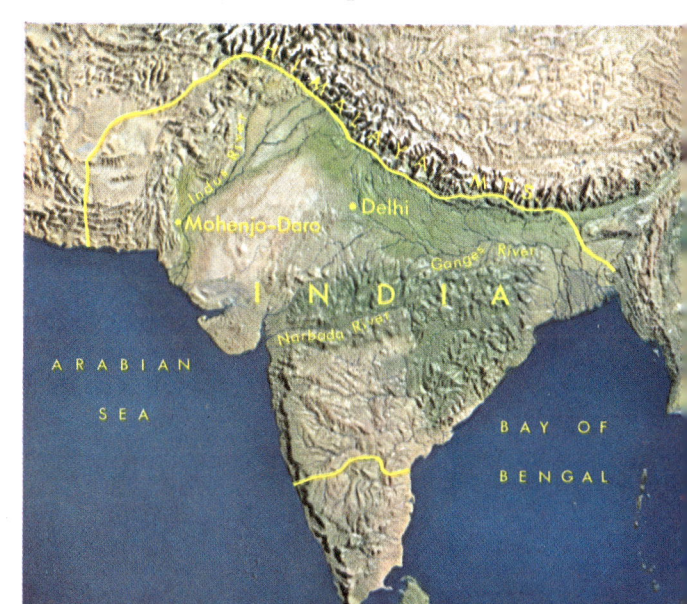

The Aryans Come into India. The mountains to the north of India are almost impossible to cross in most places, but there are a few passes through them. One of these is the famous Khyber Pass.

About 1500 B.C. people called Aryans began coming through this pass. These people seem to have come from the region around the Black and Caspian Seas. They were tall and had fair skin and long heads. They were probably related to the people who settled most of Europe.

The Aryan invasion of India did not take place all at once. It continued for many years, perhaps for several centuries. Little by little the Aryans either conquered the dark-skinned natives or pushed them south. The Aryans became the masters of the Indus Valley and then they pushed on into other parts of northern India.

The Aryan invaders found that the people they had conquered had a much more advanced culture than their own. They adopted many features of this culture.

The language of the invading Aryans was Sanskrit. This became the language of much of northern India. Later, travelers from the Near East brought knowledge of the alphabet to India. The alphabet was adapted to Sanskrit. Many writings in ancient Sanskrit have been found, and scholars know how to read them. Today, Sanskrit is not spoken anywhere in the world.

The Caste System. Before the Aryans came into India they had two classes of people, the small ruling class and the great mass of common people. When they settled in India, they made a third class of the dark-skinned people they had conquered. These people were considered lower than any of the Aryans. The Aryans were afraid that they would disappear as a race if they intermarried with the natives, so they ruled that nobody in the lowest class could marry anybody in the two higher classes.

In time, four classes of castes developed: (1) the priests; (2) the knights; (3) the traders, merchants, and farmers; (4) the laborers. In addition, there was a group of outcastes who were considered too low to belong to any caste. They were called the "untouchables" because members of the castes thought they would be defiled if they even touched these people. All non-Aryans were either in the lowest caste or were untouchables.

In time, these four castes broke down into many more. They depended largely on occupations. Today there are about 2000 or 3000 castes in India. Nobody knows exactly how many there are.

The red spot in the center of the forehead marks the women of the caste system, many of whom are well-educated today.

A man who was born into a certain caste had to stay in that caste all his life. No matter how hard he worked, he could not better himself. A person of one caste could not marry a person from another caste.

This caste system, which began many centuries ago, has persisted to our own day. The modern government of India had passed laws to soften the caste system and to do away with the untouchable class, but the laws are hard to enforce.

The system has no doubt kept India from the progress she should have made. A country makes progress when the people work hard to better themselves. But the people of India have known that there was no hope of bettering themselves.

How Ancient India Was Governed. As the Aryans spread from the Indus Valley into other parts of India, they established small kingdoms. At one time there were sixteen kingdoms in India. The kings often went to war against one another and took territory from one another, so the boundaries of the kingdoms were constantly changing.

The governments of the various kingdoms were much alike. The king and his nobles were members of the second caste, the knights. They lived in the city that was the capital of the kingdom. The king was the absolute ruler. At harvest time, he collected taxes from the farm villages. In peaceful times he might take one-sixth of the total crop, and in times of war he might take one-third.

The Indus Valley became part of the vast Persian Empire about 527 B.C. The Persians, however, left most of the power in the hands of the local kings.

Bronze statue of Siva, god of creation and destruction. The people pray to him in times of trouble, such as wars and famine.

In 327 B.C. a Macedonian King, Alexander the Great, reached the Indus and conquered the Indus Valley. He died soon after and his empire fell apart. About 321 B.C. one of the Indian Kings, Maurya, conquered most of the other kingdoms and became the emperor of most of India. This empire lasted till 184 B.C.

Most People Lived in Self-Governing Villages. Today, nine-tenths of the people of India live in small farm villages. Many of these villages are not even on a highway, but are reached by a footpath or a rough, cart road. The houses are made of dried mud and have thatch roofs. The villages have no sewers or means of disposing of waste.

A traveler who found himself in one of these villages today, could easily imagine that he was living 1000 years before the birth of Christ. The people of that time lived in the same kind of villages.

In those days each village was self-governing. A council of villagers were elected to distribute the land and collect the taxes. The kings did not bother the villages very much, as long as they paid their taxes.

The Joint-Family. When a boy married, he brought his wife home to live. If there were a number of boys in a family and they all brought their wives home and all had children of their own, there could be a large number of people under one roof. This was called a joint-family.

The father was the head of the joint-family. When he died, his place would be taken by the oldest son.

When a member of the joint-family earned some money, he would not spend it on himself. He would put it in the family fund. The father would decide when and how much money could be taken from this fund.

This system is still strong in India today. It makes the people very close to their families. It also makes them think of the group instead of thinking of themselves as individuals.

The women of the joint-family did the cooking and the housework. The men spent most of the day in the fields, caring for the crops. Children worked, too, almost from the time they could walk.

The People Were Religious. Religion has always played a big part in the lives of the people of India. Today, 85 per cent of the people in the country of India belong to the Hindu religion. This religion has developed slowly over the years. Many changes have been made in it. Its beginnings can be traced back to the Aryan invaders of 1500 B.C. The Aryans, however, adopted some of the gods of the people whom they conquered.

Hinduism is a very complicated religion. It is not possible to tell all about it in this book. We shall just look at a few of the important features of it.

Hinduism has many gods, the chief of whom is Brahma, "the Father of all." The gods are very powerful, and the Hindus have built many temples to them. The people can appeal to the gods only through the priests. The priests perform many ceremonies, and these ceremonies are considered very important. The Hindus believe that the world would stop existing if the priests did not perform their ceremonies in the right manner. It is easy to see why the priests were considered so important in ancient India, and why they formed the highest caste. They were higher even than the kings.

The joint-family governs itself almost like a nation within a nation. Some have more than one hundred and fifty members.

One of the Hindu beliefs is the transmigration of souls. According to this doctrine, the soul of a person passes at death into another creature. If a person has led a good life, his soul goes upward. That is, he is born into a higher caste. If he has led a bad life, his soul may pass into the body of a dog or pig or some other animal.

Thus, the Hindu religion is tied up with the caste system. That is one reason the caste system has such a strong hold on India.

Hindus believe that it is a sin to kill any living thing. For this reason, many of them never eat meat. Disease-bearing insects and dangerous animals have been allowed to thrive in some places because the Hindus would not kill them.

A Hindu prince named Guatama became known in India for his holiness and love of all creatures. He was called the Buddha, meaning "the Enlightened One." Buddha thought that the Hindu religion, with its many gods and ceremonies, was too complicated. He did not like the caste system. He taught that the reason people suffer is that they are greedy for power and for worldly possessions. Men could avoid this craving by following the "Eightfold Plan." This consisted of right views or understanding, right ambition, right speech, right action, right mode of livelihood, right endeavor, right thoughts, right concentration. Buddha taught that all men are created equal and that each man must work out his own salvation. He had to go through a number of lives in order to do this, Buddha said. He took the idea of transmigration of souls from the Hindus, but he did not tie it up with caste system as they did.

Hindus first worshipped in caves, then in high, domed buildings, and then in tall, pointed temples, as shown in the illustration.

Buddha did not claim to be divine, and he did not say that his ideas came from above. He meditated, but he did not pray to a Higher Being. It might be said that he did not teach a religion at all, but that he taught a way of life.

Strangely, after Buddha died many of the things he attacked as evils crept into Buddhism. Buddha attacked the worship of gods, but his followers made a god out of him, and today about 150 million people pray to Buddha.

We have read that around 321 B.C. Maurya became emperor of most of India.

His grandson, Asoka, became the second emperor. Asoka was an ardent Buddhist. He encouraged all his people to become Buddhists, and he sent Buddhist monks to Syria, Egypt, Greece, and Ceylon. Buddhism remained an important religion in India for several centuries. Then it died out in the country where it was founded. It is still strong in Ceylon, in Southeast Asia, in Korea, and in Japan.

We see, then, that the culture which developed in India was somewhat like the cultures of the other countries we have read about, but it was also different in some ways. Perhaps the outstanding features of the culture of ancient India were: (1) the importance of religion, especially Hinduism; (2) the caste system; (3) the self-governing village; (4) the joint-family.

1. How did Buddha explain suffering? Did Buddha's followers strictly preserve his teachings after his death?
2. How was Ancient India governed?

4 2

Ancient China

A Land of Many Rivers. We have read that most of the early civilizations developed along rivers: the Tigris and Euphrates in the Near East, the Nile in North Africa, the Indus in India. This was because the rivers could be used to irrigate the fields and to supply drinking water for men and cattle. Governments developed partly because men had to work together to get the water from the river to fields.

China is a land of many rivers. The most important are the Hwang Ho, or Yellow River, in the north and the Yangtze in the central area. It is not surprising, therefore, to learn that an early civilization developed in China. This land is cut off from the rest of the world by mountains and deserts, so for a long time it was not influenced very much by other civilizations.

Shang, China's First Civilization. The history of China is the story of the rise and fall of dynasties. A dynasty is a ruling house. If a king dies and is succeeded by his son or by one of his followers, the dynasty continues. When the king is overthrown and someone else seizes the throne, then a new dynasty has been started. A dynasty may be very short, or it may last hundreds of years.

The first Chinese civilization of which we have any record was the city-state of Shang, on the Yellow River. This civilization began about 1500 B.C. The period in which Shang was the most important part of China is called the Shang dynasty. It lasted till about 1100 B.C.

The king seems to have been the high priest. He pleaded to the gods for rain, for a good harvest, for success in war, and for many other things. The people also paid homage to their ancestors and begged their help in many ways. Thus, we see that ancestor worship has played a big part in the lives of the Chinese people from the very beginning.

The king and his nobles lived in the city. When they went forth, they rode in beautifully decorated chariots. Other city people were storekeepers and craftsmen. The great majority of the people were peasants who grew wheat, millet, and rice and raised cattle, sheep, pigs, and horses. Farming is still the principal occupation of China.

There was a written language, but only the most educated people could use it. It was a form of picture-writing.

We call Shang a city-state because it had one city in which the ruling class lived. Besides the city itself the city-state included the farmlands surrounding it. Such a country seems very small to us, and it is certainly small compared with today's China, but it was an important beginning.

Shang existed three thousand years ago, and that seems a long time. But we know there were men living in China long before that. Human bones found in a cave near Peking are half a million years old.

A New Dynasty and a New Form of Government. A new city-state named Chou arose in the northwest of China. Chou was not as large or powerful as Shang. The

We learned about the Shang Dynasty from the writings on turtle shells and animal bones that were buried during the dynasty.

King of Chou secured the help of barbarian warriors from lands north of China. With them, he conquered Shang in 1122 B.C. This was the end of the Shang dynasty and the beginning of the Chou dynasty, which lasted till 221 B.C. It was the longest dynasty in Chinese history.

After conquering Shang, the King of Chou went on to conquer other lands. The king then had the job of ruling not only his own people but the people of the conquered lands. Besides, he had promised rewards to the barbarian leaders who had helped him in battle. He found that the best way to answer both problems was to grant land to the leaders, provided the leaders promised to remain loyal to him. The leaders who were granted the land were called feudal nobles, or vassals. The new form of government was called feudalism.

The feudal noble owned the territory that had been granted him, and he had complete power to rule it. His commands had to be obeyed by everyone in his territory. He even had the right to take the crops of the serfs, who lived on his land, so they had nothing to call their own.

The King of Chou promised to send his army if the noble should be attacked. In return, the noble recognized the King of Chou as his overlord and promised to send him gifts of tribute. The noble promised not to attack another noble and to bring his army to the aid of the king when needed.

In the territory of each noble was a walled town. The purpose of the wall was to protect the town and the serfs who would flee there in case of an attack. In the center of the town was the mansion of the noble, surrounded by a smaller wall.

In time, some of the nobles became so strong that they ruled as if they were kings. They paid little attention to the King of Chou, who was supposed to be their ruler. The nobles went to war against one another. This last part of the Chou period is often called the Era of Contending States. In the end, the ruler of one of the states, Ch'in, overthrew all the other rulers, including the King of Chou. This was the end of the Chou dynasty, and the beginning of the Empire Government in China.

The ancient land of Chou was a feudal kingdom. The king was the overlord of many nobles. Each noble owned and ruled his part of the kingdom.

Confucius, a Famous Teacher. Confucius was a famous teacher who lived in the last half of the Chou dynasty, from 551 to 479 B.C. He was shocked to see various feudal states fighting one another. He preached law and order. He said that China should go back to the early days of feudalism when the lords lived in peace with each other and acknowledged the king as their head. The common people should always obey their rulers, and the rulers should always consider the good of the people. He said that the family was the foundation of the state. In the family, young people learned to obey their superiors.

Like Buddha, who lived in India at the same time, Confucius never pretended to be more than a man. But later he was made a god-like figure. His teachings were passed on from generation to generation. There was much that was good in his teachings. But many Chinese rulers stressed only what he said about obedience. The ruler received his power from Heaven, these rulers said, and it was the duty of the common people to obey. They did not mention that Confucius had also said it was the duty of the rulers to give good government.

Chinese Craftsmen. Archaeologists have found many beautiful objects which Chinese craftsmen made during the Shang and Chou periods. Jade, which is a certain kind of stone, was considered sacred by the Chinese. From jade they carved many objects to be used in the worship of their gods and in the worship of their ancestors. Other beautiful objects were made of bronze. Many vases show that the Chinese were among the best pottery makers of all times.

Confucius said that men should not worry about their position in life, but should worry about learning to fill it well.

A Complicated Language. In the Chinese spoken language, tones are very important. There are from four to nine tones for every sound, and each tone has a different meaning. When Chinese talk, they sound as if they were singing or chanting. It is difficult to say when the language split into different dialects, but today a man from one part of China usually cannot understand a man from another part.

During the Chou dynasty the Chinese written language took form, and it has changed very little since then. Chinese who can read and write can understand one another through writing even though they cannot speak to one another. They can also read things that were written many centuries ago. This helps greatly in learning about the way the ancient Chinese lived. There are many poems and other pieces of literature from the time of Confucius.

Like the Egyptians, the Chinese began writing by drawing pictures of everything they wanted to say.

The difficulty is in learning to read and write. The written language has 40,000 separate characters. It is necessary to know about 3000 in order to be able to read and write. The Chinese never adopted the alphabet, as so many other peoples have.

The Empire. As we have just read, the ruler of Ch'in conquered all of China and ended the Chou dynasty. It is probably from Ch'in that we get the name China. The new ruler took away the power of the nobles and made himself the absolute ruler of all China. This was the end of feudalism and the beginning of the Chinese empire, which lasted until our own century.

During the Ch'in dynasty, roads were built across the country. The Great Wall was begun. It was supposed to protect China from the barbarian tribes to the north.

The Ch'in dynasty was very important, but it did not last long. A young farmer named Liu Chi led a successful revolt against the government and became the new emperor. Because Liu Chi came from the state of Han the new ruling house was known as the Han dynasty. This dynasty ruled until two centuries after the birth of Christ. During this time China grew in area by conquering more territory. In this period the Chinese learned to make paper from the bark of the mulberry tree, hemp, and rags. This was a thousand years before the people of Europe learned to make paper.

> Mention three dynasties of China and an important accomplishment of each.

Chapter 4. REVIEW

Learning to Use New Words

Use each of the following terms in an original sentence, expressing something you have learned in Chapter 4:

peninsula	dynasty	caste
dialect	barbarian	transmigration
Sanskrit	feudal	tribute

Knowing the Important Facts

1. What were the various castes in Ancient India? How did life differ in each of them?
2. Describe the people who conquered the Indus Valley in about 1500 B.C.
3. What is the main religion of the people of India?
4. Where did civilization first develop in China?
5. Name a famous Chinese teacher who lived about 500 years before Christ's birth.

Thinking Through the Facts

1. What were some of the teachings of Confucius which might be valuable today?
2. Describe the religious beliefs of the Hindus. Why has it been possible for people in India to starve with so much cattle around?

3. Do you think Buddha's "Eightfold Plan" would be a helpful guide for you? Which points in his plan do you think are most important?
4. What was the purpose of building the Great Wall? Do you think it would be of no value or of great value in today's world? Why?

Developing a Time Sense

Arrange the following events in the proper time order:
1. Alexander the Great conquers the Indus Valley
2. Aryans invade India
3. Chinese learn to make paper
4. Confucius teaches in China
5. Shang dynasty ends and Chou dynasty begins

Unit ONE *Summary*

I Should Know That...

1. Old Stone Age men were hunters. They invented crude stone tools and discovered uses for fire. New Stone Age men became shepherds and farmers. They learned to sharpen tools by grinding them against stones.
2. The Prehistoric period ended when man learned to write and keep records.
3. Man's advance from the Stone Ages to civilized living began in the river valleys of Asia and northeast Africa.
4. The Egyptians set up one of the first strong nations, ruling a large area. They were craftsmen, builders, and traders.
5. The Babylonians prepared written laws to regulate group living. Other nations of the Near East started alphabetical writing, studied astronomy, established good systems of communication, and spread civilization to other parts of the world.
6. The Hebrews believed in one God, kept this belief alive, and prepared the way for the Redeemer.
7. The Aryans who conquered Northern India developed a village civilization and began the caste system.
8. Buddha taught a way of life which swept across India after his death and became the religion of millions.
9. During the Chou dynasty the Chinese philosopher Confucius taught the people a code of behavior that stressed education, good manners, and tradition.
10. Under the Ch'in dynasty, China was unified and the Great Wall was built to keep out barbarians.

Dates I Should Remember...

3400 B.C.—Menes united Upper and Lower Egypt
1500 B.C.—Aryans invade India
586 B.C.—Hebrews enter Babylonian Captivity
551–479 B.C.—Confucius lived in China

Some Interesting Things To Do

1. Make a scroll. Illustrate it with pictorial signs such as the Egyptians might have used. Continue this record as you study other countries.
2. Look up information on the Seven Wonders of the Ancient World. Draw pictures to illustrate those Wonders you have finished studying.
3. Pretend you are a reporter. Write a newspaper story describing one of the following events: Man's first discovery of fire; Man's first use of the wheel; The completion of the Pyramid of Cheops; The flight of the Hebrews from Egypt; The invasion of India by the Aryans; The building of the Great Wall in China.
4. Check newspapers and magazines, especially the travel section of the Sunday newspaper, and cut out articles and pictures relating to the lands you have just studied.

Books I Should Read...

Brindze, Ruth, *The Story of Our Calendar*
Gere, Frances K., *Boy of Babylon*
Meadowcroft, Enid Lamonte, *The Gift of the River*
Quennell, Marjorie and Charles, *Everyday Life in the New Stone Age*
Tunis, Edwin, *Wheels, A Pictorial History*
The *Holy Bible*. Read the story of creation and the fall of man.

TWO Civilization Comes to Europe

Chapter 5
The People of Ancient Greece

Americans should be especially interested in Europe because our civilization comes mostly from that continent. So far in this book, we have read about people who lived in Africa and Asia. That is because the first civilizations were on those continents. Now our story brings us to Europe and the rise of civilizations there.

5.1 Aegean Civilization

Crete — A Stepping Stone of Civilization. Crete is a large island in the eastern part of the Mediterranean Sea. It is not far from the end of the Greek peninsula, and this peninsula is part of Europe. Crete is also rather close to Southwest Asia and to North Africa, homes of early civilizations. It is not surprising, then, that Crete was a stepping stone by which civilization reached Europe.

Ships from Egypt, Phoenicia, and other civilized lands stopped at Crete. In this way the people of Crete learned the ways of civilization. But the Cretans did not just copy the cultures of their neighbors. They made some additions of their own.

Cretan civilization began to develop when the Egyptians were building the pyramids, about 3000 B.C. By 2000 B.C. the Cretans had great stone palaces with running water and drainage systems. Paved roads went to every part of the island. The people made beautiful pottery and jewelry. They had a form of writing. Cretan ships sailed to every part of the eastern Mediterranean.

The largest city of Crete, Knossos, was captured by warriors from Mycenae, which is on the Greek peninsula. After a time the Cretans drove out the invaders. But the warriors had learned much while they were in Knossos. Soon the people of Mycenae

The scenes of everyday life, painted on Cretan walls, show what a well-developed civilization they had.

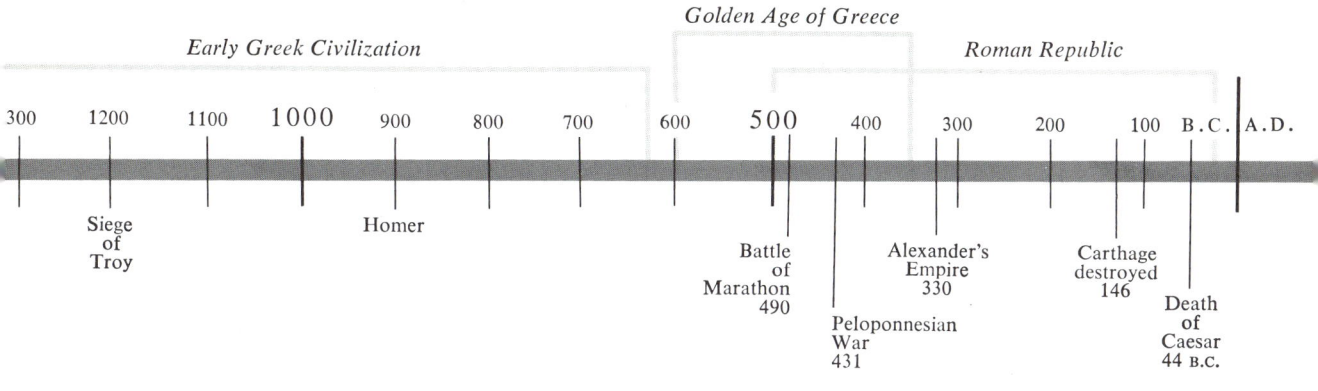

Timeline:
- 1300
- 1200 — Siege of Troy
- 1100
- 1000
- 900 — Homer
- 800
- 700
- 600
- 500 — Battle of Marathon 490
- 400 — Peloponnesian War 431
- 300 — Alexander's Empire 330
- 200
- 100 — Carthage destroyed 146
- B.C. — Death of Caesar 44 B.C.
- A.D.

Periods: Early Greek Civilization · Golden Age of Greece · Roman Republic

were making tools, weapons, and pottery very much like those made in Crete. They also built ships which sailed to many Mediterranean ports. They had a written language which was the same as the one used in Knossos. Mycenae probably had the first civilization on the continent of Europe.

Another city that was very much influenced by Cretan culture was Troy, in Asia Minor.

Knossus, Mycenae, and Troy were the centers of a civilization we call the Aegean civilization. This is because all three cities were on the Aegean Sea, a northeastern arm of the Mediterranean.

Two Famous Stories. We know something about the way people lived in the Aegean civilization about 1200 B.C. because there are two famous stories about this period. These stories are called the *Iliad* and the *Odyssey*.

The *Iliad* tells about a war in which people from Greece conquered the city of Troy. Archaeologists believe that there really was such a war, but it did not happen in the way it is told in the story. The *Odyssey* tells about the adventures of Odysseus, one of the victorious leaders who was returning from the war. The story says that he was blown off his course, and it tells his many adventures. This story is fiction rather than history, but it is interesting to read.

From the *Iliad* and the *Odyssey* we learn much about the people who lived in the Aegean civilization. We learn about their religious beliefs, the kind of weapons they used, the kind of ships they had, the kind of food they ate, and many other details of their daily lives.

The *Iliad* and the *Odyssey* were told in the form of poetry. They were said to have been composed by a man named Homer. Nobody knows who Homer was. For many centuries the stories were not written down.

The people of ancient Greece memorized and recited their songs and legends. Here Greek pupils listen to the story of Greek heroes.

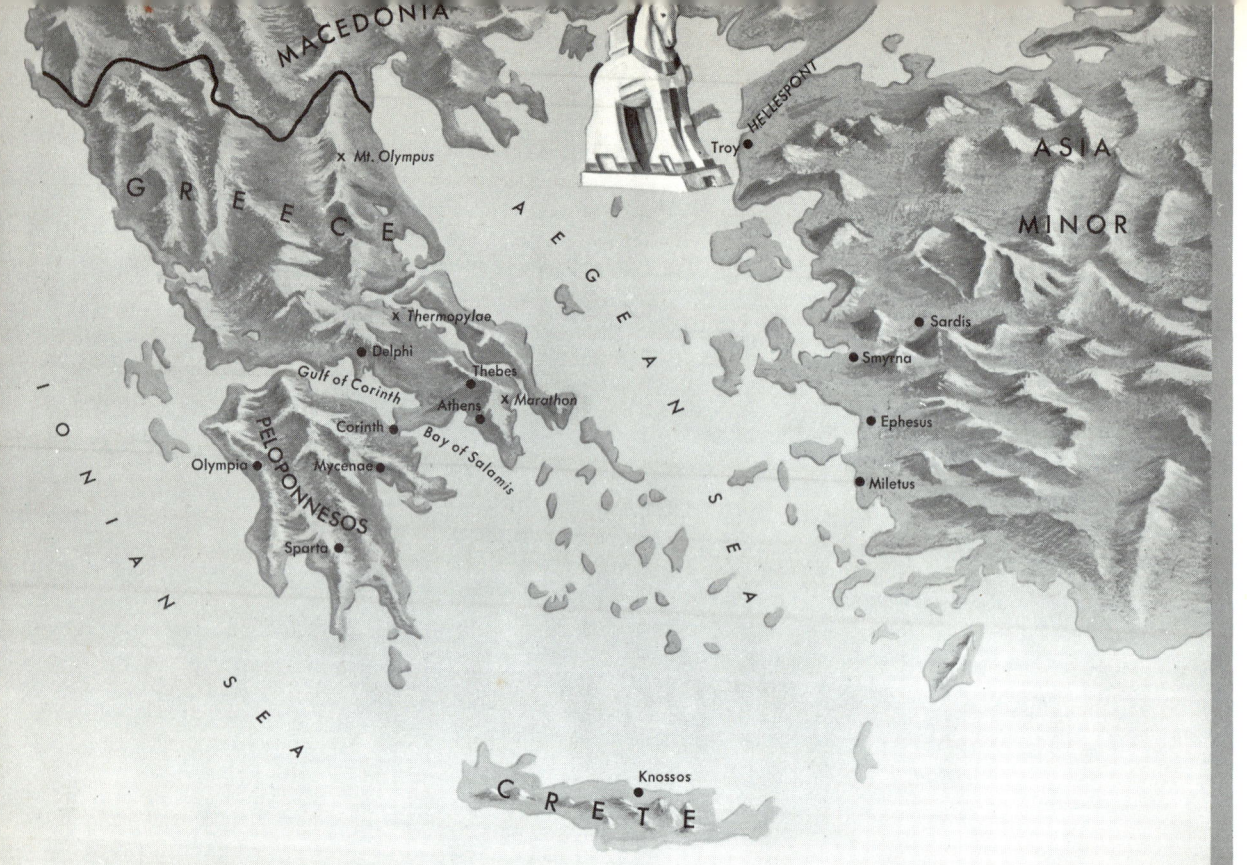

A Land of Bays, Gulfs, and Mountains. In one important way, ancient Greece was different from most of the civilizations we have already read about. With the exception of Phoenicia, all these civilizations developed in river valleys. Greece has no great rivers. It is a rugged land almost surrounded by the sea and cut by many gulfs and bays. The Gulf of Corinth almost cuts Greece in two. There are many mountains. The mountains are not high, but they were hard to cross in the days when most travel was by foot.

In the summer there is not much rain in Greece. Most of the soil is poor. It was not possible for most of the people to make their living by farming, as they did in other early civilizations.

Like the Phoenicians, many of the Greeks took to the sea and became sailors or traders. To help their trade, many Greek cities sent some of their citizens to other lands to start colonies. Some of the colonies were across the Aegean Sea, in Asia Minor. Others were in Sicily, the large island south of Italy. Others were in the southern half of the Italian peninsula. Southern Italy became known as Great Greece. There was even a colony in what is now France.

When we think of the Greek world of 650 B.C., we think not only of the Greek peninsula, but also of all places the Greeks had colonies.

They were memorized and recited. In this way they were handed down from generation to generation.

Aegean Civilization Comes to an End. About 1100 B.C. warlike people from the north moved into Greece and conquered much of the peninsula. They destroyed the city of Mycenae. We do not know very much about the next three or four centuries. There seem to have been many battles, but there was also much peaceful mixing between the invaders and the natives. The two cultures became mixed. Out of it all came what we know as the civilization of ancient Greece.

> Where were Mycenae, Crete, and Troy located? How did their location help the growth of civilization?

5 2 Early Greece

Greece Was Made up of City-States. We have seen the term "city-state" before in this book. A city-state usually contained one large city and the farms surrounding it. It had no higher government over it. It was a small independent country.

Ancient Greece had no united government. It was made up of about eighteen city-states. Often the city-states went to war against each other. In our day, we cannot imagine the city of New York going to war against the city of Philadelphia, or Toledo going to war against Detroit. In ancient Greece such wars were common.

Why did the Greeks fail to have a united country? We have already seen one reason for this. Because of the mountains, bays, and gulfs, each city was cut off from other cities. This made it hard for the cities to unite.

Another reason is that each Greek had a great love for his own city. He wished it to become larger and richer than the other cities. The cities were rivals, and no city wished to give up its independence.

Every colony became a city-state. In addition to the eighteen city-states on the Greek peninsula, therefore, there were also Greek city-states in Asia Minor, Sicily, Italy, and other places.

The Greeks Used the Alphabet. By 650 B.C. the Greeks were using the alphabet. It is believed that the Phoenicians had brought it to them and that the Greeks had changed it a bit to fit their language. After they had

Fighting among one another made the Greeks so weak that it was possible for Alexander the Great to come from the North and conquer them.

The only prize at the Olympic Games, which began in 776 B.C., was a wreath of laurel leaves from a tree sacred to Zeus.

the alphabet, the Greeks wrote about the way they lived. Many of these writings are still in existence. We know much more about the Greeks who lived after 650 B.C. than we know about the ones who lived before that time.

The Greeks Had Many Things in Common. Although Greece was divided into many city-states, the Greeks felt they had many things in common. They spoke and wrote the same language, although each section had some of its own local words. They felt that they were all Greeks no matter what their city or tribe.

The Olympic Games also helped bring the people together. These were held every four years at Olympia in honor of the God Zeus. There were contests in running, wrestling, discus throwing, and many other kinds of sports. There were also contests in oratory, poetry, and drama. Men came to the Olympic Games from every part of Greece and from the colonies. Women were not allowed to take part in the Olympic games or to watch them. If two Greek cities were at war, they declared a truce while the games were on.

Our modern Olympic Games are patterned after those of ancient Greece.

The Greeks Believed in Many Gods. The Greeks believed in many gods and goddesses. Each city had its own god, and there were other gods for all of Greece. The chief god was named Zeus. Apollo was the sun god. Aphrodite was the goddess of beauty and love. Athena was the goddess of wisdom. There were many more. The Greeks believed that the gods and goddesses lived on Mt. Olympus. The gods looked and acted like human beings, but they had much greater power than humans. Each city had a temple where the people offered sacrifices to the gods.

The Greeks also believed in fortune-tellers, who were called oracles. These oracles said they could talk with the gods and thus find out what was going to happen in the future. The oracle at Delphi was thought to be the best. People from all over the Greek world came to see the priestess, who said she could foretell the future. Her prophecies were made in words that were hard to understand. In this way, nobody could ever prove the oracle to be wrong. She could always say that her message had been misunderstood.

1. How do our Olympic Games differ from those of the Greeks?
2. Why did the Greeks develop independent city-states?

5 3
How People Lived in Sparta

Everybody Was the Servant of the Government. Of all the city-states in Greece, the two most important and best known were Sparta and Athens. They were less than a hundred miles apart, but they were different in many ways. First, let us take a look at Sparta, and then we shall take a look at Athens.

Today, we have a long word to describe the kind of government the Spartans had. That word is "totalitarian." The heads of a totalitarian government believe that the people live only to serve the state, or government. This is the opposite of a democracy, in which the government serves the people.

Sparta conquered many of the surrounding city-states. Some of the conquered people were brought to Sparta as slaves. In time, there were more slaves in Sparta than there were Spartans. Slaves took care of the farms and did many other kinds of work.

Spartan slaves called helots produced food for all Sparta. The freedmen devoted their time to military affairs.

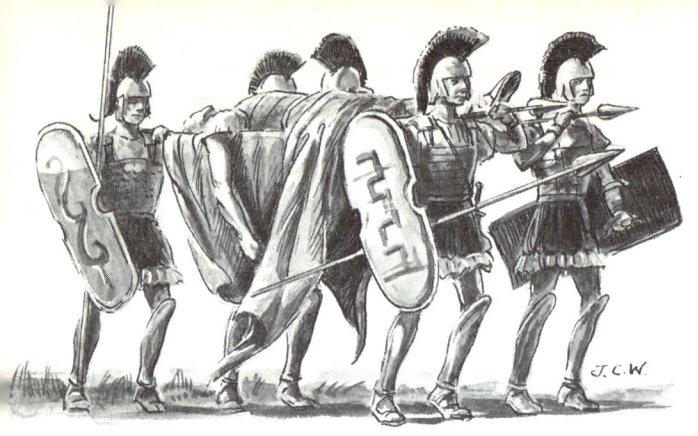

Spartan soldiers were trained to believe that it was noble to die fighting for their country.

Spartan men and boys did not have to work. They gave all their time to being soldiers.

When a Spartan baby was born, it was examined by five judges. If the baby seemed strong and healthy, it was allowed to live. If the baby was crippled or weak, it was left on a mountainside to die. The Spartans believed that a weak or crippled person would

School days. Education in Sparta taught boys to handle weapons and to build strong bodies through exercise.

be of no use to the state. A healthy baby boy would grow up to be a strong soldier. A healthy baby girl would grow up to be a strong woman who would be the mother of soldiers.

Boys Were Trained as Soldiers. When a Spartan boy was seven years old, he was taken from his parents and put in a camp with other boys his age. There he was trained to be a good soldier. He was trained to be absolutely obedient to the laws and customs of Sparta.

Their training was designed to make the boys strong and able to endure hardships and suffering. They swam in the river every day, summer and winter. They went on long marches. They practiced the use of weapons. They slept with only reeds between themselves and the hard ground. They were taught to admire brave men and despise cowards. They never ate rich foods. Usually they had only soup and coarse bread.

If a Spartan boy was caught stealing, he

was beaten severely. He was beaten not because he stole, but because he was caught. There is a story about a boy who stole a fox. When he was in danger of being caught, he put the fox under his cloak. The fox clawed and bit, but the boy did not give any sign that he was suffering. He died of his wounds like a true Spartan.

Spartan girls were trained almost as severely as the boys.

When one Spartan soldier started off to war, his mother handed him his shield and said, "With it or on it." She meant that the boy should either be victorious and come back with the shield on his arm or else he should be carried back on it, dead. It was considered a disgrace to lose a battle and live.

Most Spartans cared little about literature, art, or music. Such things were not considered important.

> Most of the Spartans were soldiers. How did Sparta obtain food and other necessities?

Greek boys had to learn to sing battle songs in honor of their country's heroes. They also had to know well the history of Greece.

54

How People Lived in Athens

Boys of Athens Trained Their Minds. Boys who lived in Athens went to school when they were seven, but they continued to live at home. They learned reading, writing, history, music, and other subjects. They learned the legends and poems of old. When they were older, they learned public speaking. They took part in many sports, but body-training was not all-important as it was in Sparta.

A boy who belonged to a wealthy family had a personal slave called a pedagogue. The pedagogue helped him with his studies, and after his lessons were over, took him to the playground where he could run and wrestle and jump with other boys.

When a boy reached eighteen, he went into the army for two years. After that he became a citizen of Athens. He was free to make his living in any way he chose. He was expected, however, to take part in the government of Athens.

57

All important matters of government were settled in a general assembly of citizens at which all could speak and vote.

Girls were not considered as important as boys. They did not go to school. Their mothers taught them how to sew and cook and keep house.

The Athenians Governed Themselves. Most of the people we have read about were ruled by kings. The Egyptians, for example, had a king called the Pharaoh. The Babylonians, the Persians, the people of India, and the Chinese had kings. These kings had absolute power. This means that the people had to do exactly what the kings told them to do. The kings could put people in prison without a trial and could even put people to death. In other countries the king did not have absolute power. He was guided and advised by a council. He was bound to observe the laws that had been accepted by the people. His power was limited. When people are ruled by a king, we say they have a monarchy.

At one time the people of Athens had a king, but they no longer had one by 650 B.C. By then, the laws for Athens were made by the assembly. Every free man of Athens who was over thirty was allowed to vote.

Most of the men who had important offices in the government were chosen by lot. During his lifetime almost every free man had his turn at holding office. Each man thought it was a great privilege to serve Athens. He served without pay.

Athens was the world's first democracy. *Democracy* is a Greek word that means "rule by the people."

In a perfect democracy every adult is free to live his life as he wishes, and every adult has a voice in the government. Athens was far from being a perfect democracy. Like Sparta, it conquered other city-states and brought many of the people to Athens as slaves. Some historians say that two-fifths of the people living in Athens were slaves. Other historians say that four-fifths of them were slaves. These slaves had no freedom, and they had no voice in the government. Women were not allowed to vote or hold public office, nor were the men who had moved to Athens from other places. Therefore, the number of free men who ruled Athens was small in comparison with the total population.

Even though the democracy was not perfect, Athens is remembered as the first place in which the people ruled themselves.

Athens Was Entirely Different From Sparta. As we look back at ancient Athens, we do not like some of the things we see. Athens conquered surrounding territory and failed to grant the people the same freedom that Athenians had. There were many slaves in Athens, and some of them were treated cruelly. We shall read later that the Athenians put Socrates to death because they did not like his ideas. With all its faults, however, Athens was far ahead of most other states of the time.

The differences between Athens and Sparta were great. The Spartans believed that each person lived only to serve the state. The people had no freedom. The men were forced to be soldiers all their lives. Boys were taken from their parents and trained by the government. Women and girls had to do what they were told. The people were hardy and brave, but they knew little about literature and music and the things that help a man to think intelligently.

The Athenians loved Athens, but they did not think they should live just for the state. They thought that the government should be the servant of the people, not the master. They thought that every free man should have a voice in the government. Athenians thought that each citizen should be free to make his living in the way he wished. The men were good soldiers, but they did not devote their entire lives to being soldiers. Athenians loved music and literature and everything beautiful and fine.

The difference between Sparta and Athens was the difference between a totalitarian government and a democracy. It is a difference still very much in evidence in our world of today.

1. Mention two types of monarchy.
2. What does it mean to say "the government should be the servant of the people, not the master"?

55

The Greeks Defeat Mighty Persia

King Darius Decides to Conquer Greece. The Greek colonies that were founded on the coast of Asia Minor grew into Greek city-states which were called the Ionian cities. King Croesus of Lydia made the Ionian cities part of his kingdom. The people of these cities did not mind this. Croesus was a wise king. He allowed the Ionian cities much freedom, and he protected the cities from their enemies.

In 546 B.C., King Cyrus of Persia conquered Lydia. Then the Ionian cities came under his rule. The people of the Ionian cities did not like this. They planned to revolt against Persia. They sent messengers to Athens, Sparta, and the other Greek cities, asking for help. Sparta refused to help. Athens and several other cities sent ships to help the Greeks of Ionia.

Cyrus died, and his son Darius became

A Greek statesman tricked Xerxes into ordering the return of his ships by sending him false information. The entire Persian fleet was destroyed.

the Persian emperor. Darius crushed the revolt. He was angry and asked who had helped the rebels. When he was told that the Athenians had helped, he said, "The Athenians? Who are they?" He had never heard of them.

Darius determined to crush the Athenians and the other Greeks. He was sure that this would not be very hard to do. Persia was a mighty empire. Greece was small and was not even a united country.

Darius' first attempt to conquer Greece ended in failure. In 492 B.C., he sent a great fleet across the Aegean Sea in the direction of Greece. A storm came up and the fleet was destroyed. This made Darius more determined than ever.

The Athenians Defeat the Persians at Marathon. In 490 B.C., Darius sent an army of 100,000 men to conquer Greece. As the army came close to Athens, the Athenians sent messengers to Sparta to ask for help. The Spartans said they could not come before the moon was full. They sacrificed to Apollo when the moon was full, and they said the god would be angry if they broke this custom. This meant that they could not come for five days. By that time they would be too late.

The Athenians were forced to face the Persians alone on a plain called Marathon. Although they were outnumbered, the Athenians won the battle. The Persians were forced to leave Greece.

The Athenian general knew that the people in Athens would be waiting to hear the news of the battle. He sent a runner named Pheidippides with the news. The runner raced the twenty-two miles of mountain road from Marathon. He gasped to the waiting crowd, "Victory." Then he fell dead.

The Athenian Fleet Saves Greece. The Persians were angry because the Greeks had defeated them. They decided to try again. This time, they took ten years to prepare for the attack. In that time Darius died, and his son Xerxes took his place.

During these ten years, a wise man named Themistocles was one of the leaders in Athens. Themistocles was certain that Athens needed a powerful fleet to protect herself. Under his leadership new warships were built.

In 480 B.C., Xerxes led an army of half a million men toward Greece. A fleet of 1200 ships sailed along the coast near the army. In northern Greece the Persians defeated an army led by King Leonidas of Sparta.

The Persians were now free to march upon Athens. Themistocles urged the people to leave the city. The Athenian ships took the people to the island of Salamis. The Persians marched into Athens and destroyed the city.

The Persian warships sailed into the Bay of Salamis to destroy the Athenian ships. Xerxes sat on a golden throne atop a tall cliff and watched the battle. He was sure that his ships would win.

But the Persian ships were too big and clumsy for the small bay. They got in each other's way when they tried to turn around. The smaller and lighter Athenian ships moved in among them, sinking one after another. Xerxes saw his great fleet defeated and much of it destroyed.

The Persians did not try again to conquer Greece. Tiny Athens, with a little help from the other Greek cities, had defeated a powerful empire.

The Battle of Salamis is one of the important battles of world history. If the Persians had won, they might have destroyed Greek civilization. This could have changed the whole history of the world, including the history of our own United States.

But Persia had been defeated. For a time there was peace. During this time, civilization in Greece reached its greatest height.

> How do you think the course of history would have been affected if Persia had conquered Greece?

56

Great Artists, Thinkers, and Writers of Ancient Greece

Greece Has a Golden Age. When the people of Athens returned to their city after the Battle of Salamis, they found it burned to the ground. Instead of being discouraged, they started to build a new city. They said they would make it the most beautiful city in the world.

The Athenians chose a wise man named Pericles for their leader. He held office for about thirty years. This period is called the Age of Pericles. It is also called the Golden Age of Greece. It was the city-state of Athens that made the age golden.

The Greeks Built Beautiful Temples. Near Athens there was a large supply of stone called marble. In the Age of Pericles this marble was used for statues, buildings, and monuments.

The buildings from which we get most of our knowledge of the beauty of Greek architecture were the temples. Because the Greeks believed that the gods protected their city-states, almost all public buildings were erected in honor of a god. The people did not worship in these temples. Each temple was the home of a god where offerings were brought to be placed before his or her statue.

The statue of Athena inside the Parthenon was forty feet high. The one outside, made of brass, was eighty feet tall.

The most beautiful of all Greek temples was the Parthenon. Pericles appointed the famed sculptor, Phidias, to build this temple on the Acropolis, a hill in the heart of Athens. The Parthenon was built to honor the goddess Athena, and its name means "dwelling of the maiden." The Parthenon had seventeen columns on each side and eight across each end. A band of carved marble extended all around the building just above the columns. The carving pictured stories of the Greek gods.

The Parthenon now stands in ruins, but from its remains and from the ruins of other temples we have been able to learn how the Greeks beautified their columns. A column is a stone post or pillar erected to support a crosspiece. The Greeks improved these plain stone pillars by carving channels down the sides of their columns. Then they placed a stone cushion, called a capital, between the top of the column and the crosspiece. The Greeks used three different styles to make their capitals beautiful. They are called the Ionic, the Doric, and the Corinthian orders.

The Athenians Loved Beauty. The Athenians built a theater on the side of the Acropolis. A half circle was cut out of the hill. Rows of seats were placed in this half circle. Each row of seats was a little higher than the row in front of it. The stage was at the bottom of the hill. In this way, everybody could see the actors. If a person could not afford to buy a ticket to the plays, he was given a ticket. The theater was enjoyed by rich and poor alike.

The Athenians loved beauty, and in the Age of Pericles they were surrounded by beauty. They had beautiful buildings and beautiful statues. They enjoyed great plays. Wealthy Athenians ate and drank from beautiful vases, cups, and bowls.

Greek houses were very plain, but the people did not spend very much time in their houses. The climate was so warm that they spent a great part of the day in the open air. A wealthy man would not build a beautiful home for himself. Instead he would pay for a beautiful building or monument which everyone could enjoy.

Greece Had Famous Writers. We have seen that the people of Athens built beautiful buildings and statues during the Golden Age. This age was also known for its writers. Other Greek cities built theaters like the one at Athens. Great writers wrote plays for these theaters. Serious plays were called tragedies. Lighter plays were called comedies. Plays were written to honor the gods, and they were given as part of a religious festival.

A man named Herodotus traveled through all the countries ruled by Persia. He questioned the people who lived in these countries. He tried to find out what had gone on in the past. He wrote down everything he could learn about the countries he visited. In Egypt, for example, Herodotus saw the great pyramids. They were already about 2500 years old by this time. Herodotus wrote a complete description of the pyramids. Herodotus also wrote the story of the wars between Greece and Persia. He could write much of this from his own memory, because he had fought in these wars. Herodotus is often called the Father of History.

Greece Had Great Thinkers. A man named Socrates lived in Athens during the Golden Age. He carved small statues for a

DORIC   IONIC   CORINTHIAN

living. He was more interested in trying to find the truth, however, than he was in carving statues. He was a lover of wisdom, or a philospher. He was an interesting talker, and he asked questions which made people think. Young and old found pleasure in gathering around him—to argue with him, and, more important, to listen to what he had to say.

Socrates did not believe in the gods and goddesses of the Greeks. His great mind told him that there was one God who created the world and watched over it. He also believed that our souls would continue to live after our death. Many of the people who talked with Socrates came to believe these things also.

Socrates was accused of insulting the gods. He was arrested and condemned to death.

Socrates' goal in life was to train young men to think for themselves and decide what kind of life was worth living.

He was given a cup of poison to drink. He was not afraid to die, because he knew that his soul was immortal. When asked where he would like to be buried, he said: "You cannot bury Socrates. You can bury my body, but you cannot bury me in a grave."

One of the followers of Socrates was a young man named Plato. Plato remembered what Socrates had taught, and he recorded these teachings. He also added some of his own thoughts.

Plato was a pupil of Socrates, and Aristotle was a pupil of Plato. Aristotle was not only a philosopher but also a scientist. He watched nature closely and wrote down what he observed.

Socrates, Plato, and Aristotle all believed in one God. Socrates and Plato believed in an immortal soul. Like other Greeks, however, they continued to worship many gods in public. They came to believe in one God through their thinking, or through reason.

In later days, great Christian thinkers and writers, such as Saint Thomas Aquinas, studied the teachings of these three Greek philosophers.

There Were Many Scientists in Greece. Long before the Golden Age, the Greeks studied the stars and learned much about the shape of the earth. In 585 B.C. a man named Thales discovered a way to tell in advance when an eclipse was going to take place.

Euclid wrote a book about geometry. Much of what Euclid wrote is still used in high school geometry books.

Hippocrates studied the human body. He said that sickness had nothing to do with evil spirits and that cures could not be worked through magic. He discovered many ways to help people. He is called the Father of Medicine.

Athens Was a City of Great Men. Most of the men who have been mentioned here were citizens of Athens, and most of them

In taking the Hippocratic oath, a doctor swears to do his best, and promises not to reveal secrets about a patient's illness.

lived during the Golden Age. These are only a few of the many Athenians who could have been mentioned. Athens was not a large city. There were probably about 200,000 people living there. A person who lived in Athens could not walk along the street without seeing famous writers, sculptors, architects, or philosophers. This was because in Athens people trained their minds, and because they loved beauty and truth.

On the other hand, not a single great thinker or artist or writer came from Sparta. This was because the Spartans trained only the body.

Athens will always be remembered for its Golden Age and for the great men it gave to the world.

1. How did the Athenians show a love of beauty?
2. Describe an Athenian temple.

Gifts of Greece

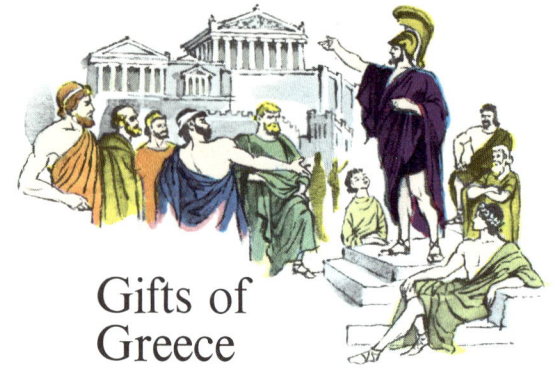

1 The Greeks developed city-states. These were small democracies in which every freeman had a vote and could hold office.

2 They produced great writers. Homer was a famous Greek poet who wrote the *Iliad* and the *Odyssey* which described Greek heroes. Outdoor theaters were popular in Athens showing Greek plays.

3 Artists and sculptors built splendid buildings and temples, such as the Parthenon. They carved beautiful statues to adorn their temples.

4 They spread culture and learning along the Mediterranean and to the countries of western Asia. Teachers, philosophers, and writers spread education wherever the Greeks conquered other nations.

5 7 Greek Ideas Spread Far

The Golden Age Comes to an End. The various Greek city-states worked together when there was danger from Persia, but they quarreled with each other when that danger was over. War broke out between Athens and Sparta. The Athenians were weakened by a plague which had swept through their city. The Spartans captured Athens. This was the end of Athens as a great city. For a time Sparta became the leading city of Greece, but Sparta had been weakened by the fighting. She did not hold her leadership for long.

King Philip Becomes the Ruler of Greece. North of Greece was a region called Macedonia, sometimes known as Macedon. The people of Macedonia were related to the Greeks, but they were not as civilized as the Greeks. A leader named Philip united all the tribes of the region and became the first King of Macedonia. Thus, Macedonia became the first nation of Europe. Today, there is no country of Macedonia. The region is divided among Greece, Yugoslavia, and Bulgaria.

King Philip formed a large army and marched into Greece. After a few battles, he had conquered all of Greece except Sparta. Thus, he united most of the Greek city-states under one government. This was something the Greeks had never been able to do for themselves.

Philip had lived in Greece, and he admired Greek culture. He did not enslave the Greeks, and the city-states kept their democratic local governments. Philip said he wished the help of the Greeks in fighting their old enemy, Persia.

Alexander the Great Conquers an Empire. Before Philip could carry out his plan of conquering Persia, he was killed. His twenty-year-old son, Alexander, became King of Macedonia and Greece. Today we call him Alexander the Great.

Like his father, Alexander admired the Greeks and their culture. He knew the *Iliad* and the *Odyssey*. He had been a pupil of Aristotle.

Alexander wished to carry out his father's plan of conquering Persia. With a large Macedonian and Greek army he invaded Asia Minor. At first he met with little resistance from the Persians.

As you remember, many Greeks lived along the eastern shore of the Aegean Sea. These people formed about one-third of the Greek world. They had long been under Persian rule. They welcomed Alexander as their deliverer. They set up democracies similar to those of Athens and other cities on the Greek Peninsula.

King Darius III of Persia gathered a huge force and met Alexander at Issus, a small

Alexander, with foot soldiers and cavalry, traveled almost 11,000 miles to conquer all the world that was known at the time.

plain at the northeast corner of the Mediterranean Sea. Alexander led his cavalry in a charge, and his foot soldiers followed. Darius turned and fled.

Alexander took most of the land along the eastern end of the Mediterranean, and thus cut the Persian navy from its ports. Then he marched into Egypt where he was again hailed as a deliverer from Persian rule. In Memphis he made sacrifices to the Egyptian gods and was accepted as Pharaoh, or king. He found an excellent harbor, and

The Gordian Knot

This knot was tied to the yoke of an ox cart. The Delphic Oracle declared that whoever could unloose it would rule Asia. Alexander cut it.

made plans for a city to be built there. The city was named Alexandria in honor of him.

Leaving Egypt, Alexander marched across southwest Asia, defeating the Persians in several battles. Babylon welcomed the conqueror, and Alexander made sacrifices to the gods of the Babylonians. Susa, the capital of Persia, fell without a battle.

Alexander's men had been away for many years, and they wanted to go home, but he pressed on into India. He conquered everything as far as the Indus River. He made Babylon his capital, and there he died in 323 B.C. He was not quite 33 years old.

The Macedonian Empire. The Persian Empire was the largest ever known in its time. Alexander's empire was even bigger. Alexander conquered the entire Persian Empire and part of India as well. He also ruled Greece and his own Macedonia. His empire covered parts of three continents. With the exception of China, Rome, Carthage, and part of India, Alexander ruled all the civilized lands of the world.

Alexander wished to make his empire strong so that it would last for centuries. In this world-state he wished all men to live as brothers. He encouraged his officers to marry women from Asia. He welcomed

More than 500,000 rolls of papyrus—the books of ancient times—were stored in the library at Alexandria.

Asians into his army where they mixed freely with his soldiers from Europe. He adopted Persian court customs and on state occasions he wore Persian robes. He did this to show the people of Asia that he respected their customs and was not trying to force Greek and Macedonian ways upon them. He knew that people of different cultures could learn much from each other.

Through Alexander, Greek culture was spread through much of the world. He built new cities along trade routes, and the people who lived in these cities were Greeks and Macedonians. Greek architects, sculptors, and teachers came into these cities.

Alexandria, Egypt, was the greatest of these cities. It took the place of Athens as the world's center of learning. It became famous for its library. It also had a university where Greek scholars, poets, and men of science taught.

Alexander's dream of a lasting empire did not come true. He left no will and named no successor. His generals fought each other for supreme power. Then the empire was divided into three parts, all ruled by Macedonians. Three dynasties resulted: the Antigonids of Macedonia, the Seleucids of Asia, and the Ptolemies of Egypt.

In all three regions Greek ideas continued to spread, and Greek was the language in which the people of different regions spoke to each other. The Greeks had been conquered, but Greek culture conquered the world.

1. How did Alexander the Great treat conquered peoples?
2. Did his behavior toward conquered peoples fit in with his dream of a world-state?

Chapter **5. REVIEW**

Learning to Use New Words

Use each of the following terms in an original sentence expressing something you have learned in Chapter 5:

truce	monarchy
oracle	architecture
totalitarian	philosopher
democracy	gulf
pedagogue	city-state

Knowing the Important Facts

1. What can we learn from the *Iliad* and the *Odyssey?*
2. Which invaders took Cretan customs and ideas back to their homeland?
3. Describe three contributions made by great artists, writers, or scientists of Ancient Greece.
4. Who were the greatest philosophers in Ancient Greece?
5. What was the contribution to world history made by Alexander the Great?

Thinking Through the Facts

1. Why was the Aegean civilization important?
2. Compare the early education of a Spartan boy with that of an Athenian boy. How does your education differ from that of either Spartan or Athenian youngsters?
3. Discuss the contributions of the following Greeks: Socrates, Aristotle, Plato, Herodotus, Euclid, and Hippocrates.
4. Why didn't Greece ever become a united country? What helped produce some spirit of unity among the separate city-states?
5. What is the place in history of each of the following: Homer, Darius, Xerxes, Pericles, Alexander?

Developing a Time Sense

Arrange the following events in the proper time order:
1. The Battle of Salamis
2. Age of Pericles
3. The writing of the *Iliad* and the *Odyssey*
4. The Battle of Marathon
5. Alexander conquers most of known world

Chapter 6
The People of Ancient Rome

Civilization spread from Egypt and Southwest Asia to the lands surrounding the Aegean Sea. One of these lands was Greece. Now we shall see how civilization came to the city of Rome, in Italy. It is the story of a little village that grew into a great city and ruled a great empire on three continents. We shall read how the people of ancient Rome took this civilization to other lands.

6·1

Early Rome

There Were Three Important Groups Living in Italy. When you look at the map, you will see that Italy looks like a boot sticking out into the Mediterranean Sea.

The Etruscans learned arts and crafts from the Greeks and passed them on to the Romans. Their pottery is among the most valuable in the world.

Like Greece, Italy is surrounded on three sides by the sea. Halfway down the boot, near the west coast, is the city of Rome.

About 800 B.C., there were three important groups of people in Italy. These were the Greeks in southern Italy, the Etruscans in the north, and the Latins in central Italy.

The Greeks had established colonies in southern Italy and in Sicily. These colonies developed into city-states similar to those in Greece. The people built temples with large columns and many beautiful statues. They had theaters and schools.

The Etruscans of northern Italy are a mystery to us. We do not know exactly where they came from or how they became civilized. They did metalwork, and they made pottery. They lived in cities and had large buildings. They had a written language, but we have not yet found out how to read their writings.

Between the civilized Greeks and the civilized Etruscans lived the less civilized Latins. They had no written language, and they did not know how to make beautiful things. They lived in crude houses and kept small farms.

One tribe of Latins lived in a village overlooking the Tiber River about fifteen miles from the sea. This village was Rome. In 800 B.C., Rome was a village of crude houses and dirt streets. Chickens, ducks, and geese ran through the streets. In that year no one would have thought that Rome would some day rule a large part of the world.

The Romans Learned From Their Neighbors. The Etruscans conquered Rome and seem to have governed the city for about two hundred years. The Romans learned many things from their conquerors. From the Etruscans they learned to work with metal. Also from the Etruscans they learned how to build the arch. This brought about a new way of building temples and palaces. The Etruscans also taught the Romans how to organize an army. It is possible that the Romans took some of their gods from the Etruscans.

Greeks from southern Italy sailed up the Tiber River to trade with the Romans. From these Greek traders the Romans learned how to use coins. The Greeks also taught the Romans how to build ships. One of the most important things the Greeks taught the Romans was the alphabet. The Romans used letters not only for writing but also for counting. You have probably learned the Roman numerals.

The Greek traders told the Romans about the gods that were worshipped in Greece. The Romans began to worship many of the same gods, but they gave the gods different names. The Greeks called their chief god Zeus, and the Romans called him Jupiter.

Although the Romans borrowed many ideas from the Etruscans and Greeks, they also clung to many things in their own culture. They kept their own language for example.

Rome Becomes a Republic. We do not know how the Romans rid themselves of Etruscan rule. We do know that in 509 B.C., the Romans set up a new kind of government. This government was a republic.

Roman Government

Although Rome was ruled by two consuls, in times of war the Senate chose a dictator to make fast decisions. The two consuls were chosen because the Romans did not want any one person to have too much power. Many features of the Roman republic are found in our own system of government.

In forming their republic, the Romans did not want any man to have too much power over them. At the head of the government there was not one man, but two men. These men were called consuls. One consul could not do anything unless he asked the other. Thus, each consul was a check upon the other one. The consuls were elected by the free men of Rome. If the Romans did not like what the consuls did, they could elect new consuls at the end of the year.

The Romans also had a Senate. The Senate had 300 members. The senators were elected by the people. We must remember, however, that only a small number of Romans were allowed to vote. The senators advised the consuls and helped them rule.

We read in the last chapter that when people rule themselves they have a democracy. Athens was a democracy. The Roman Republic was a democracy, too, but it was different from Athens. In Athens, the free men gathered together and made their own laws. In Rome, the free men elected certain men who made their laws for them.

Our United States is a republic. The voters elect the head of the government, and they elect the men who make the laws. Our government is different in many ways from the Roman Republic, but the idea of having a republic goes back to ancient Rome. Some of the words we use in government also come from Rome. We have a Senate, for example.

Dictators Ruled in Times of Trouble. In time of war, the Romans needed someone who could act quickly. At such a time, the Senate elected a dictator. The dictator could rule as he thought best, and everybody had to obey him. At the end of six months, however, he had to give up his office.

The Common People Gain More Power. When we read about Athens, we saw that it was not a perfect democracy. There were many people who were not allowed to vote or hold public office.

This was also true of Rome in the early days of the republic. The people were divided into two classes, the patricians and the plebeians. The patricians were the nobles, or the upper class. They were descended from the people who had first founded Rome. The plebeians were the common people, or the lower class.

The patricians kept control of the government. They were the only ones allowed to vote. Only patricians could become consuls or senators.

The plebeians complained that they were not being treated fairly. "We do all the hard work," they said. "We pay a large share of the taxes, and we do most of the fighting in time of war. Yet, we receive little in return. We are not allowed a voice in the government. We can be put in prison or sold as slaves if we are not able to pay our debts. We are not even allowed to marry patricians."

Cincinnatus

The Romans liked to tell the story of Cincinnatus. Rome was being attacked by an enemy and was in great danger. The Senate voted to make Cincinnatus the dictator. The messengers rushed off to find Cincinnatus. They found him plowing his fields on his little farm outside Rome. Cincinnatus hurried into Rome. He took charge of the government and directed the armies. In sixteen days he defeated the enemy. He was a great hero, and he could have received many honors. He also could have been the dictator for five and a half more months. When some men have great power, they do not like to give it up. But Cincinnatus cared nothing about honors and power. He had done his duty. He had saved Rome from its enemies. He turned the government back to the consuls and the senate. He went back to finish his plowing.

A committee of ten officials drew up laws which had to be approved by the people. We also elect officials to write our laws.

For a long time the patricians paid no attention to these complaints. Then the plebeians decided to rebel. Many of them left the city and went to live on a nearby hill. The patricians saw that they could not get along without the plebeians. There was no one to do the hard work or to fight in the army. The patricians had to give in.

The plebeians were given the right to elect men called tribunes. If the senators tried to pass a law which the plebeians did not like, a tribune could stop them. He did this by shouting "veto," which means "I forbid."

Little by little, the plebeians won more rights. They were allowed to marry patricians. Then a law was passed which said that at least one of the consuls had to be a plebeian. The plebeians won the right to vote. They also won the important right to become senators.

As the plebeians won more and more rights, Rome became more a government of the people. In other words, it became more democratic.

The Laws Are Written. In the days when the patricians controlled Rome, there were no written laws. A patrician could say the law meant anything he wished it to mean. The patricians sometimes used the law to imprison plebeians and to take away their property.

When the common people gained more power, they said that the laws must be written down so that everyone would know what they were. The laws were carved on twelve large stone tablets. These tablets were set up in the market place, which was called the forum. Now it was possible for everybody, both patricians and the common people, to know exactly what the laws said. School boys had to memorize the laws on the twelve tablets.

1. How did the common people of Rome gain more power?
2. Why are written laws important?

6 2

Rome Conquers the World

The Romans Unite All Italy. Rome was one of several city-states in Italy, just as Athens was one of many city-states in Greece. Unlike the Greeks, however, the Romans were able to unite the people of Italy.

Why were the Romans able to unite Italy, while the Greeks were unable to unite Greece? If you will look at a map of Italy, you will see one very important reason. You remember that the mountains of Greece divided the country into little sections. Now look at Italy, and see where the mountains are. To the north of Italy are the high mountains called the Alps. These mountains separate Italy from the rest of Europe. In Italy, there is one large mountain range, the Apennines. These mountains run north and south and are near the Adriatic Sea. Between the mountains and the Mediterranean Sea there is a large region that is rather flat. This region has hills, such as the seven hills of Rome, but there are no high mountains. Most of the people of Italy lived in this flat section. It was easier for the people of Italy to unite simply because their country was not divided into little sections as Greece was.

When Rome was a city-state, it was in danger from the other Latin tribes and from the Etruscans. The Romans saw that they had to conquer or be conquered. Roman armies went forth first to the nearby tribes and then to farther places. Some tribes and cities were willing to join Rome as friends and allies. Others had to be conquered. By 265 B.C., all of Italy had come under Roman rule.

Most of the people in Italy were content under Roman rule. The city-states had been fighting each other, and there had been much suffering and bloodshed. Now, the Romans brought an end to this fighting. The Romans also protected the people against enemies from outside Italy. The people were still allowed to elect the chiefs in their villages as well as the rulers of the republic.

Rome Destroys Carthage. We read in Chapter Two that the Phoenicians founded the city of Carthage on the northern coast of Africa. At first Carthage was a city-state, but like Rome, Carthage extended its rule farther and farther. Soon the Carthaginians held land on both sides of the Mediterranean Sea, as the map shows. They also held the islands of Sardinia and Corsica, which are close to Italy. They held half of Sicily, which is the island south of Italy.

Carthage and Rome grew into the two most powerful cities in this part of the world. They became great rivals.

Rome fought three wars with Carthage. These are called the Punic Wars. The wars began in 264 B.C. In the first war the Romans drove the Carthaginians from the island of Sicily. When the war was over, the people of Sardinia and Corsica revolted against Carthage. All three islands then became Roman territory.

During the journey across the Alps, Hannibal lost almost half of his men and all of the elephants.

A great general fought in the second Punic War. He was Hannibal, the Carthaginian. Hannibal formed a large army in Spain. He had 50,000 foot soldiers, 9,000 horsemen, and 37 elephants. Hannibal led this army across Spain and France and then across the snow-covered Alps into Italy. Only a very great leader could have done this. The Romans were amazed and frightened when they heard that Hannibal was in Italy. He remained there for sixteen years. At one time he brought his men to the gates of Rome. He was never able to capture Rome, however.

Meanwhile, Roman soldiers were fighting in North Africa. The city of Carthage was in danger. Hannibal was called home to protect the city, but he was not able to save it. The Romans captured Carthage, and the war was over. Carthage gave up her possessions in Spain, and she lost most of her power.

There was peace for fifty-three years. Then war broke out again. This time the Romans destroyed the city of Carthage. They put salt on the ground where the city had been so that nothing would grow there. Rome took all the territory that had belonged to Carthage. All the land surrounding the western end of the Mediterranean Sea now belonged to Rome.

Rome Becomes Master of the Mediterranean. While Rome was fighting Carthage, she was also fighting countries at the eastern end of the Mediterranean. The Romans conquered Macedonia and Greece. They now ruled the land where the first great civilization of Europe had developed. The Romans extended their sway over Asia Minor, Phoenicia, and Palestine. Egypt allied herself with Rome, and later became a Roman province. In time Rome controlled the eastern end of the Mediterranean just as she did the western end.

People sometimes said that the Mediterranean Sea was "a Roman lake." The sea is huge. Except for the oceans, it is the biggest body of water in the world. But it was completely surrounded by lands either controlled by, or allied with, Rome.

We sometimes hear it said that Rome ruled the world. This means that she ruled most of the world that was known to the Romans. They did not know what, if anything, lay beyond the Atlantic Ocean. Most of Africa was a mystery. The Romans knew that there were people in India and China, but only a very few Romans had visited these faraway lands. To the Romans, the world centered about the Mediterranean Sea. And the Romans controlled that world.

East Meets West. The lands around the Mediterranean developed a civilization which we call Western civilization. This civilization developed in Greece, and later the Romans carried it to every part of their vast empire. Meantime, other civilizations were developing in India and China.

After Alexander the Great conquered Greece, he went into Asia and conquered the Persian Empire. Then he marched into India as far as the Indus River and added part of northern India to his empire. Alexander's empire broke up soon after his death, but he left many Greeks and Macedonians in Asia. Some of them were quite close to the borders of India. There was trade back and forth between the people of India and the Greeks near their borders. Each learned something from the other. Statues made in India, for example, began to look more like Greek statues.

It might be said that Alexander's invasion of India was the first important meeting between people of the East and people of the West.

Alexander did not get to China, but there was trade between China and India, and so it is possible that the Chinese learned something about Western civilization from the Indians.

Trade Between India and the Roman Empire. After Alexander's time, trade between India and the West grew rapidly. Roman ships sailed from Egypt to India and back. The round trip usually took a little less than a year. In addition to the ships, many caravans traveled the various land routes to the empire. It took much longer to make the trip by land.

Roman merchants sold the Indians precious metals, wine, pottery, glassware, and silverware. Indians sold the Romans drugs, pearls, silks, muslins, and spices. Sometimes the Romans paid for Indian goods with coins. Large hoards of Roman coins found in southwest India show that there was a very thriving trade with Rome.

The Silk Trade With China. Trade between the Roman Empire and China was not as large as that between the Empire and India. This was because China was so much farther away. A large amount of Chinese silk did find its way into the Roman markets, however. This silk was usually taken by land caravans from China to India. In India the silk was put on Roman ships and taken to Egypt. There it was carried by land to the Mediterranean Sea where it was again put on ships. The goods changed hands every time they were transferred. Few Chinese ever got to Rome and few Romans visited China.

There Were Two Kinds of Civilization in the Roman Lands. When the Romans conquered the eastern end of the Mediterranean they conquered people whose civilization was older than the civilization of the Romans. You remember that Alexander the Great had spread Greek civilization throughout this region. Most of the people spoke Greek. They had Greek laws. They read Greek literature. They admired Greek statues. This part of the world kept its Greek civilization even after the Romans conquered it.

At the western end of the Mediterranean

Taxes were paid in money or products. Tax-collectors were businessmen who paid the government for the right to collect taxes.

the Romans destroyed Carthage and its civilization. The Roman, or Latin civilization spread through this region. In North Africa, Italy, Spain, and later in France and England, the people spoke the Latin language. The more educated people read Latin literature. Their buildings looked like the buildings in Rome. This became the Latin part of the world.

We see, then, that there were two kinds of civilization in Roman lands—Latin civilization in the West and Greek civilization in the East.

1. Why did Rome destroy Carthage?
2. Describe the extent of Roman trade with the East.

6 3
Romans Lose Their Self-Government

Life in Rome Begins to Change. Early Rome was a city of farmers. Almost all the people made their living by farming or raising sheep. Cows, sheep, ducks, and geese often walked through the dirt streets. The people worked hard all day long. They lived in crudely built houses with dirt floors. They had little beauty in their lives.

Life began to change for the Romans when they became the rulers of all Italy. Life changed even more when they became the rulers of the world.

All the lands that were ruled by Rome were taxed; therefore, great amounts of money poured into Rome. Much of this money was used to erect new public buildings. Many of the streets were paved. When the Roman soldiers conquered the Greek cities they brought many Greek statues to Rome. These statues were placed in the public squares and public buildings.

There was also a great change in the way people made their living. The Romans built paved roads through most of their lands. Almost all these roads ended at Rome. "All roads lead to Rome," was a common saying. People in other parts of the world used these roads to travel to Rome. Many Romans made their living buying and selling to these visitors. These Romans became merchants. Some plebeian families who had become powerful joined with the patricians to form a group called "the new nobility." Members of the new nobility sought out public office, and the number of public officials increased.

The merchants and public officials did not have to work all day as the farmers did. They had more time to enjoy life. The Romans built theaters like the ones in Greece. They read Greek poetry and history. They talked about the ideas of the great Greek thinkers. Rome had changed greatly since the days when it was a little farming village. Now, it was a large city with paved streets, and large public buildings, and beautiful monuments.

Some People Became Very Wealthy. As Rome became more and more powerful, some of her people became wealthy. Merchants made a great deal of money by selling supplies to the army in time of war. Army officers brought back many treasures from the provinces.

The rich people built magnificent houses. These houses had baths which were almost

The Romans added the use of concrete and the arch to what they had learned from the Greeks to build the beautiful city of Rome.

as large as our swimming pools. Public baths, which were actually clubs, attracted many Romans. The water in them was usually heated. Rich Romans spent hours in these warm baths. They had slaves to do all their work. When they traveled, they were carried in litters by slaves, or they rode in chariots.

The wealthy Romans enjoyed many pleasures and did little work to make up for their hours of play. They became soft and lazy. Many of them did not come by their wealth honestly. They grew more and more evil.

Most Romans Were Very Poor. Some of the wealthy Romans owned large farms. They had many slaves on these farms. The slaves plowed the fields and took care of the crops. They did all the other work on the farm.

The men who owned small farms did not own any slaves. They had to do all the work themselves. They had to charge higher prices for their grain and fruit. They found it difficult to make a living. Many of them had to sell their farms to the rich landowners.

A man who had to sell his farm usually took his family into the city. When he got there, he found that it was almost impossible to find work. Most of the work which had once been done by free men was now done by slaves.

Soon there were thousands of poor families in Rome. They lived in miserable dwellings. When they could not find work, they begged.

The People Are Given Free Bread and Free Entertainment. As the slaves continued to replace the free workers, the wealthy

One of the amphitheaters where Romans went to see gladiators struggle and even kill each other. It held about 80,000 people.

slave-owners grew concerned. They were afraid that the poor people of Rome would begin to envy the easy lives of the rich. They knew that this would lead to serious trouble.

The wealthy and powerful men of Rome began to give free bread to the poor people. Then, they decided that this was not enough, and they began to provide free entertainment. The people gathered in places called amphitheaters. An amphitheater looks very much like a football stadium. The shows held in the amphitheaters were very cruel. Sometimes two athletes, called gladiators, would fight each other. Usually the fight went on until one of the gladiators was killed. Sometimes people from the conquered countries were brought in to fight lions, tigers, and other wild animals. These people were usually killed by the animals.

The common people became so accustomed to receiving free bread and free entertainment that they began to think that they had a right to these things. Some men even refused to work when they had a chance. "Work is for slaves," they said. "We are free Roman citizens and do not have to work."

We can see that something had happened to the Romans since the days when they had been hard-working farmers. They had become lazy. This was true of both the rich Romans and the poor ones.

The People Sell Their Votes. The politicians of Rome saw opportunity for themselves in the people's desire for free bread and free entertainment. They spent large sums of money feeding and entertaining the poor. In return, they asked the people to vote for them.

In a democracy it is important that the people think carefully before they vote. They should learn as much as possible about the men who are running for office. They should vote for the man they think will give them the best government.

The Romans no longer did this. They voted for the man who provided the best entertainment. As a result, many unworthy men were elected to office. These men took bribes and stole money that belonged to the government. The people did not seem to care.

Many years before, the common people of Rome had struggled hard to gain a voice in the government. Now, their descendants were selling their votes for bread and entertainment.

The Gracchi Brothers Try to Help the People. There were some men in Rome who were very much worried about the way things were going. They thought that the idea of free bread and free entertainment was bad for the country as well as for the people. They believed that everyone should have the chance to earn a living.

Two of the men who felt this way were the brothers Tiberius and Gaius Gracchus. Tiberius became a tribune. He had a law passed which would provide small farms for the men who had no work. Many Romans were opposed to this law. There were riots and fights in the streets. Tiberius lost his life before his law could go into effect.

Gaius Gracchus tried to carry out his brother's program. Gaius also wished the government to build roads and public buildings to provide jobs for those who had no work. Gaius, too, lost his life.

When people are not able to rule themselves, they soon have someone ruling them. This happened in Rome. A general named Sulla had himself appointed "permanent Dictator." This meant that he did not have to give up his office at the end of six months as all the previous dictators had done. Sulla ruled as he pleased and paid little attention to the Senate. Self-government in Rome was coming to an end.

Julius Caesar Becomes Ruler of Rome. Julius Caesar was born in Rome about 100 years before the birth of Our Lord. He was very popular with the people, and he was elected to many offices. He provided many free shows, as did other men who wished to be elected.

Caesar was made governor of the Roman province of Iberia, now known as Spain. North of his province was the country which was then known as Gaul. Today, we call it France. The Gauls were fierce fighters and had never been conquered by the Romans. Caesar feared they planned to attack his province. He decided to conquer them. The war against the Gauls lasted for many years. Caesar was victorious, and Gaul became a Roman province.

Caesar became even more popular with the people of Rome when they learned that he had conquered the Gauls. Some of the senators thought that Caesar was becoming too popular. They ordered him to leave his army and come back to Rome. Because Caesar feared that his enemies in Rome might kill him or put him in prison, he took his army to Rome with him. He led his army to the edge of his province. The boundary of the province was a little stream called the Rubicon. He led his army across the Rubicon. He had disobeyed the Senate. Now, he could not turn back. Today when someone makes a very important decision from which

Caesar knew that crossing the Rubicon River would be taken as a declaration of war by the senators in Rome.

he cannot turn back, we say, "He has crossed the Rubicon."

First Caesar defeated his enemies in Rome, and then he defeated his enemies in the provinces. After that, the Senate appointed him dictator for life. Caesar had absolute power over Rome and all the lands ruled by Rome.

Caesar Proved to be a Good Ruler. If the Romans had to be ruled by a dictator, Julius Caesar was probably the best man for the job. He proved to be a wise and just ruler. He set about making the government better and making things better for the people. He insisted that the governors treat the provinces justly. He gave land to needy families. He lowered taxes. He planned to send many poor Roman families to the provinces where they could make a new start in life. He erected many new public buildings which would improve Rome and also give work to the jobless. He reduced the number of people who were fed by the government.

Julius Caesar introduced the Egyptian calendar into Rome after he made some changes in it. He introduced the idea of leap year—an extra day every four years. He named one of the months, July, for himself.

Caesar Is Murdered. Julius Caesar did not have time to do all the things he wished. One day, when he entered the Senate chamber, a group of men came up to him. They pretended that they wished to talk with him. Suddenly, they drew their knives and stabbed him to death.

Why did these men kill Caesar? Some of them were his enemies; they killed him because they wished to gain control of Rome.

Strangely enough, some of the men who killed Caesar liked him, and thought he was a good ruler. These men believed in democracy and self-government. They did not like the idea of having a dictator. They thought that if they killed Caesar the people would again control the government.

These men were mistaken. Romans never regained their self-government. The Roman Republic became the Roman Empire.

1. How did the Gracchi brothers hope to help the people?
2. What were the effects of giving the people free bread and the circus?

Chapter 6. REVIEW

Learning to Use New Words

Use each of the following terms in an original sentence, expressing something you have learned in Chapter 6:

republic	province
consul	chariot
patrician	amphitheater
plebeian	dictator
tribune	caravan

Knowing the Important Facts

1. Briefly describe Roman rule during the Republic.
2. What were some reasons the Romans were able to unite Italy?
3. What cities were involved in the Punic Wars?
4. Describe the political conditions which led to the end of the Roman Republic.
5. What were some of the contributions which Caesar made to the Roman civilization?

Thinking Through the Facts

1. Why were the Punic Wars important to Rome and western civilization?
2. How did the Romans manage to make loyal allies of the people they conquered?
3. Explain the following expressions:
   "All roads lead to Rome"
   "Rome's great gift to the world was the art of government"
   "to cross the Rubicon"
   "the Mediterranean is a Roman lake"

Developing a Time Sense

Arrange the following events in the proper time order:
1. All of Italy is united under Roman rule
2. Etruscans conquer and govern Rome
3. Republican form of government is set up by Romans
4. Julius Caesar becomes ruler of Rome.
5. The beginning of the Punic Wars

Unit TWO *Summary*

I Should Know That . . .

1. The Aegeans built one of the first civilizations that centered on sea trade.
2. The Greek city-states set up colonies and trading posts along the Mediterranean coast and soon controlled the commerce of the seas.
3. Greek city-states had close cultural ties but they never united into one country.
4. Alexander the Great united Macedonia, Greece, and the Persian Empire. His conquests brought Greek customs and ideas into western Asia.
5. Rome developed a republican government in which the wealthy people had control.
6. The Punic Wars determined that western civilization would be centered in Rome rather than North Africa.
7. The Roman Empire preserved and spread much of the culture which is considered western.
8. Rome made great contributions in government, law, architecture and road building.

Dates I Should Remember . . .

490 B.C.—Battle of Marathon
460–429 B.C.—Age of Pericles
265 B.C.—Rome unifies Italy
264–146 B.C.—Punic Wars
44 B.C.—Death of Julius Caesar

Some Interesting Things to Do

1. Bring to class pictures of national buildings, such as the Lincoln Memorial, which show the influence of Greek architecture.
2. Make a chart showing the Greek and Roman gods who represented the following: god of the sky, the sun-god, goddess of wisdom, messenger of the gods, goddess of love, god of war.
3. Choose some high spots from the history of Greece and Rome and picture these scenes in drawings.
4. Read some of the myths of Greece and Rome. You may enjoy reading "Horatio at the Bridge" by Macaulay.
5. Draw a map of the lands around the Aegean and Mediterranean Seas. Locate Crete, Troy, Athens, Sparta, Bay of Salamis, Marathon.

Books I Should Read

The *Iliad* and the *Odyssey* of Homer, as told by Jane Werner Watson
Regina Tor, *Getting to Know Greece*
Sam Epstein, *The First Book of Italy*
Caroline Dale Snedeker, *A Triumph for Flavius*

THREE   The Roman Empire

Chapter 7
A New Government for Rome

The Roman Republic had united the entire Mediterranean world under her leadership. The people had a large amount of self-government. Slowly, the people lost their self-government. When Julius Caesar became head of the Roman government, he was really a dictator, although he never called himself that. Caesar was murdered. Some of the men who plotted the killing hoped that after Caesar was dead, self-government would return to Rome. But it did not. Rome was no longer a republic; it was now an empire.

7.1 The Beginnings of the Roman Empire

The Emperor Augustus. Octavius was the nephew of Julius Caesar and also his adopted son. In his will Julius Caesar ordered that Octavius should succeed him as ruler of the Roman world. Octavius was only eighteen years old when Caesar died. For a time he ruled with two other men. In the year 31 B.C., Octavius became the sole ruler of Rome.

Octavius knew that the Romans did not want their government to be changed. He made no attempt to have himself called a king. However, the Senate gave Octavius the name Augustus, which means "honored." Before this the word had been used only for the gods. Octavius liked the name and used it all the time. We call him the Emperor Augustus. Under his rule, the Roman Republic came to an end, and Augustus was, in fact, the first ruler of the Roman Empire. Augustus ruled wisely, and the people of Rome scarcely realized that their republic had come to an end.

How the Provinces Were Governed. Most of the land ruled by Rome was divided into provinces. The provinces, in turn, were divided into dioceses. These provinces were ruled in different ways. Sometimes, Rome allowed the various lands to keep their own form of government, provided this government did nothing contrary to the wishes of the central government in Rome.

The most common way of governing a province was through a governor. In the

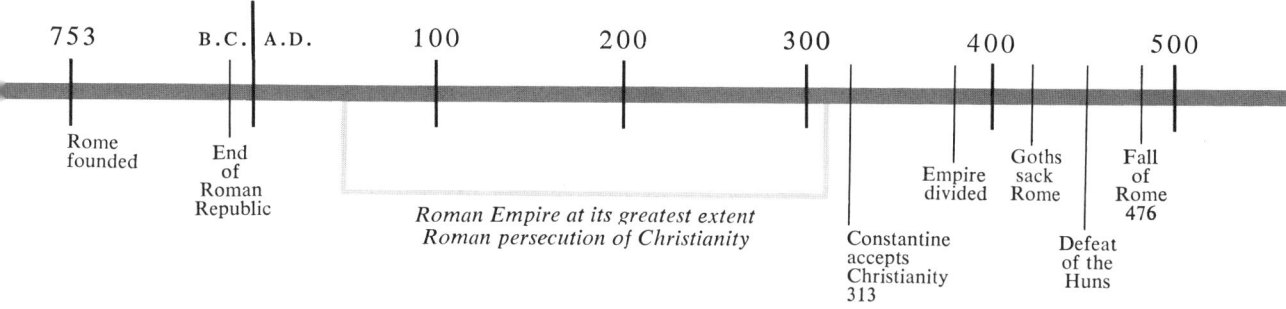

```
753        B.C. A.D.   100         200         300         400         500
 |           |    |      |           |           |           |           |
Rome       End of              Roman Empire at its greatest extent   Empire    Goths   Fall
founded    Roman              Roman persecution of Christianity      divided   sack    of
           Republic                                                            Rome    Rome
                                                              Constantine              476
                                                              accepts           Defeat
                                                              Christianity      of the
                                                              313               Huns
```

days of the Roman Republic, the governors were appointed by the Senate. Emperor Augustus appointed about half the governors himself and allowed the Senate to appoint the other half. The governor had almost as much power as a king, although he had to answer to Rome for his actions. He brought his own officials with him, and he had an army to see that his orders were carried out. The dioceses had lesser officials over them. These officials were under the control of the governor.

The "Roman Peace." Even though Roman rule had its faults, there were many good things about it. One of the best features was the Pax Romana, or "Roman Peace." This peace began in the reign of Augustus and lasted for about two hundred years. Augustus decided that Rome ruled enough territory and should not try to conquer any more. Instead, he said, Romans should use their time and energy for improving life within the Empire.

Because the Romans ruled the entire Mediterranean world, they could also bring about peace inside the empire. Before the Romans ruled this land the peoples of the different regions had fought prolonged and bitter wars. Some regions had been overrun by savage

The Roman Senate assembled to hear Emperor Augustus report on the state of the far-flung empire that he ruled.

The Vast Roman Empire

At the height of its grandeur and power, the Roman Empire covered most of the then-known world. Its provinces on three continents bordered on the Mediterranean. Caesar's legions pushed the frontiers into Britain.

tribes that raided cities and farms. In others, fierce robber bands had terrorized the people.

The Romans did not allow one province to fight another, in this way they brought about peace in their part of the world. They built paved roads throughout the empire so that Roman armies could travel over them quickly and put down any trouble. These roads were so well built that some of them are still in use today. These roads all went out from Rome, which meant that in the other direction they all went into Rome. That explains the meaning of the old saying: "All roads lead to Rome."

These roads were also used by travelers. A traveler could go over thousands of miles of well-paved roads in the Roman Empire. If he knew two languages, Latin and Greek, he could be understood almost everywhere he went. In all that distance he would never be in danger of being captured by savage tribesmen. He would probably never be bothered by robbers. He would never come to a country that was at war.

Because of the roads, there was much trade between people in various parts of the empire. Because of the roads, people were able to exchange ideas on almost every subject.

The Romans, as we have already seen, borrowed much of their civilization from the Greeks. They added certain ideas of their own. Then in the days of the *Pax Romana* they carried their civilization to the people of Western Europe, who had known very little about the Greeks.

1. How were the Roman Provinces governed?
2. Why was road building so important to the prosperity of the Roman Empire?

GLAND
RANCE
ITALY
Rome
MACEDONIA
BLACK SEA
Byzantium
GREECE
ASIA MINOR
Carthage
MEDITERRANEAN SEA
PHOENICIA
Jerusalem
Nazareth
Bethlehem
PALESTINE
Alexandria
AFRICA
EGYPT

72

Achievements of the Romans

Masters of Construction. We have already seen that the Romans built thousands of miles of paved roads. They were masters of construction in other fields as well.

In building, the Romans often used the column, which they learned about from the Greeks. They also used the arch, which they learned about from the Etruscans. An arch is usually built of bricks or stones. It has two upright sides which meet in a rounded peak. The Romans went further than the Etruscans. They learned that they could build four arches and put a curved roof over them to form a dome. We still use the arch and the dome in many of our public buildings.

The Romans used the arch to bring water into their cities. They built aqueducts. An aqueduct is a huge water trough supported by arches. The aqueduct brought the life-giving water into the cities from distant rivers or lakes. Some of the aqueducts were so well built that they are still standing.

The arch was important in building the Colosseum at Rome. The Colosseum was like one of our stadiums. It seated 50,000 people for games and shows. The ruins of the Colosseum are still standing. From them it is possible to picture what the structure looked like when it was first built.

The famous Forum of Rome was first used as a market place. Later, it was used as a place for public meetings, and was the center of Roman life. The Forum was surrounded by beautiful public buildings including the Senate House.

The most famous example of Roman architecture is the Pantheon. This was a tem-

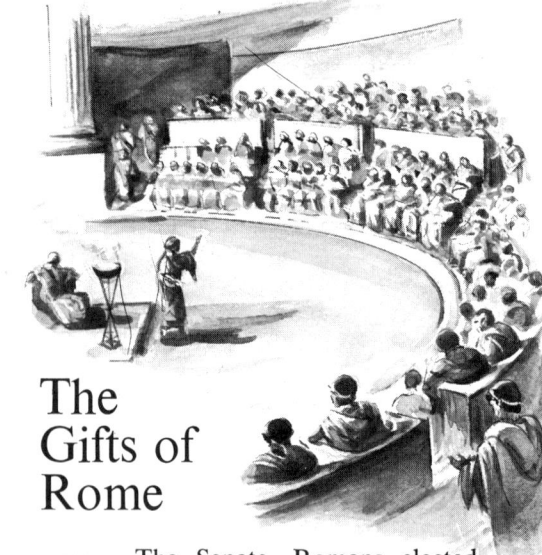

The Gifts of Rome

1 The Senate. Romans elected 330 senators to make their laws. Our own governing body, elected by the people, borrowed this idea of a republic from the Romans.

2 Roman Law. Romans could read their laws in the public Forum where they were inscribed on pillars of stone. Our Constitution is the written law of the land.

3 The Forum. In early Rome, the Forum was the market place for business. Here traders met to buy and exchange goods, and in time it became the city square where parades and speeches attracted vast crowds.

4 Roads and Aqueducts. The remains of Roman roads can still be seen in Italy and neighboring countries. These solid concrete roads enabled armies to move at a fast pace. Aqueducts and sewers helped keep Rome free from diseases.

LIMY GRAVEL — LIMESTONE SLABS — HARD GRAVEL
LARGE GRAVEL — YELLOW CLAY
WATER LINE

ple to "all the gods." It is still standing. It has a huge concrete dome with a front of Greek columns. It is the best preserved building erected by the ancient Romans.

The Latin Language. When Greek was the language of great poetry, Latin was only a dialect spoken by a few tribes living in and around the village of Rome. As Romans

*Latin became the language
of a great part of the empire.
New languages developed from ancient Latin.*

spread their power, they also spread their language. Latin became the language of all Italy, and then it became the language of a vast part of the empire. Greek was the common language at the eastern end of the Mediterranean, but even here it was usually possible to find someone who could speak Latin.

Today, many people say that we need a world language so that people of different nations can talk to each other without translators. As we see, Latin actually was such a language. It remained so for many centuries.

The Latin of everyday life kept changing in pronunciation, grammar, and vocabulary. People of different regions spoke different dialects. When the Roman Empire was later overrun by people from the outside, the various dialects mixed with the languages of the newcomers. New languages developed as a result, but the Latin influence could still be noted. Five modern languages are very similar to ancient Latin. These are Italian, French, Spanish, Portuguese, and Romanian. They are called the Romance languages. The word *Romance* comes from "Roman." In our own English language, one-third of the words are from Latin.

The twenty independent nations south of the United States are called Latin America. That is because they all use the Romance languages. In eighteen of them the people speak Spanish. Portuguese is spoken in Brazil, and French is spoken in Haiti.

Although everyday Latin kept changing, literary Latin changed very little from the time of Emperor Augustus. Even after the Roman Empire came to an end, this literary Latin remained the language of religious, scholarly, and political life. State documents, as well as scientific, philosophical, and other scholarly works, were written only in Latin. This continued for centuries after Latin had disappeared as a spoken language.

We shall read later that the Church was founded in the days of the Roman Empire and that it spread throughout the Empire. It was only natural, therefore, that Latin should become the language of the Church. Long after Latin had disappeared as a spoken language, it was still used for Church ceremonies. In recent years, the Church has dropped Latin in most services.

Literature and Art. Some of the writings of the Romans are still studied in our schools and colleges. They are studied in the original Latin, so the students must know Latin before they can read them.

Probably the best known Latin book today is Julius Caesar's account of his campaigns in Gaul and Britain. Caesar was not only a good general and a good ruler, he was a good writer as well.

Cicero was a great orator who lived at the time of Caesar. His orations were written down. They are still read and studied today.

Vergil, who was a friend of Augustus, wrote a long poem called the *Aeneid*. It tells the story of Aeneas who escaped from Troy after that city fell and later founded the city of Rome. The story is interesting fiction. We may be sure that Vergil got his idea from the *Iliad* and the *Odyssey*.

There were many other fine Roman writers, like the historian Livy and the poet Ovid.

From the Greeks, the Romans learned the art of sculpture. But Roman sculpture was different from Greek sculpture. It was more realistic, more true to life. The Greek statues usually portrayed gods and goddesses. The sculptor had never seen the gods or goddesses, so he did not make them look like anybody in particular. The Roman sculptor was usually portraying a living person such as Caesar, Cicero, or Augustus. He had the person in front of him as he made his statue. As a result some of the statues look so real you would almost expect them to talk.

A Well-Ordered Empire. We have just read about many of the achievements of the Romans. Perhaps their greatest achievement was the Empire.

In the Roman Empire there were many different nations and races. The nations had a large amount of self-government, but they were united under one strong central government. The various nations could not levy taxes on goods coming in from other nations in the Empire. Such taxes, or tariffs, have caused much trouble at other times in history. And the various nations within the Empire could not go to war against each other. The Roman Empire has showed that there *can* be peace and harmony in the world.

Laws. Laws for Rome and the Empire were made by different people at different times: the Senate, the Emperor, and judges called praetors. On the whole, Roman laws were very just.

In 529 A.D. Emperor Justinian had a group of educated men study the Roman laws and arrange them in good order. The collection is called the Justinian Code. The Code became the law for the entire Empire.

It was later adopted by many of the new nations of Europe. Today almost every free nation has a system of laws based on the Justinian Code. English law was strongly influenced by the code, and American law is based on English law.

Two of the important principles developed by Roman law are: (1) the individual has certain rights which must not be taken from him, and (2) every man is considered innocent until proved guilty.

1. Mention four important Roman writers.
2. How did Roman sculpture differ from Greek sculpture?

7 3

The Jews in the Roman Empire

Persian Period (538-333 B.C.). We last read of the Hebrews, or Jews, in Chapter 2. When we left them they had just returned to Palestine from their Babylonian Captivity. They were under the rule of the Persian Emperor.

Cyrus, King of Persia, made his triumphal entry into the city of Babylonia in 538 B.C. One of his first acts was to tell the Jews that they were perfectly free to return to their native land of Palestine. About 50,000 Jews took advantage of the offer and went back to Jerusalem and surrounding territory. They elected a council of twelve elders to manage their affairs.

Some Jews decided to remain in Babylon. These Jews faithfully clung to their religion despite the fact that they were surrounded by people who worshipped false gods.

The Jews who had returned to Palestine rebuilt their temple. The Jews of Babylon sent money to help in the rebuilding. The king of Persia also sent help.

The Jews had a great number of laws regarding religion and everyday life. Some of these laws were handed down by word of mouth. Others were written. The laws were so complicated that some men had to devote their entire lives to studying the laws and putting them into effect. These men were called scribes. Today we would call them lawyers. These scribes became very important men during the Persian period, and they remained so afterward.

The Palestine Jews were happy and prosperous during the two centuries they lived under Persian rule.

Greek Period (338-168 B.C.). Alexander the Great, King of Macedon and Greece, invaded the Persian Empire. Palestine came under his rule in 333 B.C. This began a long period in which the Jews were in touch with Greek civilization.

Alexander allowed the Jews full freedom. Some joined his army in the invasion of Egypt. After Egypt was conquered, some of these Jewish soldiers decided to live in the new city of Alexandria which Alexander founded. He made them full citizens, the equal of Macedonians and Greeks.

Alexander died in 323 B.C. One Greek leader became ruler of Egypt, and another Greek leader became ruler of Syria. Both rulers wished to control Palestine, which was between the two countries. First, Syria seized control of Palestine. Egypt sent in an army and drove out the Syrians. Then the Syrians drove out the Egyptians. This went on for 170 years. There was bitter fighting each time, and much bloodshed.

During this time many Jews moved to Egypt and Asia Minor. These Jews became eminent in science, art, and literature. A group of Jews in Egypt translated the Old Testament into Greek.

At the end of this Greek Period, Palestine was ruled by a cruel King of Syria who was determined to end the worship of God. He dedicated the temple to the Greek god Zeus, and sacrifices were offered to this god. In all the surrounding territory altars were put up to the false gods. Jews were ordered to offer sacrifices to these gods. If they refused, they were severely punished.

The Machabean Period (168-63 B.C.). In 168 B.C. the Jews revolted against the Syrians. Judas Machabeus became leader of this revolt. In 165 B.C. the troops of Judas Machabeus entered Jerusalem. The temple was restored to the worship of God. This was the beginning of the Machabean Period which lasted till 63 B.C. The struggle against Syria continued during the first years of this period. Then Syria gave up the fight. Palestine was independent. It was the last time the country was to be independent until our own century.

Although Palestine was independent, it was not always at peace. There were two factions within the Jewish religion, the Pharisees and Sadducees. Each faction tried to obtain control of the temple, and each faction tried to select the king. There were many civil wars.

In 63 B.C. a great struggle was going on between the two factions. No end of the struggle seemed to be in sight. The leaders of both sides agreed to take their problem to the Roman general, Pompey. Pompey took advantage of the situation and seized control of Palestine. This was the beginning of a long period of Roman rule.

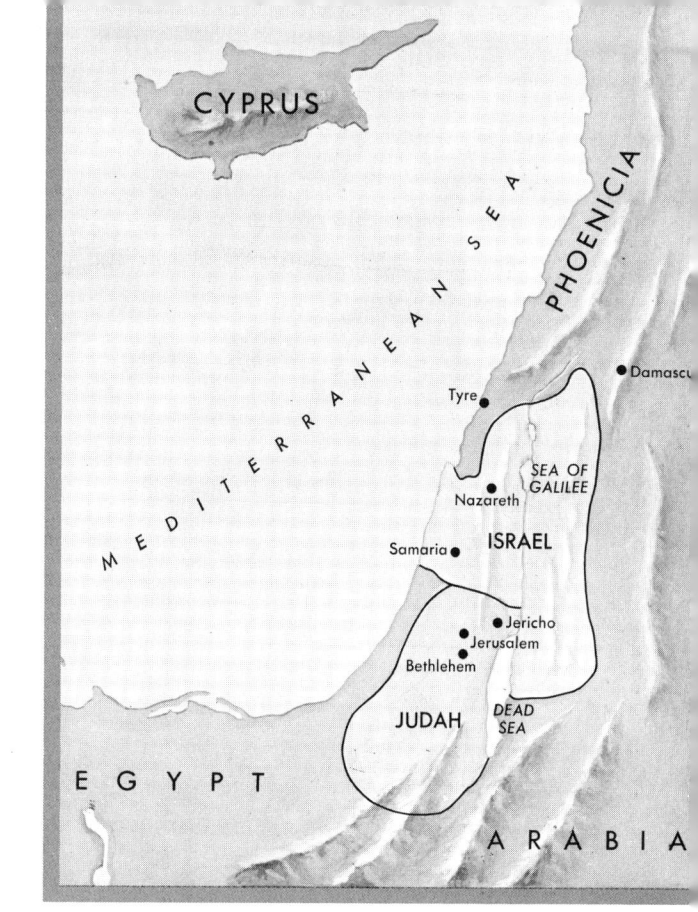

Early Roman Period (63 B.C.–39 A.D.). After Pompey had conquered Palestine he took a number of Jewish captives with him to Rome. It is not known whether these were the first Jews to live in Rome. We do know that there were a large number of them in Rome by the time Our Lord died. In other parts of the empire there were also many Jews. There were five times as many outside of Palestine as there were in Palestine itself. However, we are principally interested in the Jews of Palestine.

A man named Herod became King of Palestine, or Judea, in 37 B.C. Herod was not a Jew, either by race or by religion, but he was put into power by the Romans. Herod tried to win the friendship of the Jews by worshipping in the temple and also by taking a Jewish wife. He rebuilt the temple and did many other things for the Jews. In history, he is known as Herod the Great. Herod's bad qualities outweighed his good qualities, however. He was ruthless with anyone he suspected of being his enemy. He had numerous people put to death, including his own son. He died in 4 B.C.

Our Lord was born sometime before Herod died. This means that a mistake has been made in figuring the year of Christ's birth. Instead of being born in 1 A.D. as we would expect, He was born before 4 B.C.

Herod the Great was a cruel ruler. Put in power by the Romans, he punished and killed many people.

When King Herod heard that Jesus was to be King of the Jews, he determined to destroy Him. This caused the massacre of the Holy Innocents, and it also caused the Holy Family's Flight into Egypt.

Herod was succeeded by his son, Archaelaus. This king made himself so unpopular with the Jews that they begged the Emperor Augustus to remove him. Augustus did so. The Jews were happy that they had rid themselves of their king, but they soon found that their troubles were not over. After that, they were ruled by procurators sent from Rome. These procurators were not Jewish by either race or religion, and some of them were enemies of the Jewish faith. The Jews were unhappy under their rule. They felt that they were a conquered people. Every last sign of Jewish independence had disappeared.

The procurator from 26 A.D. to 36 A.D. was Pontius Pilate. It was under him that Our Lord was crucified.

Another Herod comes into the story here. He was the son of Herod the Great and the brother of King Archaelaus, who was deposed. Herod was the ruler of Galilee, the northern part of Palestine. He is sometimes called King Herod, but he never had the title of king. He ruled Galilee from 4 B.C. to 39 A.D. It was in Galilee that Our Lord lived most of His life.

This second Herod asked the Emperor Caligula to make him a king. This angered the emperor, and he had Herod banished from Palestine in 39 A.D. It is thought that Herod was murdered soon after that.

Over Herod was the Roman procurator, Pontius Pilate. He was the procurator of all Palestine, which included Galilee. Over Pilate was the governor of Syria. And over the governor of Syria was the Roman Emperor, who at that time was Tiberius.

Palestine Jews at the Time of Christ. There are some words we should know when we read about the Palestine Jews at the time of Christ. We know about *priests*. They are our religious guides and teachers. They perform religious ceremonies which no one else can perform. The Jews had priests, too, although they did not do exactly the same things that priests do now. At the head of the priests was the *high priest,* the most important religious official in Palestine. During the latter part of the Machabean period, the king was also the high priest. This was not surprising in a land where religion and government were tied together so tightly.

At one time the priests told what the different religious laws meant. In time, this work was taken over by the *scribes.* We read about them earlier in this chapter.

The *Sanhedrin* was the supreme court of Palestine. It made judgments in both religious and political matters. At times, it was very powerful. At other times, strong rulers took away much of its power. The Romans usually left it much power. We don't know exactly who were members, but we know that priests and scribes were members. The trial of Our Lord was conducted by the Sanhedrin. Its president was Caiphas, the high priest. We don't know whether the high priest was always the president.

The *Pharisees* and the *Sadducees* were the two opposing parties in Palestine. It would be a mistake to think that they were like the Democratic and Republican parties in

The most important religious official in Palestine was the high priest. Here a priest performs a ceremony.

the United States. Our parties are concerned with running the government and have very little to do with religion. The parties in Palestine were concerned mostly about matters of religion. Since religion and government were tied together, however, the parties were also interested in government. Each party tried to get a majority in the Sanhedrin. When there was a struggle to decide who the ruler of Palestine would be, the Pharisees were usually on one side and the Sadducees on the other. It was a struggle between the Pharisees and the Sadducees that brought the Romans into Palestine.

Today, it is a little difficult to tell what the Pharisees and the Sadducees quarreled about. We know that the Pharisees wanted to keep to the Jewish way of doing things, while the Sadducees favored Greek culture. The Sadducees believed only in the written law, while the Pharisees believed that the Jews should also consider the law that had been handed down by word of mouth.

By the time Jesus was born, the Pharisees had more influence than the Sadducees. They no doubt helped the Jewish religion in some ways. They made the Jews think more about God and about religion. But many of the Pharisees had come to think of themselves as better than ordinary Jews. They called themselves the "pious ones."

The Jews as a whole hated the rule of the Romans. Other peoples were fairly happy under Roman rule, but not the Jews. Other peoples worshipped many gods, and so did the Romans. The gods of the Romans did not seem very different from their own gods. But the Jews worshipped one God, and this made them different from all other peoples. They knew that the Romans did not understand or respect their religion. The Jews also had a long history. They knew about the glorious days of King David and King Solomon. They longed for a return of those days.

The prophets had told the Jews that a Messiah, a Saviour, was coming. This was written in their Scriptures. But the Jews did not understand the Scriptures. They thought the Messiah would be an earthly king. They thought He would deliver them from Roman rule. They thought that He would be their earthly king and bring back the glories of Solomon and David. That is why most of them did not recognize the Messiah when He came.

1. What Jewish leader helped Palestine to become independent?
2. How did Palestine come under Roman rule?

Chapter 7. REVIEW

Learning To Use New Words

Use each of the following terms in an original sentence, expressing something you have learned in Chapter 7:

province	dialect
scribe	Sanhedrin
reign	procurator
Pax Romana	Pharisee
aqueduct	Sadducee

Knowing the Important Facts

1. What kind of government did Octavius start? Why did it prosper?
2. What were the results of the Pax Romana?
3. Make a list of Roman achievements in architecture, literature, language, and law.
4. Name the principal leaders of the Hebrews from the Babylonian Captivity to the time of Christ.
5. How did the Pharisees differ from the Sadducees?

Thinking Through the Facts

1. Why were the Romans able to rule such a large empire without much difficulty?
2. Describe the importance of Latin to the Roman world and its place in today's world.
3. Why was the Justinian Code important? What were two principles it developed? How did the Code influence modern law?
4. Describe the role of the Hebrews in keeping alive the belief in one God.
5. Explain the religious and political situation which existed in Palestine at the time of Christ's birth.

Developing a Time Sense

Arrange the following events in the proper time order:
1. Beginning of the "Pax Romana"
2. "Justinian Code" reorganizes Roman law
3. Palestine is ruled by the Roman governor Pontius Pilate
4. The Emperor Augustus rules the Roman Empire
5. Machabean Period of Jewish history

Chapter 8
Christianity in the Roman Empire

When the Roman Empire was at its height, the most important events in all history took place. Christ, our Redeemer, was born, established His Church, died for the sins of mankind, rose from the dead, and sent the Holy Spirit down upon the Apostles. Then the Apostles went forth to spread the word of Christ throughout the world. Later, the Church spread to every part of the Empire.

8 1
The Rise of Christianity

Christ's Life and Mission. Emperor Augustus wished to know how many people there were in the Roman Empire. When a government counts its people, we say it takes a census. Today, a census is a door-to-door count of people. Augustus did not do it that way. He ordered everyone to go to the town of his ancestors to be counted.

The Hebrew prophets had foretold that the Saviour would be of the house of David. Mary, the mother of Jesus, and Joseph, His foster father, were descendants of King David. Therefore, they had to go to Bethlehem, David's birthplace, to be counted. There Jesus was born in a stable, because there was no room in the inn.

Jesus spent most of His life in Nazareth, in Galilee. When he was thirty years old, He began preaching and teaching. He announced the kingdom of God, founded His Church, and claimed He to be the Son of God. He worked many miracles. He cured the sick, the blind, the lame. He even raised dead people to life. Jesus' message and miracles won many followers among the Jews.

Jesus also aroused fear and envy among priests, Pharisees, and other Jewish leaders. "If we let him alone as he is," they said, "all will believe in him, and the Romans will come and take away both our place and our nation" (John 11:48). So they planned and plotted to put Him to death.

Betrayed by the Apostle Judas, He was condemned by the Jewish council as a blasphemer for claiming to be the Son of God.

Jesus frequently talked to the people about the Kingdom of Heaven, and what they must do to live there with Him.

Before Pontius Pilate, the Roman procurator of Judea, He was accused of leading the nation astray. He was charged with "forbidding the payment of taxes to Caesar, saying he is Christ a king" (Luke 23:2), thus setting Himself against Caesar (John 19:12).

Pilate found Jesus not guilty of any of these charges. Yet he gave in to Jesus' accusers. On a cross on Calvary Jesus died the death of a common criminal. Three days later He gave His greatest sign by rising from the dead. His final command to His Apostles was to preach His Gospel to every creature and to make disciples of all nations throughout the world.

The Growth of the Church. All of Our Lord's preaching and teaching were done in the little country of Palestine. People in other parts of the world had never heard of Him or of the Church which He founded. After His death, His Apostles and other missionaries, such as St. Paul, carried His

Roman Persecutions

1 Early Christians. The early Christians had to endure much persecution. The Roman government thought the Christians were disloyal and often ordered that Christians who refused to give up their religion should be put to death.

2 To the Lions. The Colosseum was often used for contests between lions and men. It was in this arena that spectators watched lions tear Christians and criminals to pieces.

3 Fire of Rome. In 64 A.D. a tremendous fire, which lasted for six continuous days, destroyed the greater part of the city of Rome. Nero blamed the Christians for the fire and used this excuse to persecute them.

message to every part of the Roman Empire and beyond. St. Peter himself, took the word of Christ into the city of Rome. The first missionaries found that there were many people eager to hear what they said, and some of these people came into the Church.

In July of the year 64 A.D., a fire destroyed a large part of the city of Rome. Many Romans believed that the emperor Nero had started the fire for his own amusement. Nero was afraid the people would rise up against him. To protect himself, he said that the Christians had started the fire. Many pagan Romans were ready to believe this because they did not like the Christians anyway.

This started a great persecution of the Christians. Some Christians were thrown to hungry lions. Others were cruelly tortured until they died. The next 250 years saw many persecutions of the Christians.

Persecution Comes to an End. A powerful Roman named Constantine was friendly toward the Christians. He became a Christian just before he died.

In the year 312 A.D., Constantine was waging war with a powerful rival. They were fighting to see who would become emperor. In a vision or in a dream, Constantine saw a cross in the sky. On the cross was written: "In this sign thou shalt conquer." Constantine immediately took the cross as his badge. Although his men were outnumbered three to one, they won an important battle. Constantine became an emperor.

The following year, 313 A.D., Constantine and his co-emperor issued a new law. This is called the Edict of Milan. The law said that the Christian religion should be equal to the pagan religion and that Christians were no longer to be persecuted.

There was great rejoicing among the Christians. Two and a half centuries of persecution had come to an end. Now the Christians were free to practice their religion openly and without fear.

4 **The Catacombs.** To escape persecution in the cities, Christians hid in catacombs which were burial grounds used by Romans. There they celebrated Mass, sang hymns, and listened to readings from the Holy Scriptures.

1. How did the persecutions of Christians in Rome begin?
2. What was the Edict of Milan? When was it issued? Who issued it?

99

The Roman Empire Becomes Weaker

The Emperors Who Followed Augustus. After going through a long period of persecution, the Christian religion was made the religion of the empire. The number of Christians grew rapidly after that, and the number of pagans in the Empire became smaller and smaller.

While the Church was making great progress within the Empire, the Empire itself was becoming weaker.

It is hard to say just when the Empire started to lose its strength. Perhaps this happened before the birth of Our Lord. As we know, thousands of people in the city of Rome had no work and had lost their interest in the government. They voted for the men who would give them the most food and free entertainment. Then Julius Caesar came to power, and self-government came to an end.

Caesar was succeeded by his nephew who became the Emperor Augustus. While Augustus was Emperor, Our Lord was born.

Augustus was followed by four members of his family. These four emperors were called the Julio-Claudians. They ruled from 14 to 68 A.D.

The first two emperors in this line were good rulers. They were Tiberius and Claudius. Christ's crucifixion and death took place while Tiberius was emperor. Palestine was far from Rome, and Tiberius probably knew nothing about the trial and crucifixion of Jesus. Under the next emperor, Claudius, the Romans added part of the island of Britain to the Empire. (The country of England would later develop on this island.)

The next two emperors of this line were quite different from the first two. Caligula acted like a madman. He once appointed his favorite horse to a position in the government. Nero had his wife and mother murdered. He ordered the first persecution of the Christians. Nero committed suicide in 68 A.D., and this ended the line of Julio-Claudians.

There was a struggle for power after Nero's death. There were four emperors in one year. The last of the four was Flavius Vespasius. He restored order and established the Flavian dynasty. The Flavian emperors gave the Empire good government.

Rome Reaches Her Peak Under the "Five Good Emperors." The next five rulers are known as the Antonine line. They reigned from 96 to 180 A.D. They have been called the "five good Emperors." Under them, Rome reached the height of her wealth and power. Two of these emperors are worth special mention.

Hadrian reigned from 117 to 138 A.D. He traveled widely throughout the Empire. He improved the government of the provinces. He started new cities and restored old ones. Postal service was improved. New laws protected slaves from cruel treatment. No longer could a master put a slave to death. For these laws Hadrian truly deserves to be called a "good Emperor."

In Germany, Hadrian erected walls to keep out invaders. A wall was built across the narrowest part of the island of Britain to protect the Roman part of the island.

This was called Hadrian's Wall. Parts of it are still standing.

The last of the "good emperors" was Marcus Aurelius, who ruled from 161 to 180 A.D. He was a philosopher and scholar. He was a peace-loving man, and would have liked to spend most of his time with his books. But the Germanic tribes from northern Europe attacked the Empire, and he led his troops against them. While taking part in the Germanic campaigns, he wrote his *Meditations*. This is a book explaining his views on life and showing a great love for all mankind. No emperor was more devoted to the welfare of his people.

A Century of Civil War. The Roman Empire was a good government in most ways, one of the best the world has ever known. But there was one problem that the Romans were never able to solve. This was the problem of choosing an emperor. This problem caused much trouble and much bloodshed. The generals of the Roman army had great power, because they had armed soldiers under their command. They used this power to put their favorites on the throne. Often a general would declare himself to be emperor. Sometimes generals fought each other, and there were many wars within the Empire. Such wars are called civil wars.

Emperors of Rome

The Roman emperors were heads of the government and had all legislative, judicial, and military authority. The emperors also had an army to support their authority. The emperors were thought to rule by divine guidance.

1. Augustus was the first emperor of Rome and his reign was known as the Golden Age of Rome. Some of the best writers of the time wrote during this era: Vergil, Ovid, Horace, and Livy.

2. Nero was a very cruel emperor who persecuted the Christians. After his death, Rome was ruled by several wise and good emperors.

3. Hadrian was a good and generous emperor who appreciated literature and other forms of art. He carried on a building program, including Hadrian's Wall built by the Romans.

4. Marcus Aurelius was a loyal and devoted emperor who was a student by nature. He spent his last years trying to save Rome from its enemies.

5. Septimius Severus was very interested in law, and important changes in Roman law go back to his reign. He tried to protect weak people from the strong and treated his armies very well.

Across the Empire, civil war and invasion left a trail of bloodshed and ruin.

When Marcus Aurelius died in 180, his son Commodus became emperor. He was not at all like his father. He led an evil life and spent all the money in the Empire's treasury. He was murdered after he had reigned twelve years. A period of civil war followed. After much bloodshed, Septimius Severus was made emperor in 193. On his deathbed he is said to have told his sons: "Make the soldiers rich and don't trouble about the rest." The Empire had come upon sad days.

The line of Septimius Severus ruled until 235. In the next fifty years there were twenty-six emperors. All but one of these emperors died violent deaths. During all this time the Romans were killing each other and destroying each other's property. At the same time powerful forces were attacking the Empire from the outside.

Other Problems within the Empire. Many things were going wrong within the Roman Empire. Because of the civil wars and the wars against the enemies on the outside, a vast number of soldiers was needed. These soldiers had to be paid. They had to have food, clothing, and places to live. All this cost a great deal of money. Taxes went up and up. Many landowners did not have enough money to pay their taxes. Some paid in wheat, fruit, and other farm products. Some had to give up their land.

Most of the land was coming into the hands of a few rich and powerful men. These men had many slaves who could do the work on a farm. The small landowners did not have slaves. They could not compete with the large slave plantations. A small landowner soon found himself forced to give up his land to a large landowner. He became a *colonus*. This means that he was given a small patch of land which he was allowed to farm. In return, he had to perform many tasks for the landlord. He would work in the landlord's fields, erect buildings for him, repair his roads and fences, and do many other kinds of work. He became little better than a slave. If the land was sold, he stayed on his patch of soil and worked for the new owner.

Later, when we read about the Middle Ages, we shall see that Europe had the feudal system at that time. Under this system, the largest class of people were serfs. They were "bound to the land" and not allowed to leave the estates of their landlords. We can see that this system had its beginnings in the Roman Empire, before the Middle Ages began.

A farmer who did not wish to become a *colonus* might run away to the city. There he would find it almost impossible to find a job. He would join the large mob of people who had no work and who lived on free food passed out by the government. As the number of unemployed grew larger, it became more expensive to feed them. This, too, caused the taxes to be increased.

To make matters worse, the money system became confused. Less precious metal was put into the coins, and so they became less valuable. Prices became very high. Many people could no longer pay for the goods they needed.

With the constant civil wars, the attacks from outside, the high taxes, the increasing number of unemployed, and extremely high prices, it did not seem that the Roman Empire could last much longer. But its days were not yet over.

Diocletian Tries to Stop the Decay of Rome. Diocletian became emperor in 285 and ruled until 305. He was a strong emperor and brought the period of civil wars to an end for a time. He strengthened the armies that were protecting the borders. To stop the rising prices, he fixed the prices for which various goods could be sold. If anyone tried to charge higher prices, he was punished. Diocletian also fixed the wages which should be paid to workers. He tried to establish a system by which the emperor could be chosen without having one of the political parties start a civil war.

Some of Diocletian's measures were partly successful, and some were complete failures. His measures probably stopped the decline of the Empire for the time being. In the end, they probably only helped the Empire's downfall, because many new government officials had to be appointed to enforce his new laws. This meant spending more money and raising the taxes once more.

During most of his reign, Diocletian did not bother the Christians. As he became older he came under the influence of advisers who hated Christians. In 303 a new persecution began. Many Christians were thrown into prison, tortured, and killed. The persecution continued after Diocletian gave up his throne in 305. It was the last great persecution of the Christians in the Roman Empire.

The Reign of Constantine. Emperor Diocletian resigned in 305. His system for selecting a new emperor did not work. In 310 there were five men who claimed to be emperor. Civil war broke out again. Constantine and another man defeated the others and shared the rule for a time. In 324 Constantine became the only emperor.

We have already read something about Constantine. We know that in 313, before he was the only emperor, he made Christianity the equal of other religions.

In 332 Constantine decreed that no *colonus* could leave the soil and that the children of a *colonus* had to stay on the soil just as their fathers did. He also decreed that workers of various kinds must stay in their line of work and that the children must do so also.

Constantine Moves the Capital. Constantine decided not to rule from Rome which had been the capital of the Empire for centuries. He moved to the city of Byzantium, at the eastern end of Europe, near Asia. At first he called the city New Rome. This was soon changed to Constantinople, which means "Constantine's City."

Constantine had several reasons for this change. While the western, or Latin, part of the Empire became weaker, the eastern, or Greek, part remained strong. Constantine wished this part to remain strong, and he thought he would be better able to keep it strong if he lived there.

Ships could reach Constantinople only through a long narrow channel. This made the city easy to defend. The channel also had a fine harbor. From the harbor ships could sail to many ports in Europe, Africa, and Asia.

There was still another reason why Constantine wished to move. Rome had been a pagan city for centuries. Statues of the pagan gods and temples to the gods could be seen throughout the city. Many of the people were still pagans. Constantinople was smaller than Rome and had fewer reminders of a pagan past. Constantine hoped to develop it into a great Christian city.

After Constantine's death, Constantinople did become the great Christian city he had dreamed about. We shall read later that Constantinople was conquered by the Turks, who were Mohammedans. Today, it is a Mohammedan city, and the name has been changed to Istanbul.

The Empire is Divided. Constantine died in 337. In the fifty-eight years that followed, the Empire remained united. Sometimes the emperor in Constantinople ruled the entire Empire. Sometimes he shared his power with an emperor for the western part of the Empire. When there was an emperor in the west, he ruled from Ravenna rather than Rome. Rome was never again to be so powerful.

Theodosius ruled from 379 to 395. He ruled the entire Empire, east and west. Theodosius said that after his death the Empire should be divided between his two sons. When he died in 395, one son became emperor of the Western Empire, and the other son became the ruler of the Eastern Empire. Except for a brief period, the two parts of the Empire were not united again.

1. Who were the "five good Emperors"?
2. Why was Hadrian's Wall built?
3. Describe the life of a colonus.
4. How was the Roman Empire divided after the death of Theodosius?

3

The Church After Persecution

Rome, the Center of Christianity. After Constantine left Rome, the people of Rome did not have any important government officials to turn to when they were in trouble, so they turned to the Bishop of Rome, the Pope. At times, the Pope seemed to be not only the spiritual ruler of the Christian world, but also the highest official of the city of Rome. And Rome became known as the center of the Christian world instead of the capital of the Empire.

The Bishops Meet at Nicea. After the Edict of Milan, the Church was no longer persecuted by the Empire, but it faced new problems. Certain Christians refused to believe all the truths taught by the Christian Church. Christians who do not believe all the teachings of the Church are called heretics. Beliefs that are not in accordance with the Church's teachings are called heresies.

One of the early heretics was a priest named Arius. He taught that Christ was not God. He won many followers.

With the approval of Pope Sylvester,

Constantine called a meeting of all the Bishops of the Church. One of the principal purposes of this meeting was to discuss the doctrine that Arius was teaching. Constantine said that he considered heresy "more dreadful and more painful than any war."

The meeting was held at Nicea in Asia Minor, in 325 A.D. It is called the Council of Nicea. This was the first general council of the Church. The Bishops declared that Christ is God and that all Christians must believe this doctrine.

The Fathers of the Church Explain the Christian Religion. When Constantine ended the persecution of the Church, only about one in every ten persons in the Empire was Christian. This meant that nine out of ten people were still pagans. These pagans knew very little about the Christian religion.

Germans from northern Europe were moving into the Empire. These Germans knew nothing about Our Lord's teachings. Many heretics were teaching wrong ideas about the Christian religion. The Church now needed great writers and thinkers who could explain the Christian religion and defend it against heretics.

The men who explained the doctrine of Christianity in the important years after the Edict of Milan were called the Fathers of the Church. These men were brilliant thinkers and writers. The Church has also given certain of these Fathers the title "Doctor of the Church." They received this honor because of their holiness and their skill in explaining Christian truths.

Four of the Doctors of the Church lived in the eastern part of the empire. They wrote in Greek. They are called the Greek Doctors. They are Saint Athanasius, Saint Basil the Great, Saint Gregory Nazianzen, and Saint John Chrysostom. *Chrysostom* means "golden mouthed." Saint John was given that name because he was such a good preacher.

There were also four Latin Doctors. They lived in the western part of the Empire and wrote in Latin. They are Saint Gregory the Great, Saint Ambrose, Saint Augustine, and Saint Jerome.

Saint Gregory the Great was the Pope, but he found time to do much writing. Saint Ambrose was the Bishop of Milan in Italy. He is known for his books, and also for the hymns that he wrote. Saint Jerome's great-

To state the principal beliefs of the Church, the Bishops wrote a Creed which is even now being used at Mass. It is called the Nicene Creed.

est work was revising the Latin translation of the four Gospels. Besides this work, Saint Jerome completed, with the exception of a few books, a translation of the Old Testament from the Hebrew. Saint Jerome's version of the Old and the New Testaments is called the Latin Vulgate.

The writings of these great Doctors of the Church were read and studied throughout the civilized world. Later writers and scholars were helped by referring to these writings which are still widely read today.

The Christian Religion Becomes the Religion of the Empire. Constantine had ended the persecution of the Church. The emperor Theodosius the Great, who reigned from 379 to 395 A.D., went further. He made the

Pagan temples were turned into churches. The Christians assembled for public worship on Sundays and other holydays.

Christian religion the religion of the Empire. Little by little, the old pagan temples were closed. The feast days of the Church became holidays.

At the beginning of the fourth century Christians were in fear of being put to death for their religion. At the end of the fourth century, their religion was the religion of the Empire.

1. How did Rome become the center of Christianity?
2. Who was Arius? What did he teach?
3. Why was the council of Nicea called?
4. Name the Latin and Greek Doctors of the Church.

The Fall of the Western Empire

The Germans. In the northern part of Europe were many tribes whom the Romans had never been able to conquer. The Romans built forts along the border to protect the Empire from these people.

What shall we call these people? Sometimes they are called barbarians. When we use the word "barbarian" today, however, we usually mean someone who is at least half savage. Many of the people who lived in northern Europe were barbarians in this sense, but others were quite civilized. Therefore, "barbarian" does not seem quite the right word to describe all the tribes who lived beyond the outposts of the Empire.

Sometimes these people are called Teutons, or Germans. Perhaps that is a better name for them. When we call them Germans, however, we should not think that they are the same as the people who live in Germany today. Today's Germans are descended in part from these Germans of old, but so are people in France, Italy, Spain, England, and other countries of Western Europe.

The Germans who were farthest from the Empire usually lived in houses made of rough logs. They wore the skins of wild animals. The men carried spears and shields. They were good warriors and good hunters. They raised crops and cattle, and so they had reached one stage of civilization. They worshipped the sun, the moon, fire, and other things which were important to them in their daily lives. We get the names of the week from the German gods and goddesses. Sunday is the sun's day. Monday is the

The German tribesmen were good hunters and fierce fighters. Many had become Christians before entering the Empire.

moon's day. Wednesday is named for Woden, the chief god. Thursday is named for Thor, the god of thunder.

Many of the Germans who lived near the Empire traded with the Romans. They learned about the use of coins from the Romans, and they learned many other things. They lived very much as the Romans did.

Roman writers tell us that the Germans were tall and blond and had blue or gray eyes. They were probably not any taller than the average American of today, but they seemed tall to the Romans, most of whom were rather short.

Germans Come into the Empire. The first Germans who came into the Empire did so in a peaceful manner. They came because they were invited.

The Romans did not have enough men for their armies. The jobless who roamed the city streets did not make good soldiers. The other people were needed for work on the farms and for many other kinds of work. Therefore, young Germans were invited to join the Roman army. These young men often brought their families with them. Soon there were many Germans living in the Empire.

Some of the Germans became officers in the Roman army. Some even became generals. We know that the generals in the Roman Empire were powerful men. They often decided who would be emperor. The Germans were becoming a powerful group within the Empire.

Rome Is Captured by Germans. In the fourth century, a fierce race called the Huns came out of central Asia into northern Europe. The Huns were the most terrible in-

Savage horsemen from Asia invaded Europe, conquering tribe after tribe. The Huns destroyed cities, which contained porcelain art treasures.

vaders Europe had ever seen. They had invented reins and the stirrup, so they could ride horses into battle. This gave them a big advantage over their enemies, most of whom were on foot. When they rode into battle, they carried the heads of their enemies on lances, as if to tell their foes what would happen to them.

Both the Romans and the Germans were afraid of the Huns. The emperor Valens invited a group of Germans called Visigoths (West Goths) into the Empire. He told them he would supply them with food if they would help defend the Empire against the Huns. The Visigoths accepted the invitation.

After the Visigoths were in the Empire for some time, they decided they didn't like the way they were being treated. Fighting broke out, and the Visigoths defeated the Romans. The emperor Valens was killed in a battle with the Visigoths at Adrianople in 378.

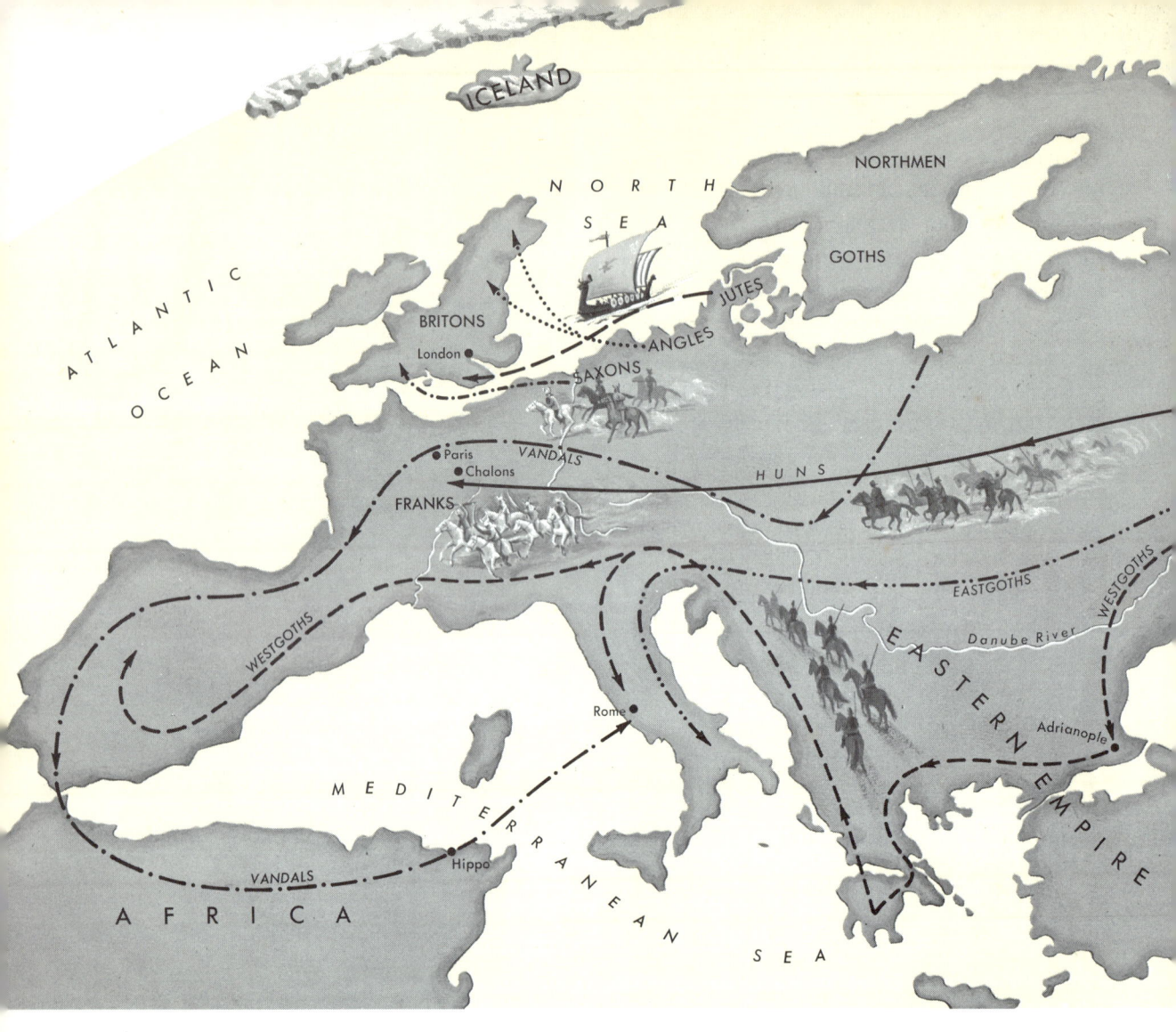

For a time there was peace between the Visigoths and the Romans. Then the Visigoths went to war again. This time they marched into Italy. In 410, under the leadership of Alaric, they captured the city of Rome.

People in every part of the Empire were shocked when they heard that Rome had fallen to the Visigoths. No one had been able to capture the city in more than 800 years. Even the great general Hannibal of Carthage had not been able to capture it. The people of Rome had been so proud of their city that they called it the "Eternal City." They had thought it would last forever. Now it was in danger of being destroyed by the Visigoths.

People who were still pagans said, "As

long as Rome was a pagan city, nobody could conquer it. Rome became weak when the people became Christians."

St. Augustine heard these arguments. That is one reason why he wrote the *City of God*. He said in this book that no man-made city could last forever, no matter how strong it seemed. He said that people who led good Christian lives would some day live in the City of God, which is infinitely superior to any man-made city, and that it would last forever.

The Germans Spread over the Western Empire. The Visigoths made peace with the Western emperor. They left Italy and went into southern France and into Spain. Both these places had been Roman provinces. Here they started a Visigoth kingdom. The king of the Visigoths, said he was loyal to the emperor. Actually he did as he pleased, and the emperor had no control over him.

Germans called Vandals had moved into Spain. When they were driven out by the Visigoths, the Vandals moved into North Africa and started a kingdom there. St. Augustine, Bishop of Hippo, died while his city was being beseiged by the Vandals. In 455 the Vandals crossed the Mediterranean Sea into Italy and captured Rome. This was the second time the city had been captured in forty-five years. After stealing much and destroying much, the Vandals went back to Africa. Today, when a person destroys something for no good reason, we call him a vandal.

German tribes moved into every part of the Western Empire. The Franks conquered northern Gaul. This region became known as the country of the Franks, or France.

After taking Germany, the Huns moved into Italy. It was Pope Leo I who finally stopped Attila at the gates of Rome.

The Ostrogoths (East Goths) moved into southern Italy. The Lombards went into northern Italy. This section is still called Lombardy. Angles and Saxons and Jutes took over the part of Britain which had belonged to the Empire.

While the Germans were taking control of Western Europe, people called Slavs were taking over much of Eastern Europe.

Pope Leo I Saves Rome from the Huns. It was fear of the Huns that had brought many Germans into the Empire. Shortly after the Vandals had captured Rome, the Huns began moving through Italy. The emperor fled from Ravenna. The people of Rome were terrified. They feared their city would be captured for the third time, and this time by the fierce Huns.

Pope Leo I went to meet Attila, the leader of the Huns who was called the "Scourge of God." After talking with the Pope, Attila made peace. Rome was saved. Attila died soon after, and his followers settled down in peace.

The Western Empire Comes to an End. The power of the proud old Roman Empire was almost gone. North Africa and most of Western Europe were ruled by German kings who paid little or no attention to the emperor. In Italy itself most of the generals were Germans. These generals were more powerful than the emperor. In 476 A.D. a German general named Odoacer removed the emperor from the throne. Odoacer made himself the king of Italy.

Sometimes we say that the year 476 A.D. marks the end of the Western Empire. Actually, as we have seen, the Empire had lost most of its power long before this. Still, 476 A.D. is a convenient date to remember.

Odoacer said that he was loyal to the Eastern emperor in faraway Constantinople. Actually, he ruled as he pleased, and so did his successors.

The Eastern Empire was still in existence. Thus, we might say that part of the old Roman Empire still remained. The Eastern Empire, however, had always been more Greek than Roman. As far as the West was concerned, the Roman Empire had come to an end.

What Caused the Fall of the Western Empire? The people who lived in the Western Empire greatly outnumbered the Germans and Slavs who invaded the Empire and brought it to an end. Why were these "outsiders" able to conquer the once-powerful Empire?

In this chapter we saw that there were many troubles inside the Empire. The people had no power at all. All power was in the hands of the army generals and the emperors they supported. In the cities there were thousands of jobless people. The jobless were unhappy, even though they received free food and entertainment. They saw no hope for their own future or the future of their children and grandchildren. Most farm workers had become little better than slaves. Workers were tied to their jobs, and children had to follow the occupations of their fathers. People who owned large amounts of land had to pay very high taxes. Money had gone down in value, and prices were extremely high. There were many civil wars, with great loss of life and property. A deadly decay was gnawing at the inner life and strength of the Western Empire. It was the decline that went before the fall.

With conditions so bad, most people had little love for the government of the Empire. When the Germans came in and took over the government of various sections, the people did not mind. They felt that conditions could not be any worse than they already were. They had lost the will to fight. And so the Western Empire fell.

1. Mention three conditions that contributed to the fall of the Western Empire.
2. How did the Germans first come into the Empire?
3. List four days of the week and the German gods each was named after.
4. Who was the "Scourge of God"?

Chapter 8. REVIEW

Learning To Use New Words

Use each of the following terms in an original sentence, expressing something you learned in Chapter 8:

census	colonies	province
persecution	serf	barbarian
martyr	empire	creed
edict	heretic	vandal

Knowing the Important Facts
1. How were the Christians treated before and after the rule of Constantine?
2. What were some reasons for the decay of the Roman Empire?
3. Tell where invading tribes settled in Europe.
4. Of what service were the "Doctors of the Church" to the Christian world?
5. What was the effect of the Edict of Milan?
6. Which Empire, East or West, lasted longer?

Thinking Through the Facts
1. Why did Constantine favor the Christians?
2. Why did Constantine move the capital from Rome to the East?
3. Why did Nero persecute the Christians?
4. Why did the Romans have trouble choosing an emperor?
5. Why did the Huns have a great advantage in battle?

Developing a Time Sense
Arrange the following events in the proper time order:
1. The Council of Nicea
2. Visigoths capture Rome
3. The Edict of Milan
4. The end of the Western Empire

Unit THREE Summary

I Should Know That...
1. The Roman Empire gave the Mediterranean world over two centuries of peace and prosperity.
2. The Roman Empire declined as a result of civil war and internal decay.
3. The Roman Empire made great contributions to Western Civilization in government, law, literature, architecture, and road building.
4. Latin provided the foundation for several modern languages.
5. The Jews held to their belief in one God through centuries of exile, slavery, and rule by non-believers.
6. By the end of the Fourth Century, Christianity had become the official religion of the Roman Empire.
7. Invasion by German tribes, led to the fall of Rome in 476.
8. After the Fall of Rome, the Western Empire was divided into German kingdoms.

Dates I Should Remember...
31 B.C.–476 A.D.—The Roman Empire
31 B.C.–14 A.D.—The Rule of Augustus
about 4 B.C.—The Birth of Christ
395 A.D.—Roman Empire divided into two parts, Eastern and Western
410 A.D.—Rome captured by Visigoths under Alaric
455 A.D.—Vandals sack Rome
476 A.D.—End of the Western Roman Empire

Some Interesting Things to Do...
1. Locate the following places on a map. Find articles in a current newspaper or magazine which refer to them. Why were they important in Roman history?
   Rome   Britain
   Constantinople   Palestine
     (Istanbul)   Spain
2. Select three of the following men who made news in Roman times, and write a short biography of each:
   Hannibal   St. Augustine
   Julius Caesar   Gregory the Great
   Octavius   Attila
   Constantine   Hadrian
3. Make a model of a famous Roman building or an aqueduct. Can you explain how water was brought to the city in an aqueduct? Why were some of them so high above the ground?
4. In an encyclopaedia or large dictionary find the Latin words from which we got our names for the months of the year.

Books I Should Read...
Clarke, Egerton, *St. Peter the First Pope.*
Foster, G., *Augustus Caesar's World.*
Guerber, H. A., *The Story of the Chosen People.*
Wilmot, Buxton, *Norse Heroes.*

FOUR **The Middle Ages (500-1500)**

Chapter 9

Western Europe Rebuilds

Today, many historians give the name "Middle Ages" to the thousand-year period that followed the fall of the Western Roman Empire. They call it "middle" because it came between "ancient times" and "modern times."

There are no exact years that mark the beginning and end of the Middle Ages. We might say that they began in 476 when the last Western emperor lost his throne. We might say they ended in 1492 when Columbus discovered America. To help you remember it easily, consider the Middle Ages as lasting from about 500 to 1500.

9.1 The Byzantine Empire

Justinian Tries To Restore the Roman Empire. When the Western Roman Empire came to an end in 476, the Eastern Roman Empire lived on. In time, it became known as the Byzantine Empire. Its capital was the city of Constantinople. It included most of the land around the eastern end of the Mediterranean Sea. Latin continued to be the official language of the Empire, later, Greek became the official language.

Christianity and civilization were in great danger in Western Europe, but they remained strong in the Eastern Empire. Throughout the Eastern Empire there were magnificent churches, amphitheaters, schools, libraries, and paved roads. Most cities in Western Europe were in ruins, but Constantinople remained a busy, wealthy city. Merchants came there from thousands of miles away to buy and sell silks, rugs, spices, and many other things.

Justinian was the emperor from 527 to 565. We have already read something about Justinian. He was the emperor who had all the Roman laws gathered into one code. Today, the laws of a number of Western nations are based on the Justinian Code.

Justinian dreamed of restoring the old Roman Empire. To some extent, he succeeded. After many wars, his armies won control of Italy, Sicily, southern Spain, and much of North Africa. This was not as much territory as the old Roman Empire controlled when it was at its height, but it was

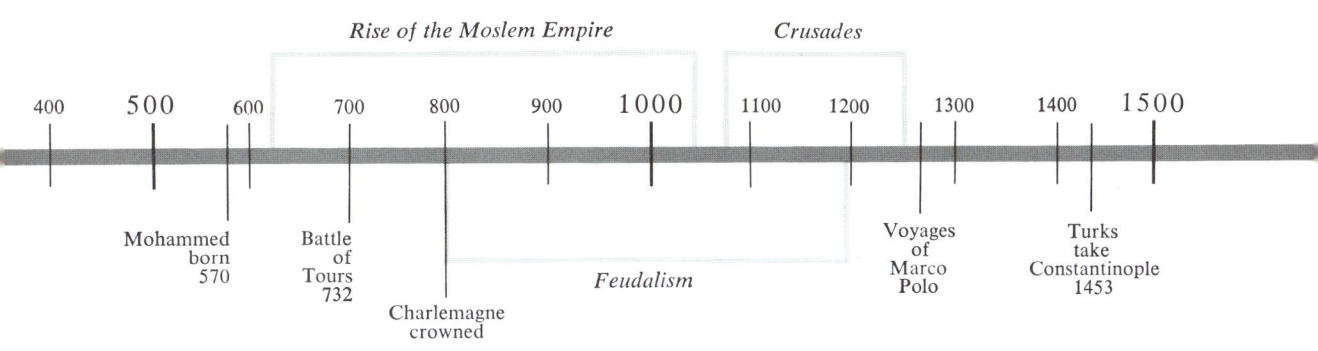

| 400 | 500 | 600 | 700 | 800 | 900 | 1000 | 1100 | 1200 | 1300 | 1400 | 1500 |

Rise of the Moslem Empire — *Crusades*

- Mohammed born 570
- Battle of Tours 732
- Charlemagne crowned
- *Feudalism*
- Voyages of Marco Polo
- Turks take Constantinople 1453

The Byzantine Empire was the stronghold of Christian civilization at the start of the Middle Ages.

more than the Byzantine Empire would ever again control.

In the capital city of Constantinople, Justinian built the beautiful church, Hagia Sophia (Holy Wisdom). Its great central dome seems to hang from the sky. Its inside walls are adorned with glass mosaics backed with gold. They are masterpieces of Christian art. Over the centuries, Hagia Sophia has been used both as a Christian church and as a Moslem mosque. Today, it is a museum visited by tourists from all over the world.

Dome-shaped Saint Sophia, built by Justinian, shows the difference between Eastern and Western architecture—curves instead of steeples.

A Split in the Church. As time went by, many of the Christians living in the Byzantine Empire wished a larger voice in the government of the Church. They said that the Archbishop of Constantinople should have almost as much authority as the Pope. The emperors agreed with this, because they could control the Archbishop of Constantinople while they could not control the Pope.

The various Popes did not agree. They said that they were the successors of St. Peter, and it would not be right to give up any of the power that Christ had bestowed on them.

In 1054, the bishops of the Eastern Empire held a meeting and declared that they no longer accepted the Pope as head of the Church. This is known as the Eastern or Greek Schism. The word "schism" means split or division. The church in the Eastern Empire became known as the Orthodox Church. It still had the Mass, the sacraments, ordained priests, and consecrated bishops, but it no longer considered the Pope as the Supreme Head. This schism has lasted to this day. There are many members of the Orthodox Church scattered throughout the world. They are found mostly in Greece and in other parts of Southeast Europe. At one time there were many Orthodox Christians in Russia. Nobody knows how many there are in Russia today, because the Communist government of that country is an enemy of all churches, including the Orthodox.

Today, Roman Catholic and Orthodox leaders are seeking ways to end the Eastern Schism. Their efforts are part of a worldwide movement to reunite all Christians.

Wild bands of Turkish horsemen overran the southeastern part of Europe, bringing the Roman Empire to an end and threatening Western Europe.

The Eastern Empire Becomes Weaker. Justinian had greatly enlarged the Byzantine Empire, but the wars had caused great losses in lives and in money. The Empire became weaker. The emperors who came after Justinian lost territory to the Lombards, the Visigoths, the Slavs, and the Moslem Arabs. By 700 the "empire" contained only the city of Constantinople and a little surrounding territory. In 1453, Constantinople fell to the Turks. This was the end of the Byzantine Empire. It had lasted almost a thousand years after the fall of the Western Roman Empire.

We Owe Much to the Byzantine Empire. Western civilization owes much to the Byzantine Empire. Much of the civilization of Western Europe had been lost as a result of the German invasions. The Byzantine Empire protected Western Europe from invaders while it was rebuilding its civilization. The Byzantines also kept the writings of many great scholars of the past. They preserved many valuable paintings and statues. Missionaries from the Byzantine Empire brought Christianity and civilization to the Slavs of Eastern Europe.

What caused the Eastern Schism? How does the Orthodox Church resemble the Roman Catholic Church?

9-2
Europe Faces New Problems

What Would Happen to Western Europe? It is hard to imagine the great change in Western Europe after the fall of the Western Empire. The Empire had brought the Roman Peace to Western Europe. The Empire had brought big cities and paved roads. It had brought beauty and learning. It had brought law and order.

Now all that was swept away. There was no longer any peace. After the various German tribes defeated the Romans, they began fighting each other. In the fighting, many cities and buildings and bridges were destroyed. Most of the Germans who moved into the empire did not know how to read or write. They did not appreciate the beautiful statues and buildings left by the Romans. They knew nothing about the system of laws the Romans had drawn up. For a time, it looked as though civilization might come to an end in Western Europe.

The Church Undertook Two Great Tasks. The Western Roman Empire was gone, but the Christian Church remained. It was the only large organization that was left in Europe. It faced two great tasks:

1. It must convert the Germans who had overrun the former Empire.

2. It must save what was good in Roman civilization.

Except for short periods, there was constant warfare in Europe between the invading tribes for many centuries. The Church acted as peacemaker.

The Church did not seem very strong when it undertook these two tasks. Many priests had been killed, and many churches had been destroyed. The Roman roads were gone, and it was hard for a bishop to get in touch with his priests. It was hard for the priests to reach the people. Many of the Germans distrusted and hated the Church.

The picture was not entirely black, however. There were three bright spots on the map. They were the Eastern Empire, Ireland, and the kingdom of the Franks.

Ireland Remained a Christian Country. Back in the days of the Roman Empire, a young Roman citizen named Patrick was kidnapped. This was around the year 400 A.D. Patrick was taken to Ireland. There he was sold as a slave. For six years, Patrick tended the flocks for his master. He loved the Irish people, and he learned to speak their language. Patrick was a Christian. He longed to teach the Irish people about God.

Patrick escaped from Ireland. For many years, he studied and prepared to be a missionary. He became a priest and a bishop. Then he went back to his beloved Ireland. Before he died, he had succeeded in bringing nearly all the Irish people into the Church.

Ireland was one country of Western Europe which was not overrun by the Germans. Churches continued to stand. There were few schools left on the continent of Europe, but the Irish monasteries had many good schools. Scholars from all over Europe came to Ireland. The country became known as the "Isle of Saints and Scholars."

After the fall of the Empire, missionaries from Ireland went forth to convert the people in all parts of Western Europe.

Training young men to become priests was one of the early endeavors of Saint Patrick. He became Ireland's first Bishop.

The Franks Become Christians. Along the Rhine River lived a group of German tribes who were called Franks. In 481 a fifteen-year-old boy became king of one of these tribes. The boy's name was Clovis. In time, Clovis united all the tribes of Franks under his rule. He became the king of the Franks.

Clovis next conquered most of Gaul, or what is now France. Gaul had been conquered by Julius Caesar four centuries earlier. It had been part of the Roman Empire. The people spoke Latin, and most of them were Christians. Clovis was kind and just to the people of Gaul. He did not treat them as conquered people. He made them the equals of his own Franks. He allowed them to practice their religion.

Clovis' wife, Clotilda, was a Christian. One day Clovis was in danger of losing an important battle. He promised that if he won the battle he, too, would become a Christian. He did win, and he kept his promise. He and 3000 of his followers were baptized on Christmas Day in 496 A.D.

The kingdom ruled by Clovis continued to grow. It included France, the Netherlands, Switzerland, and a large part of Germany.

Clovis brought law and order and peace to his region. He welcomed priests and bishops. He helped build churches. To some extent, the kingdom of the Franks had taken the place of the old Western Empire.

Clovis united the Church and the state so that both worked to bring peace and order to the kingdom.

Because of the support received in the kingdom of the Franks, the Church was better able to bring the word of Christ to all Western Europe.

1. How did the conversion of the Franks and the Irish help save western civilization?
2. What do we call the centuries between ancient and modern times?

9 3

Europe Becomes a Christian Continent

Monks Devote Their Lives to God. The Church was helped in its work of rebuilding Western Europe by communities of monks and nuns which grew up in various parts of Europe. St. Benedict played an important part in establishing these communities.

Saint Benedict lived in Rome shortly after the fall of the Roman Empire. He had been born to a noble family. Benedict was disgusted with the lazy, sinful lives which the people led. He went off to live by himself. He lived in a cave. He ate plain food, and he wore coarse clothes. He spent most of his time praying and thinking about God. A man who lives by himself in this way is called a hermit. There were many other holy hermits throughout Europe at the time of Saint Benedict.

Other men came to Saint Benedict. They said they would like to devote their lives to God. Saint Benedict drew up a set of rules to guide himself and his followers. His followers were called monks. The place where they lived was called a monastery. The head of each monastery was called an abbot.

Saint Benedict founded a number of monasteries. The most important one was at Monte Cassino, in southern Italy. Today, after more than fourteen hundred years, a monastery still stands upon Monte Cassino.

The motto of Saint Benedict's monks was "to labor is to pray." They spent much time praying, singing hymns, and thinking about God. They also did much work. They raised their own food. They made their own clothes. They did all the work about the monastery. Their work was a form of prayer. It was done for the love of God.

Monks took vows of poverty, chastity, and obedience. This means they could not own anything, they could not marry, and they had to obey their superiors. The monks wore plain robes so that they would all be dressed alike and would not take pride in their clothes. Some became priests.

Besides praying and working on the farms, the monks copied the writing of great scholars to preserve it for future use.

Monks and Nuns Start Schools. Monasteries spread throughout Europe. Each monastery had a school. At first, these schools were for young men who wished to become monks. People who lived near the monasteries asked if they could send their boys to these schools, even if the boys did not intend to become monks. The monks allowed them to do so. Here, the boys learned about the Christian religion. They also learned to read and write. They learned history, science, and numbers.

Saint Benedict's sister, Saint Scholastica, used his rules for a group of women. These women became known as nuns. The place where they lived was called a convent.

Following the Rules of St. Benedict, nuns devote each day to praying, teaching school girls, working in the convent and fields, and studying.

Some convents had schools for girls, just as the monasteries had schools for boys.

For years, the only schools in Europe were the ones taught by monks or nuns. Because of these schools, there were always some educated people in Europe. The schools kept the years after the fall of the Roman Empire from being completely dark. In passing on the knowledge of the past, they helped save civilization.

Some of the monks became missionaries. They traveled throughout Europe preaching the word of Christ. Wherever they went, they brought civilization with them.

The Monks Copy Ancient Writings. The ancient Greeks and Romans had written many beautiful poems. Some had written histories. Greek and Roman scientists had made valuable discoveries and had written about them. The parchments recording these discoveries could be lost or destroyed. There was danger that the learning of the Greeks and Romans would be lost to the world. The monks prevented this from happening. They copied the ancient writings word for word. They did this with a quill pen or a brush made from a feather. There were no printing presses or typewriters in those days. You can imagine what a difficult task this was. How would you like to take a pen and copy this book word for word? By providing schools and keeping learning alive, the monks helped save civilization.

Saint Boniface Works in France and Germany. The Popes sent missionaries throughout Western Europe. These missionaries brought the sacraments to people whose ancestors had become Christians in the days of the Roman Empire. They also converted some of the Germans. One of the greatest of these missionaries was Saint Boniface, called the Apostle of the German people.

Saint Boniface was a member of a noble family in England. He became a monk, and was later consecrated a bishop by Pope Gregory II. Boniface worked in the lands that are now France and Germany. In France, most of the people were Christians, but many of them had no priests or bishops or churches. Boniface founded many new dioceses in France. He consecrated bishops for these dioceses. He brought priests to the country. He built new churches and monasteries.

Boniface also worked among the pagan Saxons in what is now Germany. The pagans had a great oak tree which was dedicated to their god, Thor. They thought the tree was sacred. Saint Boniface took an axe and started to chop it down. The pagans stood by and watched. They were sure that Thor would punish Boniface. To their amazement, the tree crashed to the ground. Nothing had happened to Boniface. When they saw this, some of the Germans lost their belief in the pagan gods. Many became converts to Christianity.

Some of the pagans refused to give up their religion. They hated Boniface. One day a group of pagans rushed up to Boniface. The leader brought his sword down on Boniface's head. Boniface died a martyr for the Church.

St. Boniface had a chapel made from the wood of an oak he had chopped down, and dedicated it to St. Peter, Prince of the Apostles.

Christianity Spreads through Europe. While Boniface and many others were converting the German tribes in Western Europe, other missionaries worked among the Slavic peoples of Eastern Europe. This is the region that is now made up of Russia, Czechoslovakia, and Poland. The two principal missionaries in this region were the Greek monks, Saint Cyril and Saint Methodius. These two monks brought not only Christianity but also civilization to the Slavs. Saint Cyril made up an alphabet for the Slavs and taught them how to use it.

The work of the missionaries was so successful that by the year 1000 almost everybody in Europe had become a Christian.

1. Why were monasteries founded?
2. How did they help Western Europe?
3. Describe the life of St. Benedict and his followers.

9 4

The Moslems Threaten Christian Europe

Mohammed Starts a New Religion. While Europe was slowly rebuilding, a new threat to European civilization rose in the Near East. In the year 570, a boy named Mohammed was born in Mecca. Mecca was one of the few cities in Arabia, a country of vast deserts.

When Mohammed was born, most Arabs belonged to wandering tribes. They traveled from place to place, looking for water for themselves and their flocks. The Arabs were pagans. They worshiped many gods.

Merchants carried goods across the Arabian desert by camel trains. Mohammed made his living by guiding camel trains. He

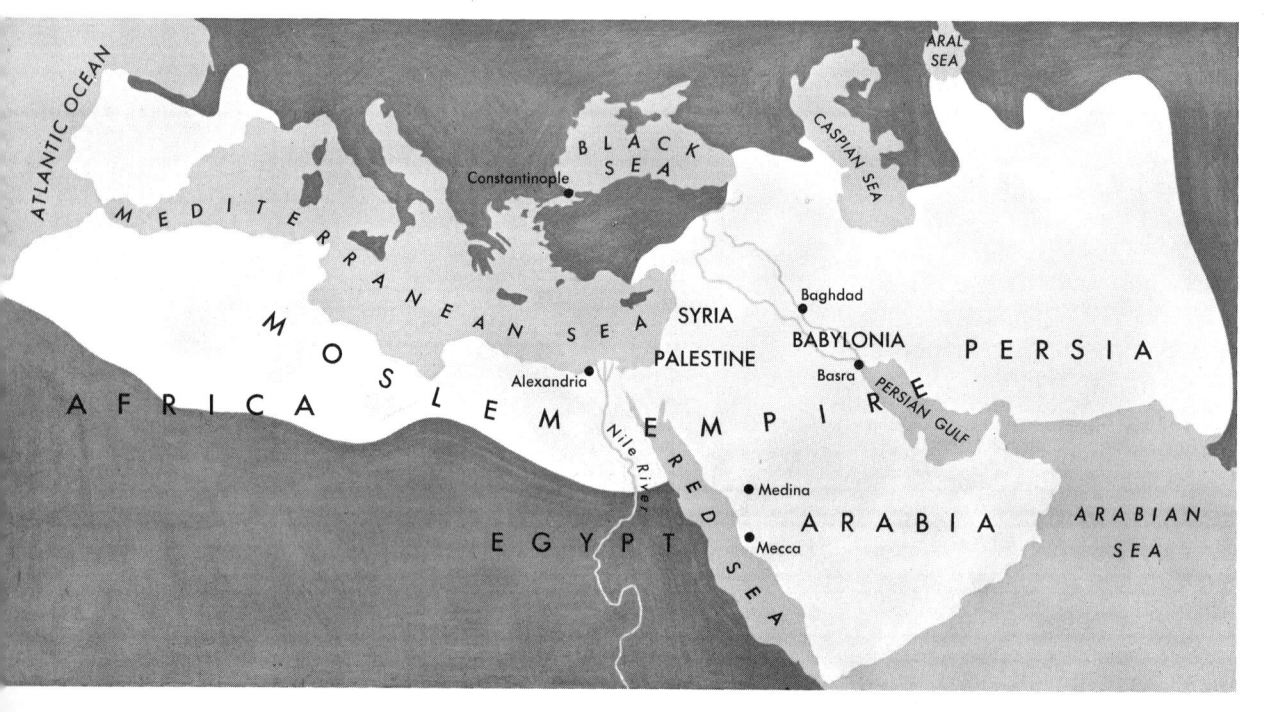

Since he was not welcome in Mecca, Mohammed gathered his followers and journeyed to Medina, where he continued to spread the Moslem religion.

met many merchants from other countries. Some of the merchants were Christians, and some were Jews. From these merchants, Mohammed learned to believe in One God.

Mohammed did not become either a Christian or a Jew. He told the Arabs that God had chosen him to start a new religion. At first, the Arabs did not like Mohammed's teachings. In 622 A.D., Mohammed and his followers had to flee from Mecca to the neighboring city of Medina. This is called the *hegira,* or flight. The hegira is the date from which the whole Mohammedan world reckons time, as we do from the birth of Christ. Later, Mohammed gained thousands of followers. His followers, known as Moslems, called their religion Islam, which means "surrender."

The Arabian word for God is "Allah." The motto of the Moslems is "There is no God but Allah, and Mohammed is His prophet." According to the Moslems, Christ was not God. Christ was a prophet but not as great a prophet as Mohammed.

After Mohammed died, his sayings were collected in a book called the Koran. The Moslems consider the Koran a sacred book. It tells the Moslems how to live and how to pray.

The Moslems Build an Empire. The Moslems believed that any man who died fighting for his religion would immediately go to paradise. They had no fear of dying, therefore, and they became fierce fighters. First the Moslems gained control of all Arabia. Then they began conquering other regions. They took Palestine and Syria away from the Eastern Empire. They conquered Persia. Next they attacked Egypt. By the year 700, the Moslems had conquered all of northern Africa and most of western Asia. The Moslems were now ready to attack Europe from two directions.

The Moslems Fail To Take Constantinople. In 717, a great force of Moslems attacked Constantinople, the capital of the Eastern Empire. If you look at the map, you will see that Constantinople is the gateway to Europe in the east. If the Moslems had taken this city, they could have swept on through most of Europe.

The defenders of Constantinople bravely held out through a siege that lasted a month. Then they drove the Moslems back. The city was saved. The Moslems could not enter Europe from that direction.

Charles Martel Defeats the Moslems in France. In 711, the Moslems crossed over from Africa and conquered Spain. They did this by defeating Roderick, the last king of the Visigoths. The Visigoths had settled in Spain two and a half centuries before. With the conquest of Spain, the Moslems were in Europe. They had been defeated in Eastern Europe, but they were more successful in Western Europe.

From Spain, the Moslems went into the country that is now France. It was here that Clovis had founded the Christian kingdom of the Franks. The leader of the Franks at this time was a man named Charles. He was such a good warrior that he was called Charles Martel, which means Charles the Hammer. In the year 732, the Franks, led by Charles Martel, met the Moslems in a great battle. The battle took place at Tours. The Franks were dressed in suits of armor. The Arabs wore turbans and long, flowing robes, and rode swift horses. Time after time the Arab horsemen charged the lines of the Franks. It was like riding into a wall of iron. After a battle that lasted all day, the Moslems withdrew. They remained in

Fall of Constantinople. After the Moslems failed to take the city, the Mohammed Empire ceased to spread. Within twenty-seven years, the Moslems were driven from France.

126

Spain, but they failed to conquer any more of Europe.

At one end of Europe, the Moslems had been defeated by the Christians of the Eastern Empire. At the other end, they had been defeated by the Christian Franks.

The battles of Constantinople and Tours are two of the most important battles of history. They saved Christian Europe.

The Moslems Develop a Rich Civilization. Mohammed's first followers were neither civilized nor well educated. Mohammed himself could not read or write. As they conquered other lands, however, the Moslems learned about the civilization of other people. They learned what the Egyptians and Persians knew about astronomy and other sciences. They learned to read the works of the Greek philosophers. They learned to erect beautiful buildings. The Moslems came to know much more about arithmetic and medicine than did the people of Europe.

In India, the Moslems learned to write numerals much like the ones we use today. The Romans, as you know, had used letters for numbers. The numerals made it much easier to work arithmetic problems. The people of Europe later learned the numerals from the Arabs, and today we call them Arabic numerals.

The Moslems introduced many new types of food into Europe such as rice, sugar, peaches, melons, oranges, and lemons. They also brought several breeds of sheep and the spirited Arabian horse. The Europeans were glad to obtain tapestries, muslin, silk, carpets, and heavy tent cloth from the Moslems.

About 800, the city of Baghdad on the Tigris River became the capital of the Moslem Empire. This was a beautiful city. You have probably read some of the stories from the *Arabian Nights* which took place in or near Baghdad. Among the best known are "Sinbad the Sailor," "Aladdin and His Wonderful Lamp," and "Ali Baba and the Forty Thieves." These stories appeal to old and young and are read widely.

The Koran contains the words of God which Mohammed wrote down. It is used in Moslem worship, and as a book to be studied in school.

1. What are some of the teachings of the Moslem religion?
2. Why were the Moslems fierce fighters?
3. How did Mohammed learn about the belief in One God?

9 5

The Pope's Kingdom

Pepin Becomes King of the Franks. After the reign of Clovis, the Franks had many weak kings. During this time, the mayor of the palace took on many of the king's duties. Charles Martel was mayor of the palace when he defeated the Moslems in 732.

When Charles Martel died, his son Pepin became mayor of the palace. It seemed to Pepin that he should have the title of king because he was doing the work of a king. He asked Pope Zacharias about this, and the Pope agreed. Pepin set aside the do-nothing king. At a meeting of the nobles, he was made king. Saint Boniface anointed Pepin.

At this time in history, the Pope became a temporal ruler of the central part of Italy, as well as a spiritual leader of the people.

The Pope Becomes the Ruler of the Papal States. The people of Rome were left without a strong government when the Roman Empire in the West came to an end. The Eastern emperor in Constantinople claimed to be the ruler of Rome. He was too far away, however, to be a very good ruler. He was not able to defend the people of Rome against their enemies.

The people turned to the Pope as their protector. He organized an army and gave Rome a government. He did these things because there was no one else to do them. He was still loyal to the emperor in Constantinople.

Some Germans called Lombards moved into northern Italy. They started a kingdom there. In 752, the Lombards marched forth to capture Rome. The Pope's army defeated them. Two years later, the Lombards again threatened war. This time their army was much more powerful. The Pope knew that he could not defeat the Lombards without help. The Pope asked the emperor at Constantinople to help him. The emperor was not able to do so. The emperor gave the Pope permission to ask help from Pepin, king of the Franks. Pope Stephen II went to the court of Pepin to ask for help. Pepin marched into Italy with a large army. The Lombards were driven from central Italy, and Rome was saved.

Pepin then did a very important thing. He said that Rome and a large part of central Italy, which he had taken from the Lombards, belonged to the Pope. He said that the Pope should rule this section. Pepin said that he would protect the Pope's kingdom from its enemies.

Charlemagne established Palace Schools where children learned to read and write. He believed in education, and recommended that the clergy teach the people.

This act was called the Donation of Pepin. It marked the beginning of the Papal States, a country ruled by the Pope. The Papal States, as they came to be known, lasted from 754 to 1870, more than 1100 years.

1. What were two results of the Lombard Invasion of Italy?
2. How did Pepin become King of the Franks?

96 The Emperor Charlemagne

Pepin's Son Becomes King of the Franks. After Pepin died, his son Charles became king of the Franks. Charles was such a great man that he was known as Charlemagne, which means "Charles the Great."

After Charlemagne became king, the Lombards once more made war against the Pope. Charlemagne came to the Pope's rescue. He defeated the Lombards. Charlemagne then made himself king of the Lombards as well as king of the Franks. Thus, he added northern Italy to his territory.

Charlemagne had to fight many wars to make his kingdom safe from its enemies. He defeated the pagan Saxons. Charlemagne added their country, Saxony, to his kingdom. He also conquered the country that is now Austria. He marched into Spain and took the northern part of that country from the Moslems.

By this time, Charlemagne's kingdom included what is now France, Germany, Switzerland, Austria, Holland, and Belgium. It also contained parts of Hungary, Yugoslavia, Romania, Poland, Italy, and Spain.

Charlemagne Is Made Emperor. On Christmas day, in the year 800, Charlemagne was kneeling at Mass in old St. Peter's in Rome. Suddenly, Pope Leo III placed a crown on his head and a cloak on his shoulders. Then the Pope declared that he had crowned Charlemagne "Emperor of the Romans."

Charlemagne issued a bulletin proclaiming that every town should have a school. He wanted all his people to have at least an elementary education.

The Pope's action did not give Charlemagne any new power or any new territory. However, it was important because the Pope showed that he thought Charlemagne had taken the place of the emperors of the West.

Under the Pope's plan, Charlemagne and his successors would keep peace in Europe as the old emperors had kept the Roman Peace. The Pope and emperor would work together. The Pope would rule in spiritual matters, and the emperor would rule in civil matters. The new emperor would protect the Church and the Pope. The emperor would always be crowned by the Pope. He would be a wise man and a good Christian.

Later, this empire became known as the Holy Roman Empire. The idea behind the Holy Roman Empire was a good one, but it did not always work out as well as the Pope had hoped.

Charlemagne Ruled Wisely. Although Charlemagne was called emperor of the Romans, his empire was quite different from the old Roman Empire. The rulers were Germans, not Romans. Most of the people spoke German, not Latin, although the educated people spoke Latin as well as German. The capital city was not Rome, and it was not even in Italy. The capital was Aachen in northern Germany. This town is often called by its French name, Aix-la-Chapelle.

Charlemagne showed in many ways that he was a good ruler. He knew that his empire was too big for him to rule without help. He divided it into counties, much as the Romans had divided their empire into provinces. He appointed a noble to manage each county. This noble was called a count.

Charlemagne sent inspectors to see whether the counts were doing their work and to see whether they were being just to the people. The counts acted as judges in disputes. They used troops to keep order.

Charlemagne was very much interested in education. He himself learned to speak Latin as well as German. In Aachen, he founded the Palace Schools. The head of this school was Alcuin, a famous scholar from England. Charlemagne also tried to have a school in every village. Unfortunately, he was never able to carry out this plan completely. However, spelling, handwriting, and grammar improved throughout the empire.

The emperor sent missionaries into every part of his empire. The Saxons and many other pagans under his rule became Christians. Charlemagne was also very generous in his gifts to the Church.

Christianity and civilization owe an enormous debt to the genius of Emperor Charlemagne. Soldier, ruler, promoter of learning, patron of religion, he is one of the truly great men of history.

The Empire Is Divided. After Charlemagne died in 814, his son Louis the Pious divided the empire among his three sons.

The western part of the empire went to Charles the Bald. This region later became known as France.

The eastern part of the empire went to Louis the German. This section of Europe later became known as Germany.

Lothaire, the oldest of the three brothers, received northern Italy and also the land between the sections given to his brothers. The latter section is known as Lorraine. Italy is cut off from the rest of Europe by the Alps. There were no mountains, however, to cut off Lorraine from France and Germany. Charles and Louis went to war, and many of the battles were fought in Lorraine. For centuries, this region remained a battleground between France and Germany.

We see, then, that we can trace the beginning of France and Germany back to the time when the vast empire of Charlemagne was divided among his three grandsons.

New Languages Appear. The Romans had never conquered the land that went to Louis the German. Here, the Franks, Saxons, and other German people continued to speak their own languages. From them, we get the modern German language.

Julius Caesar had conquered Gaul, which later became France. Many Romans had then moved into Gaul. The Latin language was spoken throughout Gaul. When the Franks conquered Gaul, they brought their language with them. Many Franks learned to speak Latin so that they could talk with the people already living in Gaul. For the same reason, many of the Romans learned the language of the Franks. From the combination of these languages comes the modern French language.

The Romans had also ruled Italy, Spain, and Portugal. When the German tribes moved into these regions, their languages became mixed with Latin. That is how the Italian, Spanish, and Portuguese languages were formed. Some words in these languages are almost alike in sound and spelling.

French, Italian, Spanish, Romanian, and Portuguese are sometimes called the Latin languages because they come largely from Latin. They are also called Romance languages. The word *Romance* comes from "Roman."

1. Why did the Pope, Leo III, crown Charlemagne "Emperor of the Romans"?
2. How was Charlemagne's empire divided after his death?

Chapter **9. REVIEW**

Learning To Use New Words

Use each of the following terms in an original sentence, expressing something you have learned in Chapter 9:

Clovis	Allah	orthodox
hermit	schism	Byzantine
abbot	Gaul	Moslem

Knowing the Important Facts

1. List at least four reasons why Western civilization owes gratitude to the Byzantine Empire.
2. What were some of the problems the Christian Church faced after the fall of the Roman Empire? What were three bright spots in the otherwise dim picture of the period?
3. Describe the works of three men who helped make Europe a Christian Community.
4. What new religion developed in the near East? Who was its founder? How much territory had the followers of this religion conquered by the year 700?
5. How did Charlemagne strengthen his empire?
6. How did the Papal States come into being?

Thinking Through the Facts

1. How can you account for the wide appeal and amazing spread of Mohammed's religion?
2. How did the Christian Church preserve the culture and learning of Rome?
3. How did the Moslems develop a rich civilization? How have they contributed to the Western way of life?
4. Why was Charles, King of the Franks, called Charles the Great or Charlemagne?
5. How did Pope Leo III hope to re-establish the Roman Peace?

Developing a Time Sense

Arrange the following events in the proper time order:
1. The Battle of Tours
2. The fall of Constantinople
3. The beginning of the Moslem religion
4. Pope is no longer accepted as head of the Eastern Church
5. Charlemagne is crowned emperor by the pope

Chapter 10

How People Lived in Feudal Times

There was great confusion in Western Europe after the fall of the Western Roman Empire. With the help of the Church, Christianity and civilization were saved in Western Europe. Then Charlemagne united much of Western Europe under his rule. He was crowned emperor by the Pope. For a time it looked as if Charlemagne's empire would take the place of the old Western Roman Empire. People hoped that Western Europe would be united in the new empire and that there would be law and order. But Charlemagne's empire came apart when he died. Once more, there was no strong ruler in Western Europe. How could the people protect themselves from enemies and robbers?

Out of this confusion the feudal system developed. We already know something about feudalism. We read that China had this system long ago.

10 1

The Growth of Feudalism

The People Needed Protection. When the Roman Empire was at its height, there was law and order throughout much of the known world. Roman soldiers saw that the *Pax Romana* was kept. A man could travel thousands of miles without being bothered by robbers or pirates. And he would not come to a place where a war was being fought.

This was changed as the Western Empire became weaker and finally fell. For a time, Charlemagne's empire brought some law and order, but this did not last long. The Northmen sailed along the seacoasts and

The peasant had to work on the noble's land about three days a week, and more during harvest time. For this service the noble protected him.

rivers of Europe. They raided farms and villages. Hungarians drove from the east into Germany, France, and Italy. Moslems conquered Spain and threatened the rest of Europe. Bands of robbers roamed the countryside.

The people of Europe were frightened. Who would protect them from all these dangers? Not the kings; the kings were not strong enough.

The People Turned to the Nobles. There were many men in Europe who ruled vast tracts of land. These men were called nobles, or lords.

The nobles got the land they ruled in various ways. The usual way was for a king to award land to a man for doing battle. Then this land was handed down from father to son. Every time a lord died and his son took his place, the son had to promise to be loyal to the king. Thus, he became a *vassal* of the King. After the vassal had made the promise of homage, the king would give him the right to rule his *fief*. The fief was the land entrusted to the noble.

Each great noble was a vassal of the king. The great nobles had lesser vassals of their own, and these, in turn, might have vassals of *their* own.

The nobles built castles from which they could defend themselves against attack. The nobles also had fighting men called knights.

When the common people saw that the kings were not powerful enough to protect them, they turned to the nobles for protection. The common people came from the farms and from the cities and lived in villages close to the castle. They agreed to work for the noble in pay for the protection he gave them. These common people were called *peasants*. Most of the peasants were *serfs*. This means they were not allowed to leave the *manor* on which they lived. A manor was the land ruled by a noble.

This system of vassals, serfs, knights, fiefs, and manors was called feudalism. The feudal period was a time of powerful nobles, many of them more powerful than the kings. It was a time when most common people led hard and uncomfortable lives and were little better than slaves.

There Was Little Travel and Little Trade. There was much travel and much trade during the days of the *Pax Romana*. The word *trade* means "buying and selling." Farmers brought their crops into the city to sell them. While they were in the city, they bought goods from far-off places. If they had enough money, they could even buy beautiful silks from China. There was much travel because

Hunting season. The king and his nobles frequently could be seen riding through the fields, hunting deer, fox, or fowl.

men had to carry the things that were bought and sold. Roman merchants sent ships to ports all along the Mediterranean to buy and sell goods. Merchants also traveled over the many fine roads of the Roman Empire. These merchants brought back news of the things they had seen. There must be cities when there is much trade. The Roman Empire had many cities. Here the ships loaded and unloaded their cargoes. Here people came to buy and sell in the many market places.

Life was quite different in the feudal period. There was very little trade. Moslem pirates seized Christians who dared sail on the Mediterranean. Robbers preyed on merchants who traveled on land. Roman cities had been destroyed or deserted. Roman roads had been abandoned and were filled with cracks and overrun by weeds. Roman money no longer had any value.

Because there was no trade, each manor had to be *self-sufficient*. This means that each manor had to produce the things it needed. The people on the manor had to provide their own food, shelter, and clothing. Life was much simpler than it had been in Roman days. There were no beautiful silks from China. There were no spices from India. Food, shelter, and clothing were very plain, especially for the serfs.

Because there was no travel, people knew very little about other parts of the world. Most serfs never left the manor on which they had been born.

Many Roman cities had been destroyed by the Roman invaders and had never been rebuilt. In the cities still standing, the people had no way to make a living. So, hundreds of people left the cities to live on a manor. They gave up their freedom and became serfs because that is the only way they could make a living. Great cities seemed to be a thing of the past. Life in the feudal period was quite different from life in the days of the *Pax Romana*.

1. Mention three ways in which life in the feudal period differed from life in the days of the *Pax Romana*.
2. Why did travel and trade decrease after the Fall of the Western Empire?

10·2
Lords and Knights

The Castle Was a Fort. Each great noble built a castle which was a fort and also a home for him and his family. The people who lived on land belonging to a noble came to the castle in time of war. The first castles were built of wood, but the later ones were built of stone.

Usually, a noble built his castle on top of a high hill. If there was no hill, a ditch, or moat, was dug around the castle. This moat was filled with water. In times of peace, visitors to the castle crossed the moat on a drawbridge. When the castle was being attacked, the drawbridge was pulled up.

The castle was surrounded by a strong, thick wall. This wall was too high to climb and too strong to batter down. On top of the wall, there were many narrow openings.

When the castle was being attacked, the defenders shot arrows through these openings. Through openings, the defenders also dropped heavy stones and poured hot tar on the enemy. You can see that it was almost impossible at that time to capture a castle that was well defended.

Inside the castle was a large, open space called the courtyard. When the castle was being attacked, the people of the neighborhood gathered in the courtyard. Often they brought pigs and cattle so that they would have food in case the attack went on for a long time.

Around the courtyard were many smaller buildings. These were used as storehouses and stables.

BARRA

DRAWBRIDGE

Inside the courtyard was another wall which gave added protection to the inner court. In this inner court was the keep, or donjon. The castle itself was a tall, thick-walled building where the noble and his family lived. Close by was the chapel.

The castle was not a comfortable place to live. It was often cold and damp. It had very little furniture.

The Great Hall Was the Living Room and Dining Room. The main room of the castle was the great hall. This hall was a combined living room and dining room. It had a large fireplace to keep it warm. The noble and his family spent much of their time in this hall. Here, they usually entertained their guests.

The noble often had feasts in this hall. After the feast, the guests might be entertained by a wandering minstrel. In some parts of Europe, these minstrels were called troubadours. The minstrels and troubadours sang songs about beautiful ladies and great heroes. Many of the songs were about Charlemagne and one of his warriors, Roland.

The Fighting Men Were Called Knights. Each noble needed a number of fighting men to protect himself from other nobles. These fighting men were called knights.

When a knight rode forth to battle, he wore a heavy metal suit. This was called a suit of armor. The armor protected him from the arrows and spears of his enemies. The armor was so heavy that it was difficult for a knight to climb on his horse. Often he had to be seated on the horse by ropes and pulleys. Only the strongest horses could carry knights who were wearing armor.

The knights also carried shields to protect themselves from their enemies. For weapons, the knights had swords, lances, and spears. Each knight wore a family coat of arms. To tell one knight from another, a picture of a bird, a flower, or an animal was painted on his armor.

Knights were always members of noble families, but not all members of noble families could become knights. Before a young man could become a knight, he had to be trained for many years, and he had to pass many tests. The education of a knight began at the age of seven. He was taken from his home and sent to the castle of some famous nobleman. He served the lord as a page until he was fourteen years old. He was taught many things: to be a good Christian, to use arms well, to ride a horse. At the age of fourteen, he became a squire. He could now accompany his knight to war. At the age of twenty-one, if he had been a good page and squire, he was ready to undergo the ceremony that prepared him for knighthood.

After spending the night in prayer, the young squire who was about to be knighted

Knighthood

Knighthood flourished in the feudal age of great stone castles. A knight was a mounted man-at-arms clad in bright armor. A heavy metal suit covered him from head to foot. An iron helmet with a movable visor guarded his face. His weapons were a long lance and a shining sword. On his left arm he bore a shield to ward off blows in battle. The shield carried the family coat of arms, with a bird, a flower, or an animal to mark one knight from others in his household. The knight's steed wore protective armor and mail, over which was a richly colored silken covering.

The Making of a Knight

1 A nobleman's son began training to be a knight at the age of seven. He became a page to some lord and lady. He waited on table and ran errands. He studied religion, music, and the code of chivalry. He learned to ride and hunt.

2 At fourteen a page became a squire to one particular knight. For seven years he cared for his knight's horse and polished his armor. He learned to use the lance and the sword.

3 He accompanied his master everywhere. He rode forth with him to battle. The squire also cared for him if he was wounded.

4 A squire, if worthy, was made a knight at twenty-one. The ceremony of knighting began with an all-night vigil of prayer. Next morning the squire confessed, heard Mass, received Holy Communion, and took the knight's vows. Then before knights and ladies, the lord struck him on the shoulder, saying, "I dub thee knight. Be brave and loyal."

The Tournament

After a knighting, the lord usually held a tournament. A tournament featured contests of skill and courage between two knights or groups of knights. It was both sport and training for war. Knights from near and far took part. On his helmet each knight wore his fair lady's scarf. In combat he strove to bring honor to her as well as glory to himself.

went to Mass and then took the vow of knighthood. This vow expressed the ideals of chivalry. The knight-to-be solemnly promised to speak the truth always, to keep the Faith, to be brave and honorable, to maintain the right, to protect women, to help those in trouble, and to be merciful to the weak.

The Knights Took Part in Tournaments. How did the knights and nobles amuse themselves? Hunting was a favorite sport of the nobles. Every castle was located near a large forest. Here, the nobles rode on horseback and hunted boars, deer, and other wild animals. Another favorite sport was hawking. Lords and ladies had hawks, or falcons, which were trained to catch pheasants, quail, and other birds. When the falcons were not bringing down other birds, they perched on the wrists of their masters or mistresses. They had chains about their legs and hoods over their heads.

Tournaments were the principal sport of feudal days. The knights would ride toward each other with their lances raised. Each knight tried to strike the shield of another knight hard enough to knock him off his horse. Sometimes just two knights took part in a contest of this kind. Sometimes there would be many knights on each side. Lords and ladies watched and cheered from their seats in the pavilion. We would call this the grandstand. The common people were often allowed to come to watch tournaments, but they were not allowed in the pavilion.

1. How did a young man prepare for knighthood?
2. Do you think you would have enjoyed being a feudal lord or lady? Give reasons for your answer.

10 3
The Church and Knighthood

The Church Introduces the Laws of Chivalry. One of the worst features of the early Middle Ages was the constant fighting among the nobles. Each noble was served by many knights. These knights were trained to fight; fighting was their business. When two nobles had a quarrel, they often sent their knights into battle. Sometimes many lives were lost in these battles.

The Church wished to put an end to this fighting, but it was not able to do so. Although the Church could not stop the fighting completely, it was able to prevent much of it.

One of the ways the Church stopped some of the fighting was by introducing the laws of chivalry. These were the laws which all knights were expected to obey. The beautiful vow which a young man made when he became a knight was introduced by the Church. Under the laws of chivalry, knights were supposed to fight only for worthy purposes. They were taught always to help widows and orphans and people who were weak and helpless.

The Peace of God Limited the Places Where Fighting Could Take Place. Another means by which the Church tried to prevent fighting was the Peace of God. Under this rule, knights were forbidden to fight near churches, monasteries, and other holy places. They were also forbidden to attack people who were not armed.

The Right of Sanctuary Saved Many Lives. A man who was fleeing from his enemies was safe if he could reach a church. The knights who were pursuing him were not allowed to force him to leave a church. This was called the right of sanctuary. The priest would question the man very carefully. If the man proved his innocence, he would be freed. If it looked as though he might be guilty, he was delivered to the authorities for a fair trial. The lives of many innocent people were saved in this way.

The Truce of God Forbade Knights to Fight on Certain Days. By the Truce of God, the Church at first forbade fighting on Sunday. The Truce lasted from Saturday evening to Monday morning. Later, the truce lasted from Wednesday evening to Monday morning. The Truce also said that there should be no fighting during Lent, Advent, the harvest season, and many other times. In the end, fighting was forbidden during about three-fourths of the year.

What happened if a knight decided not to pay any attention to the Peace of God or the Truce of God? Such a person might be excommunicated. He would not be allowed in a church, and he would not be permitted to receive the sacraments. Other people were forbidden to speak to him or do business with him. This was a severe punishment which all knights wished to avoid.

1. Why was the Church able to help control fighting during the feudal period?
2. Explain how the right of sanctuary operated.

The Fugitive. The Right of Sanctuary, at first, was limited to a church. Later, it extended to the churchyard, so that the person would not have to live in the church.

10 4

The Common People

The Serfs Belonged to the Soil. The lords spent much of their time hunting and hawking and managing the affairs of the manor. The knights spent most of their time training for battle. Who did all the work on the manor? The work was done by the common people, or peasants.

Near each castle or manor house was a little village. The peasants lived in this village. The village had narrow dirt streets which were usually filled with rubbish. The houses were made of rough timber and had thatched roofs.

A few of the peasants were freemen. This meant that they were allowed to leave the manor and look for work somewhere else. They seldom did this. There were few cities to go to, and very few jobs in those cities. Work on all the manors was very much the same, so there was little reason to change.

Long hours of hard work was the lot of the serf. Lacking was the modern farm equipment to make their work bearable.

Most of the peasants were serfs. A serf had little freedom. He could not leave the estate on which he had been born. If someone else bought the estate or took it over by force, the serf worked for the new owner. We say that the serf was "bound to the soil." This means he went with the property, no matter who owned it. He could not move away.

Although the serf had little freedom, he was not a slave. The noble could not sell a serf as a Roman master could sell his slaves. Nor could a serf be moved from the land on which he worked. The same family of serfs would stay on the same land for hundreds of years, from one generation to another.

The Serfs Worked for Themselves and the Lords. The farmers of feudal times did not know very much about fertilizers and about taking care of the soil. They did know, however, that soil soon became worn out if used year after year. To prevent this, the fertile land on the manor was divided into three large fields. Only two of the three fields were planted each year. Therefore, each field was given a rest every third year. This practice was known as the three-field system.

The three fields were divided into long, narrow strips. Each family of serfs was given several of these strips in each field. In this way, no one serf worked all the good land or all the bad land. A serf spent much of his time in going from one strip to another and from one field to the next.

On these strips, the serfs raised the things which they needed for themselves. They worked on their own land about three days a week. Part of what they raised on their own land had to be given to the lord.

The serf also had to work about three days a week for the lord. He helped in the fields that belonged to the lord. He also helped build roads and do other jobs about the manor. In this way, the serf paid for his land and for the protection which the lord gave him.

The Life of the Serf Was Not Easy. In many ways, the serf lived a hard life. His house was small and uncomfortable. It had only the ground for a floor. There were no windows. The only chimney was a hole in the roof. The serf usually slept on straw spread out on the dirt floor.

The serfs wore simple clothes made of rough, homespun cloth. They wrapped pieces of cloth around their legs to keep them warm in winter. Instead of wearing shoes, they wrapped their feet in heavy cloth and strapped on wooden soles.

The food was very simple. It was mainly porridge, soup, salt pork, fish, and black bread.

Usually, the serfs were not allowed to leave the manor. Most of them had never been more than a few miles from home. Most of them could not read or write.

The serf was not allowed to hunt in the lord's forest. When the serf ground his wheat, he had to use the lord's mill, and he had to pay for doing so. He also had to pay for making bread in the lord's mill. If he went across a river, he had to pay for using the lord's bridge. There was no money, so all these payments had to be made either in crops or in work.

If a serf was accused of a crime, he was tried in the lord's court. He was tried by a jury of his equals—other serfs.

Could a Serf Gain Freedom? There were a few serfs who tried to escape from their lords. If a serf could run away and not be captured for a year and a day, he was a freeman. This was not easy to do, because no other lord would take a strange serf onto his manor. If an escaped serf went to a town, he would have a hard time finding work.

Sometimes, a lord granted a serf his freedom because of an unusual service he had performed. A serf was usually given his freedom if he wished to become a priest or a monk in the service of God's Church.

The Church declared many holy days, so that the serfs would have a holiday and a festival singing and dancing on the village lawn.

It was unusual, however, for a serf to secure freedom. Most serfs went on living and working on the manor on which they had been born.

Religion Was Important to the Peasants. There is no doubt that the peasants of the feudal period lived hard lives. They did have some consolation from their religion, however. Almost all the peasants were Christians. Each little village had its church and its priest. The priest told the peasants that if they served God in this life, a much better life would be awaiting them.

Most of the peasants' fun centered about the church. There was no work for them on Sundays or on holy days. After Mass on these days, the peasants gathered in an open place in the village. They danced, sang, and played games. You have probably seen some European folk dances and have heard some folk songs. Most of these go back to the villages of feudal times.

> What do we mean when we say the serfs "belonged to the soil"?
> How does this differ from belonging to an individual as a slave?

Chapter 10. REVIEW

Learning To Use New Words

Use each of the following terms in an original sentence, expressing something you have learned in Chapter 10:

feudalism	peasant
noble	manor
vassal	serf
fief	armor
knight	chivalry

Knowing the Important Facts

1. What were the main reasons feudalism developed in Europe?
2. How did most nobles acquire their fiefs? What duty did the noble owe the king?
3. What were the duties of a knight? How did a boy prepare to be a knight?
4. Mention four attempts the Church made during the Middle Ages to establish peace.
5. What classes of society existed in the age of feudalism?

Thinking Through the Facts

1. Why did the medieval manor become a self-supporting unit?
2. Why might we call the Middle Ages, the "Age of the Castle"?
3. How did life differ for a serf and a knight?
4. Explain the rules the Church set up to try to control fighting in the Middle Ages.
5. Explain why the system of crop rotation was necessary on medieval farms. How did it differ from today's crop rotation?

Chapter *11*

The Crusades Change Europe

In the year 1095, the people of Europe took part in a great war, in an attempt to rescue the Holy Land from the Moslems. This war was called the First Crusade. Many other crusades followed. The Crusades changed the habits of the people of Europe and the course of history.

11 1

The Crusades

The Holy Land. We have read about Palestine several times in this book. Palestine is a small land at the eastern end of the Mediterranean Sea. Our Lord was born in Palestine and spent most of His life there.

Palestine is often called the Holy Land because it contains so many places associated with the life of Our Lord. Christians like to go to the Holy Land and pray at the shrines sacred to the memory of Christ. In Jerusalem, they make the Way of the Cross, following the same route Our Lord took when He carried His Cross. At the Holy Sepulcher, they pray at the spot where Our Lord was buried. People who go to the Holy Land to pray and to pay homage to Christ are called pilgrims.

The Moslem Turks Take the Holy Land. We know that Palestine was the home of the Jews when Our Lord was born. We also know that it was part of the Roman Empire. In 66 A.D., the Jews revolted against the Romans. The Romans put down the revolt after great bloodshed. Jerusalem, the principal city of the Holy Land, was destroyed. The Jews scattered to every part of the then-known world. Jerusalem was later rebuilt, but it was no longer a Jewish city. When the Roman Empire was divided, Palestine was part of the Eastern, or Byzantine, Empire.

The German tribes swept over the Western Empire, and it came to an end. The Church in Western Europe faced a great task of rebuilding. But the Byzantine Empire remained strong, and it remained Christian. The Holy Land enjoyed peaceful days under Christian rule. In the very early Middle Ages, just after the fall of the Western Empire, most of the pilgrims were from other parts of the Byzantine Empire.

In the seventh century, the Moslem Arabs conquered many lands and built a vast empire. Some of the conquered land was taken from the Byzantine Empire, and this included Palestine. Thus, the Holy Land came under non-Christian rule.

While the Arabs ruled Palestine, many of the people of Western Europe were becoming Christians. The feudal system had brought a certain amount of law and order to Western Europe. Some nobles, priests, and bishops made pilgrimages to the Holy Land. The Arab rulers permitted them to do this.

Not many peasants could become pilgrims to the Holy Land. They did not have the time nor the wealth to make such a trip. As we know, most peasants seldom left the manor on which they had been born. When the pilgrims returned to Western Europe they told about what they had seen in Palestine. This made many people feel close to the Holy Land.

In 1071, people called Turks took much of eastern Asia from the Arabs. This included the Holy Land. Like the Arabs, the Turks were Moslems. Unlike the Arabs, the Turks hated the Christians. They captured large numbers of pilgrims and made slaves of them. Other pilgrims were robbed, and some were killed.

The Turks had conquered land very close to Constantinople, the capital of the Byzantine Empire. The city was in danger of being captured by the Turks. By this time, the Byzantine Empire was small. Emperor Alexius was afraid he did not have enough soldiers to defend his land from the Turks. He asked Pope Urban II to help him.

The Pope Calls for a Holy War. Pope Urban II did not like the fact that the Turks might soon capture Constantinople and destroy the Byzantine Empire. The Christians of the Byzantine Empire no longer acknowledged the Pope as their head, but there were strong ties between the Christians of the West and the Christians of the East. Also, the Byzantine Empire was like a wall between the Moslems of Asia and the Christians of Europe. If that wall should be destroyed, the Moslems might overrun Europe.

Pope Urban decided to act. He sent word to the nobles and bishops of Western Europe to meet him in the town of Clermont in south central France. The meeting was held on a broad plain just outside the town. It was in the autumn of 1095.

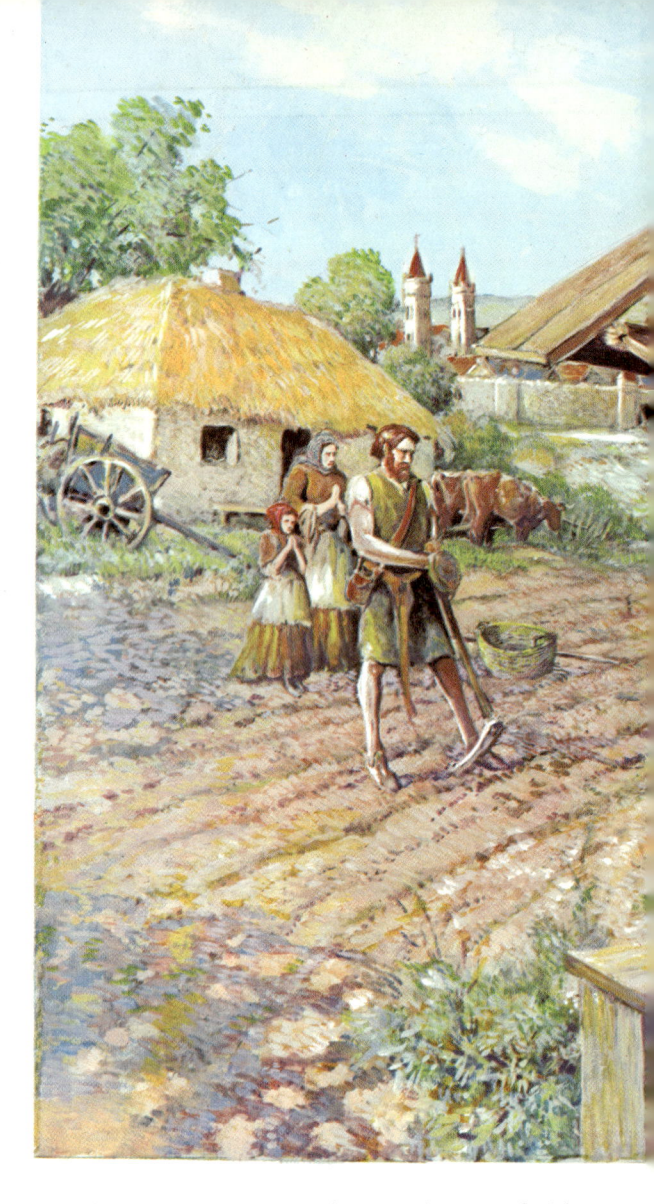

The crowd grew silent as the Pope began to speak. He told the people about the terrible dangers faced by pilgrims who traveled to Jerusalem. He told them that their fellow-Christians in the Byzantine Empire faced a great danger. He said that all Europe would be in danger if Constantinople

Off to the Crusades. Most of the Crusaders were Frenchmen. They travelled by horse and by foot to carry on a war to recapture the Holy Land.

fell. The Pope pleaded with lords and knights to forget their wars with one another and to unite in a great campaign against the Moslem Turks.

The Pope's words stirred the crowd. Someone shouted, "God wills it!" Soon the cry was taken up by the crowd. "God wills it! God wills it!"

The people who were at the meeting went to their homes and told others what had happened. Soon, the cry "God wills it!" was heard all over Western Europe. It became the motto of all those who took part in the holy wars of the next two centuries.

The Crusaders Capture Jerusalem. Plans were made for a great war against the Moslem Turks. The war was called a Crusade,

The Crusaders had to roll high ladder towers to the walls of the city, then fight their way over the walls and on through the streets of the city.

from a Latin word that means "cross." The soldiers who took part in the Crusade wore a cross made of red cloth. They were called Crusaders. Nobles, knights, and thousands of peasants became Crusaders.

Why did so many men wish to become Crusaders? There were many reasons. Some merely wished to get away from home and see more of the world. Some longed for adventure. Some nobles saw a chance to gain wealth and land. But many went because the Pope had asked them to go, and because they felt they were doing the will of God.

The First Crusade was led by great nobles. One of these was Godfrey of Bouillon. The Crusaders gathered their forces in Constantinople. Some of them reached Constantinople after a long, tiring march of many months. Others came by sea. In Constantinople, they were joined by soldiers of the Byzantine Empire.

From Constantinople, the First Crusade made a long dangerous march across Asia Minor. Thousands of soldiers were killed in battle, and other thousands died from disease and starvation. Only a few thousand of the original tens of thousands were alive when they reached Jerusalem. These forgot their suffering when they saw the Holy City. They fell to their knees and kissed the ground. With tears in their eyes, they shouted "Jerusalem, Jerusalem!"

After several weeks of fighting, the Crusaders took Jerusalem on July 15, 1099.

The Crusaders wished to make Godfrey of Bouillon the king of Jerusalem. Godfrey refused to take this title. "I will not wear a crown of gold in a city where Our Lord wore a crown of thorns," he said. Instead, he called himself the Defender of the Holy Sepulcher.

Many of the Crusaders went home after Jerusalem had been captured. But some remained to defend Jerusalem and the rest of the Holy Land. Those who remained were joined by new soldiers from Western Europe.

Second, Third, and Fourth Crusades. Little by little, the Turks won back most of the land the Crusaders had taken from them. About fifty years after the First Crusade, the Christians in Jerusalem were afraid their city would again fall to the Turks. They begged the Pope for help. St. Bernard, a French monk, inspired men by his preaching to join a new Crusade. The Second Crusade was not well organized. It returned in defeat.

A Moslem named Saladin became the ruler of Syria, Egypt, and the Valley of the Two Rivers. Saladin thought that Jerusalem had been unfairly taken from the Moslems. In 1187, he declared a "holy war," and his forces captured most of the territory held by the Crusaders. This included Jerusalem.

To regain Jerusalem, the Third Crusade was organized. It was led by the three greatest rulers in Europe: Frederick Barbarosa of Germany, Philip Augustus of France,

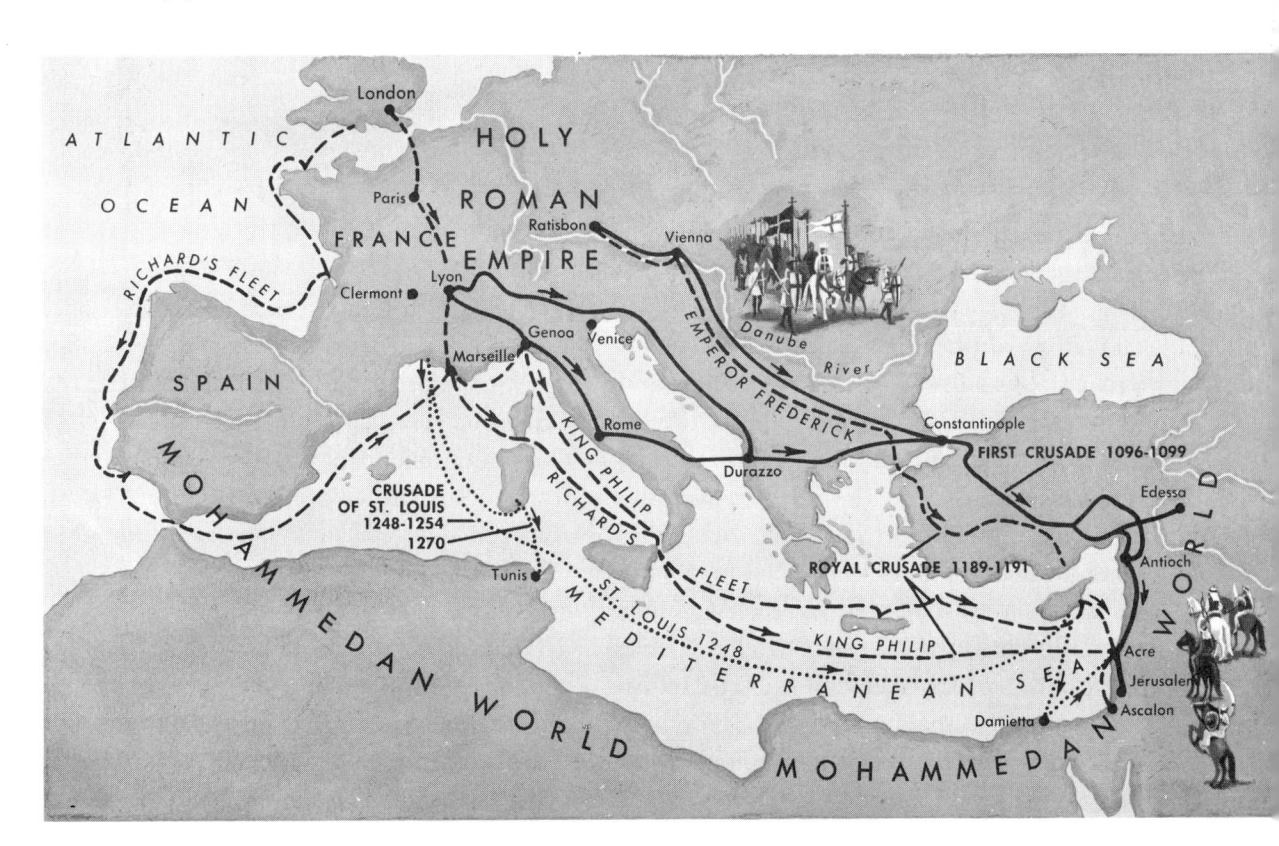

Kings, nobles, peasants, and even children joined the ranks of the Crusaders who traveled hundreds of miles and failed to take the Holy Land.

and Richard the Lion-Heart of England. Frederick was drowned in Asia Minor, and many of his followers returned home. Philip and Richard quarreled, and Philip returned to France.

Richard fought bravely, but his forces were no match for those of Saladin. Many Crusaders were captured by the Moslems. Saladin treated the prisoners kindly. Those who were wealthy were allowed to return home after they paid a ransom. Those who were poor were allowed to return home without paying a ransom.

Saladin agreed to a truce which would permit pilgrims to visit Jerusalem.

The Fourth Crusade was a shameful one. It never reached the Holy Land. In 1202, against the orders of Pope Innocent III, the Crusaders seized the great Christian city of Constantinople. They destroyed many great works of art and sent others back to Western Europe. The city and the land around it were divided among various nobles of Western Europe.

This almost marked the end of the Byzantine Empire. After a few years, there was once again an emperor on the throne, but the Empire was only a shadow of what it had once been. The Empire had been weakened and almost destroyed, not by its enemies, the Moslems, but by the Crusaders who were supposed to be its friends.

The Children's Crusades. Stephen was a twelve-year-old-boy who lived in France. He said that God had told him that only innocent children could drive the Moslems out of the Holy Land. Thousands of French children followed his lead. Some died on the way, but about 30,000 children reached Marseilles in the southern part of what is now France. Few of these children were more than twelve years old. Some of them were girls.

In Marseilles, unscrupulous men loaded the exhausted, half-starved children into old, rotted ships, and said they were taking them to the Holy Land. Two of the ships sank, and the children drowned. The other children were taken to Egypt and sold into slavery.

Nicholas, a German boy, heard about Stephen's preaching, and he started a similar crusade. Thousands joined him. He led his young crusaders over the Alps to Rome. More than two-thirds of them died during this difficult journey. In Rome, Pope Innocent III received the children kindly and told them to go home. Most of them were too worn out to make the return journey. They found homes in various villages along the way and never returned to their homes in Germany.

Fifth, Sixth, and Seventh Crusades. The Moslems were divided and weakened when the Fifth Crusade was held in 1228 and 1229. They agreed to free Jerusalem. They soon regained control. This led to the Sixth Crusade in 1249, under King Louis IX

The Children's Crusade. One of the greatest tragedies of all time was the misdirected zeal of thousands of children who thought they could help to capture the Holy Land.

of France. He was later declared a saint. Louis was captured and released when a large ransom was paid. Louis was also one of the leaders of the Seventh Crusade which was held in 1270. He died of the plague, and the Crusade failed.

Were the Crusades a Complete Failure? The Crusades had three principal objects: (1) to rescue the Holy Land from the Moslems, (2) to save the Byzantine Empire from the Moslems, and (3) to protect Western Europe from the Moslems. The holy wars covered a period of almost two hundred years. Their cost was great in lives, in wealth, and in time. When they were over, the Holy Land was still in the hands of the Turks. Part of the old Byzantine Empire still stood, but it had been greatly weakened by the Crusaders themselves. The Crusaders, therefore, failed in their chief purpose.

It is believed, however, that the holy wars saved Europe from being invaded by the Moslem Turks. In that sense, then, the Crusades were a success.

Later, the Turks sent a great fleet against Europe. They were defeated in the famous naval battle of Lepanto.

Whether they were or were not successful, the Crusades brought about great changes in Europe. These changes affected the lives of millions of people. We shall see later that these changes helped lead to the discovery of America.

1. Why were the European Christians anxious to help the Orthodox Christians of Constantinople?
2. What is a pilgrimage? Why were pilgrimages undertaken?

11 2

Trade and New Towns Weaken Feudalism

The Crusaders Find Wonderful Things in the Near East. We know that the people of Western Europe lived very simply in feudal times. They knew little about the world, because most of them never traveled far from their own homes. The peasants lived in plain houses, wore plain clothes, and ate plain food. Even the nobles lived simply. Their castles were large, but they were also cold and bare. The nobles had better food than did the peasants, but even the best food was not very good. Most people of Western Europe did not know that it was possible to live more comfortable lives.

Then the Crusades began. Thousands of men who had never been more than twenty miles from their own homes journeyed thousands of miles to Constantinople and to the Holy Land. This part of the world is called the Near East.

In Europe, the Crusaders had seen nothing but castles, manor houses, and the ugly little villages of the peasants. Their eyes opened wide when they saw Constantinople. Here, they saw a city of a million people, with paved and lighted streets, great parks, hospitals, theaters, well-trained police, fine palaces, and excellent schools.

"Why can't we have cities like this in our countries?" the Crusaders said to each other.

In the markets of the Near East, the Crusaders saw many wonderful things. They saw diamonds, rubies, emeralds, pearls, sapphires, and other precious stones. They saw

The Crusaders discovered a new world of arts, crafts, and luxuries in the Near East, samples of which they brought back to Europe with them.

beautiful glass and china. They saw rugs woven in magnificent colors. Gorgeous silks and other fabrics were displayed. There were dyes which made the plainest cloth beautiful.

The Crusaders learned that Arab traders had brought many of these wares to the Near East from India, China, and other faraway countries.

The People of Europe Want to Buy Goods from the Near East. When the Crusaders returned to Western Europe, they told their families and friends about the wonderful things they had seen. They also showed them samples which they had brought home. The people who had remained at home shared the amazement of the returning Crusaders. They were interested in all the goods of the Near East, but they were especially interested in the spices.

You may wonder why the people of Europe were so interested in spices. Pepper, cinnamon, nutmeg, cloves, and ginger probably do not seem important to you. The people of the Middle Ages, however, felt that they were very important. There were no refrigerators in those days. Spices helped keep the food from spoiling. In addition, the people had little variety in their food. Spices gave food a different flavor.

"Where can we buy these spices, these dyes, and the other wonderful things you have brought home with you?" people asked the Crusaders.

They soon found that they could buy supplies of these Eastern goods from Italian merchants.

Italian Merchants Carry Eastern Goods to Europe. Even before the Crusades, merchants in the Italian cities of Genoa and Venice had been carrying on trade with the Near East. The merchants sold the goods mostly to the people of their own cities. The

The new products and new ideas which the Crusaders brought home encouraged people to travel and see other places in the world.

people in other parts of Western Europe did not know about the goods. But after the Crusades, almost everybody in Western Europe knew about them. The Italian merchants found themselves with more and more customers. They sent more and more ships to the Near East.

Other merchants bought the goods from the Italians. These merchants carried the goods up rivers and along roads to people who lived far from the seacoast. For the first time since the days of the Roman Empire, the people of Western Europe were buying and selling in large amounts.

Roads which had not been used since Roman days were repaired and used again. With good roads, people traveled more than they had before. Life in Western Europe was beginning to change.

Towns Established. New kinds of workers were needed when trade increased in Western Europe. Men were needed to load and unload products on ships and wagons, sell goods in the market places, deliver goods to the people who bought them. These workers lived close together in towns. The towns were much larger than the little peasant villages. Towns were established on the seacoast where goods were brought in from

The Crusades helped to solve the unemployment problem. Trade brought new jobs, and roads had to be built to transport goods.

The town marketplace, filled with colorful products from all over the world, became a much more interesting place to go shopping.

different countries. Other towns were established along the rivers and roads on which the goods were carried.

Men who worked all day loading or selling goods did not have time to make the things they needed. They also had wages with which to pay for these things. Craftsmen started shops in the towns. The craftsmen included goldsmiths, weavers, dyers, bakers, glassmakers, shoemakers, blacksmiths, and many other kinds of skilled workers.

This was a change from the time before the Crusades when about one-tenth of the people belonged to noble families, and the other nine-tenths were peasants who made their living by farming. A "middle class" was developing. This class consisted of merchants and craftsmen.

The Towns Win Their Freedom. From reading the last chapter, we know that most of the land in Western Europe was ruled by powerful nobles. The new towns, therefore, grew up on land owned by the nobles.

A noble was pleased when a town grew up on his land. He could collect taxes from the merchants and craftsmen. He was also pleased to have craftsmen nearby who could do work for him. He could buy, at a reduced price, the many goods being sold in the market place.

The people of the towns, however, did not like to be ruled by nobles. They wished to rule themselves. Whenever they could, the people of a town secured a charter from the lord. A charter was a written agreement between the lord and the people. In a charter, a lord usually agreed to give the townspeople a certain amount of self-government. In return for this right, the people gave the lord a sum of money.

155

Seeking a Charter. Townspeople demand a share in governing the town which formerly was in the supreme control of the nobles.

As time went on, the towns became stronger and stronger. The nobles found they had little control over the towns. The kings often helped the towns to get their freedom, because the kings wished to weaken the power of the nobles.

The towns continued to grow. Sometimes, towns became more powerful than the nobles who had once ruled them. Serfs ran away from the nobles and hid in the towns. If they were not found for a year and a day, they became freemen. After that, they would secure work loading or selling goods, or perhaps they would become craftsmen.

Nobles were losing some of their power, serfs were becoming fewer, the middle class was growing. The new trade and the new towns had struck a great blow at feudalism. All this had been brought about largely by the Crusades.

1. How were goods brought from the Near East to Western Europe?
2. Why did the nobles first encourage the growth of towns?
3. Why was the power of the nobles weakened as the towns became stronger?

Chapter 11. REVIEW

Learning To Use New Words
Use each of the following terms in an original sentence, expressing something you have learned in Chapter 11:

Crusade	spices
pilgrims	merchant
peasants	craftsmen
Saladin	middle class
ransom	charter

Knowing the Important Facts
1. What did the Crusades hope to achieve? In what way did they fail? In what way did they succeed?
2. What were the Children's Crusades?
3. How did the Arab rulers of Palestine treat Christian pilgrims?
4. Why did Pope Urban II call for a Holy War?
5. Name three leaders of the Fourth Crusade.
6. What did the Crusaders see in the markets of the Near East?

Thinking Through the Facts
1. Why did so many men wish to take part in the Crusades?
2. How did a middle class develop in Europe?
3. Why were the people of Europe excited about the reports of the Crusaders?
4. Why were the Italians in a good position for trade with the Near East? How did towns benefit from this new trade?
5. How did the growth of towns affect feudalism?
6. Do you think the Crusades helped to strengthen the Church?

Developing a Time Sense
1. Children's Crusades are organized
2. Pope Urban calls the First Crusade
3. The Crusaders take Jerusalem
4. Richard the Lion-Heart defeated by Saladin

Chapter 12
Thirteenth Century Europe

We shall take a look at Western Europe in the years between 1200 and 1300. These one hundred years are known as the thirteenth century. There were still nobles and castles and serfs in Western Europe in the thirteenth century, but we shall not read about these. We shall read about a Europe that had changed, a Europe that seemed to be awaking from a long sleep. We shall read about towns and craftsmen, schools and universities, great saints and famous scholars, noted travelers and common people who accomplished great things.

12 1

How People Lived in the Towns

We Visit a Thirteenth Century Town. Towns had become numerous by the thirteenth century. We will understand this century better if we visit a typical town of the time. Let us imagine that we are back in the year 1250, walking along a dusty road.

As we walk along the road, we see many farms and gardens. People are working in these fields, plowing and planting. Some of them wave at us as we go by. We don't see any farmhouses, as we would in our country today. These people work in the fields during the day, but their homes are in the town. They are safer from robbers and from enemies in the town.

As we come closer to the town, we see that it is surrounded by a large wall. The wall contains watchtowers, from which watchmen can see many miles of countryside. The road we are walking on leads to a large pair of gates in the wall. The gates are open now. If the watchmen in the towers should see an enemy coming, they would give the alarm. Then the people from the fields would run through the gates into the town. The gates would be closed. The men of the town would prepare to keep the enemies from climbing the wall.

But all is peaceful now. We come closer to the town. Beyond the wall, we see the tiled roofs of many houses. The highest building in the town is the cathedral.

Because it is daylight, we walk through the big gates. If it were night, the gates would be closed and locked.

The first thing that we notice as we come into town is that everything seems very crowded. The streets are narrow. The houses are very close together, with little or no space between. All the people want to live inside the wall of the town, and there is no way of stretching the wall. Because of this, little space is wasted in the town.

We notice a strange thing about the houses. The second story of each house extends over the street. In some places the second stories of facing houses almost meet over the middle of the street. This means that little sunlight gets through.

The streets are not paved. Because the weather has been dry, the streets are dusty. In rainy weather, they would be muddy.

We who have come from twentieth century America are shocked to see the streets littered with garbage and rubbish. People have no other way to get rid of their trash. What won't burn is thrown into the streets. The people do not know about germs. It is small wonder that various diseases often sweep through the towns.

We pass boys who are bringing water from the town well. The houses have no running water.

Houses have wooden walls and tile roofs. Merchants and craftsmen have their stores or shops in the front of their houses on the ground floor. They live in the back or on the second floor.

In the center of the town, we see some larger buildings made of stone. One of the buildings is the town hall. Here the mayor and other officials meet to decide the affairs of the town. We are told that some of the buildings are guildhalls. We will learn more about guilds a little later. The biggest building of all is the cathedral. It is not yet completed, but we can already see that it will be beautiful.

The cathedral bells ring a warning. We see that the sun is going down. It is time for us to go to the inn where we will spend the night. Soon it will be dark, and there are no street lights. People are not allowed on the streets after dark.

The guards are closing the gates of the town which will remain closed until morning.

RIVER

HOSPITAL

ABBEY

INN

TOWN HALL

MARKET SQUARE

CATHEDRAL

INN

CONVENT

LOCAL SHIPPING

Workers Take Great Pride in Their Work. As we walk about the town the next day, we visit many craftsmen in their shops. A shoemaker is working on a pair of shoes. It seems to us that the shoes are ready to be worn, but the shoemaker continues to work on them. He picks up a shoe and examines it carefully. Then he trims a small piece of leather off the sole. He examines it again and trims off a little more.

"Why do you keep working on that pair of shoes?" we ask. "The man that you are making them for would be satisfied. You could start working on another pair and earn more money."

"Yes, but I would not be satisfied," the shoemaker replies. "I want to turn out a perfect piece of work, or as nearly perfect as I can make it."

In another shop, a blacksmith is working on a hinge. He tells us that it is to be used for the cathedral door. It is a beautiful piece of work.

"Why do you spend so much time on one hinge?" we ask. "Surely, a plain hinge would hold up the door just as well as this fancy one will."

"Yes," replies the blacksmith, "but this is for the door of God's house. It must be the best hinge I know how to make. It is not enough for a hinge to be useful. It must also be beautiful."

As we think about these two workmen, we begin to understand something important about the thirteenth century. It is a time of great religious faith, and a time when people think that every task should be done well. When even ordinary things like shoes and hinges must be made well, we may be sure that big things are done well, too.

There are many things we don't like about life in the thirteenth century: the dirt, the inconveniences, the diseases. But we can see why some historians say that the thirteenth was one of the greatest of centuries.

The People Enjoy Festivals, Fairs and Plays. "What do people do for amusement?" we wonder. "There are no automobiles, no movies, no radio, no television. How do people spend their spare time?"

We learn that there is not much spare

Perfection. The workers of this day, particularly those who worked on the construction of a cathedral, were satisfied only with excellence in their products. Are you?

At first, plays were recited by priests in churchyards. Later, men from the Guilds acted them out at fairs, or on traveling stages in the center of the town.

time. Just as there are no movies or television for amusement, neither are there any tractors, thrashing machines, automatic washers, or vacuum sweepers to help people with their work. All work must be done by hand. On an ordinary day, men, women, and children work from the time they get up in the morning till they go to bed at night.

On special occasions, however, when there is spare time, the people have no trouble amusing themselves.

On every important holy day, there is a festival. No one works on that day which begins with a Mass at the cathedral. After Mass, there is a procession through the streets. Men carry floats showing scenes from the lives of Our Lord and the saints. Others carry beautiful banners. Everyone wears his gayest, fanciest clothes. When the procession is over, the people gather in front of the cathedral. Musicians play gay tunes. The people play games. They dance and sing.

Most towns hold a fair once a year in a large field outside the wall. Merchants from other places set up tents and sell all sorts of wonderful goods. Entertainers come to the fair and tell jokes, do tricks, or display their dancing dogs and bears.

Many plays are given throughout the year. The shoemakers might give a play one time, the blacksmiths another time, the butchers still another time, and so on. The stage is an outdoor platform. Most of the plays tell stories about the Bible.

1. Describe a town of the Middle Ages. Why were the houses so close together?
2. What was the subject of most plays given in the Middle Ages?

161

12 2
The Craftsmen and Their Guilds

It Took Many Years to Become a Master Worker. Let us pay another visit to our friend, the shoemaker. We see that he has no machinery, and that all his work is done by hand. This takes a great amount of skill.

"How long did it take you to learn this work?" we ask.

"It took me a long time," he answers. "When I was a boy, my father thought I might like to be a shoemaker. He took me to a shoemaker who was a friend of his, and I became the shoemaker's apprentice. This means that I lived with him and helped him with his work. He did not pay me any money, but he gave me a place to live. He also gave me my food and clothing."

"How long were you an apprentice?"

"Seven years. Then I became a journeyman. This meant that I could work for daily wages. However, I was still not allowed to have a shop of my own. During this time, I traveled about the country, working for many different shoemakers."

"How did you finally get your own shop?"

"I had to become a master workman to do that. Before becoming a master, I was given a strict examination. The examination took place in the hall that belongs to the shoemaker's guild. I brought in a pair of shoes that I had made all by myself. A group of master shoemakers looked over my work very carefully. I waited anxiously while they inspected the shoes, and I said some prayers. Then, the men smiled at me and told me

Guild Hall

Men in the Middle Ages often joined together in guilds. A guild was a group of people who did the same kind of work. Each guild had its own hall. Meetings were held in guild halls to discuss the problems and work of the members.

The members of a particular guild usually lived in the same street or part of a city. They marched together in parades, attended the same church, and contributed money to fellow members in need. They set up rules for their guild so that products and prices would be the same.

Types of Guilds

There were guilds for every profession, including guilds for hatters, shoemakers, wheelmakers, glassmakers, bakers, and coopers.

From Apprentice to Master

1 To learn a trade, a boy became an apprentice of a master. During this time he worked diligently and lived with the master's family.

2 After several years, the apprentice proved his right to start working on his own and became a journeyman. As a journeyman or skilled workman he received a wage. When he had saved enough to start his own shop, he had to show that he was worthy of advancement.

3 The final step to becoming a master was to produce a "masterpiece." If the masters of the guild approved it, he became a full-fledged master craftsman.

that I had passed the test. I was now a master shoemaker. I could start my own shop.

"The pair of shoes that I made for the test was called my masterpiece. It was the work that made me a master."

"And now you have apprentices of your own," we say.

"Yes, I have two apprentices." He nods at two boys who are working in his shop. "And I also have a journeyman to help me."

"Do all workers become masters in the same way?" we ask.

"Yes, in very much the same way. I happen to be a shoemaker, but if I were a weaver, a coppersmith, a tailor, or any other kind of worker, the story would be very much the same. Each worker is an apprentice and a journeyman before he becomes a master."

The Master Workers Belonged to Guilds. When the shoemaker told us how he became a master worker, he mentioned the shoemakers' guild. Guilds were important not only in the thirteenth century, but also all through the Middle Ages. In some places, the guilds survived long after the Middle Ages were over.

A guild was like a club or society. All the blacksmiths of a town formed one guild; the master weavers formed another, and so on.

Many of the guilds owned large buildings where they held their meetings, put on plays, and did many other things. These buildings were called guildhalls. Some of the guildhalls built in the Middle Ages are still standing in England, France, Germany, Belgium, and other countries of Western Europe.

Each guild had its patron saint. The carpenters, for example, might call their guild the Guild of Saint Joseph, because Saint Joseph was a carpenter. They would place a large statue of Saint Joseph outside their guildhall. The members would try to model their lives after the life of Saint Joseph. On his feast, all the carpenters would go to Mass together. Then, they would march in procession through the streets. On a major feast, like the feast of Corpus Christi, all the guilds would join in one great procession.

When a journeyman passed his test and became a master, he was ready to join a guild. Before he could join, he had to promise that he would always do his best work. He also promised not to charge too high a price for his work. If he broke his promise, he could be put out of the guild. This meant that he would not be allowed to work at his trade. We see, then, that the guilds did not try to get high prices for their members. They were more interested in seeing that their members did good work for fair prices.

The guilds performed many works of charity. They helped their members when they were in need. The also helped other people. If a member of a guild became sick and could not work, the guild gave him money to support himself and his family. If a member died, the guild supported his widow and his young children. Some guilds built schools. Others built hospitals for the poor.

1. How did a boy of the Middle Ages prepare to be a master craftsman? What proof of his skill did he have to furnish to the guilds?
2. Who belonged to the guilds? What good works did the guilds perform?

12.3

Great Churches and Cathedrals

The People Find a New Way to Build Churches. The first Christian churches were built in the days of the Roman Empire. They looked very much like other Roman buildings.

Later, the monks improved upon the building methods of the Romans. They substituted stone roofs for wooden ones. They erected thicker walls and heavy columns to support the added weight. Windows were few and were very small, because windows weakened the walls. As a result, churches were dark and gloomy.

The builders of the late Middle Ages wished to build churches that would express the joyous faith of the people. They developed a new type of architecture which was called Gothic. Heavy pillars were replaced by graceful columns. Windows were enlarged and filled with a new kind of art—pictures done in stained glass. There were tall steeples which seemed to be reaching toward Heaven. The heavy stone roof was supported from outside the church by buttresses.

The people loved the beauty of this new architecture. The cathedrals were their Bible. Most people of that time could not read. The pictures on the stained glass windows, the wood carvings, and the statues, told them stories from the Bible. In this way they learned what they could not read in words.

Everybody Helped Build the Churches. More great churches and cathedrals were built in the thirteenth century than in any other hundred years in history. In France alone, the people built 80 cathedrals and nearly 500 large churches in the years between 1170 and 1270. The same thing was

A cathedral is a miracle wrought in stone. It is a monument of the faith of many hearts and the work of many hands.

The Great Cathedrals

The people of the Middle Ages built beautiful cathedrals. Cathedrals represented the pride and high ideals of the Christians. The Christians made contributions through their skill and craftsmanship. Stained-glass windows told the story of the saints and the early Church.

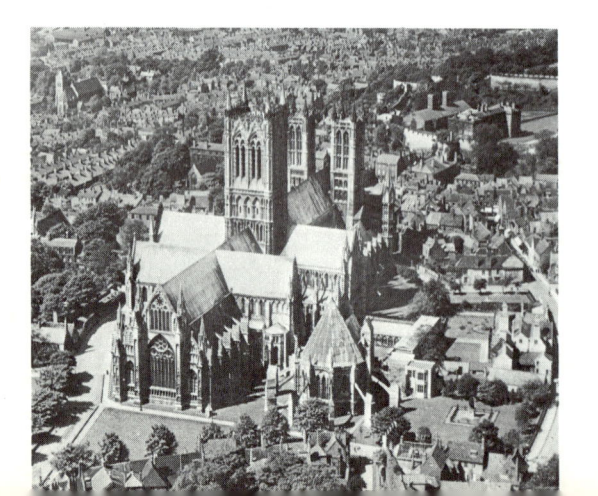

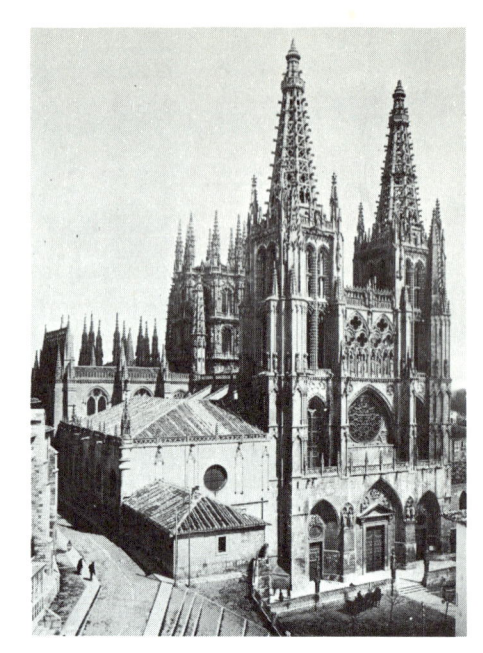

Cathedrals of Europe
Burgos in Spain (above)
Cologne in Germany (upper left)

Milan in Italy (above)
Lincoln in England (lower left)

Basilica. Early Christian churches copied the Roman law courts or basilicas. These churches had few windows and were rather dark. Two long rows of columns supported the wooden roof.

Romanesque. Rounded domes and arches made churches of Romanesque architecture more graceful than those of Basilica design. But the walls of these churches were very thick and the windows were quite small.

Gothic. Pointed arches and graceful pillars decorate Gothic cathedrals. Many colorful stain glass windows make the interior of the church light.

happening all over Western Europe.

In some cases everyone actually helped build the churches. When the great Cathedral of Chartres was built, scholars, nobles, and common people worked together. They harnessed themselves to wagons and dragged huge blocks of stone and giant tree trunks. Noble ladies helped poor farm women mix mortar. All the people worked in silence and prayed as they worked. Kings and nobles donated money for the churches and cathedrals. The guilds donated stained glass windows.

Sometimes the people did not build the cathedrals themselves. The greater part of the work was done by skilled craftsmen. The people were still very much interested and contributed money and goods to provide materials and to pay the workmen.

Many of the men who designed the beautiful windows for the churches and carved the beautiful statues are not known to us. They did not sign their names to their work. They did not care about receiving credit or praise. They wished only to honor God.

There is a story told about one artist who climbed a high ladder every day and worked on a dark corner of the ceiling. Somebody asked: "Why do you go to so much trouble when few people will even see what you have done?"

The artist answered: "God can see what I have done just as well as He can see the great painting over the altar."

1. Describe the early Christian churches. How do they contrast with the churches of the thirteenth century?
2. What do we mean when we say thirteenth century cathedrals were the "Bible of the people"?

12 4

Schools, Scholars, and Teachers

The Shops Were Also Schools. Suppose that a boy of the thirteenth century wished to become a cabinetmaker, a shoemaker, a weaver, a coppersmith, or some other kind of craftsman. How would he learn this trade? We already know the answer to this question. The boy would become an apprentice to a master worker. He would learn his trade while he was working at it. Each shop, therefore, was also a school.

Monastery schools. Religious orders gave many courses in the arts and sciences for boys who planned to go on to universities.

We know that these shops must have been very good schools. Most of the men who did such beautiful work on the cathedrals received their training as apprentices. Boys who were apprentices learned more than just their trade. They also learned about their religion. They learned numbers so that they would be able to keep their accounts when they had shops of their own. Some of them also learned to read and write.

Monasteries and Cathedrals Had Schools. Not all boys of the thirteenth century wished to become craftsmen. Some wished to become teachers, or doctors, or lawyers. Some wished to become scientists and study the world about them. Others wanted to become writers or philosophers. Where would these boys go to school?

A boy who did not wish to become a skilled worker might go to a monastery school. We know that for centuries almost every monastery had a school. Such a boy might also go to a cathedral school.

Innocent III, who was Pope at the beginning of the thirteenth century, was very much interested in schools. He called a meeting of the bishops and cardinals. This meeting was called the Fourth Lateran Council. In 1215, the Council ruled that every cathedral must have a school. The council also named certain courses which must be taught at these schools.

Many towns that had no cathedrals had schools supported by the guilds.

Universities. Some of the cathedral schools grew into universities. Three of the famous universities of the thirteenth century were at Paris in France, at Oxford in England, and at Bologna in Italy. There were many others. Young men from all over Europe attended the universities. The courses at the universities were taught in Latin, although this language was no longer spoken in everyday life. The students had to learn Latin before they could enter the universities.

There were no printed books, such as we have today. Teachers taught from rolls of parchment which had been written on with black ink. Early universities had no libraries, although later ones did. To learn, the students had to pay close attention in class. They sat on low benches or on the floor and listened to their teachers talk, or lecture. They took notes on each lecture and studied from them.

Saint Albert the Great. Young men who studied at the universities of the thirteenth century had some excellent teachers. One of the best was Saint Albert the Great. He was such a brilliant man that he has been called the "wonder of his age." Saint Albert was a Dominican friar who rose to a high position in his order. Albert was not interested in high positions, however. He wished to teach and to study. He taught at many universities.

Albert knew more about botany than any other man of his time. Botany is the study of plants. Albert studied the plants and wrote a book about them. For the next 300 years, this was the best book on botany that could be found anywhere in Europe.

Albert also studied animals, the stars, and our earth. He said that there was a North

"In science," said St. Albert, "do not accept the statements of others, but examine the reasons things happen."

Pole and a South Pole, and that it was very cold at both poles. He said that there were probably animals with thick fur living at the poles. He also said that there were probably people living between the equator and the South Pole. At that time, no one from Europe had visited any of these places. Centuries later, explorers found that Albert had been right.

As Albert studied the earth and the stars, he decided that the earth was round. A great many people at that time believed the world was flat. They did not believe Albert when he said it was round. Later, all educated men decided that Albert was right. This knowledge led to the discovery of America.

Most men become experts in only one or two things. Albert was an expert in many things. He excelled in different branches of science. He also excelled in the study of religion. He studied the writings of the Greek philosopher Aristotle. He wrote a book about the ideas of Aristotle.

Roger Bacon Was a Great Scientist. When Saint Albert the Great taught at the University of Paris, one of his students was a young man named Roger Bacon. Roger Bacon later became a Franciscan friar. He taught at the universities of Oxford and Paris.

Like Saint Albert, Roger Bacon became famous in many fields. He wrote about religion, languages, mathematics, and many other subjects. He is remembered especially for his work in science. Roger Bacon believed in performing experiments. If he wanted to know something about chemistry, he would put different chemicals together to see what happened. If he wanted to learn more about gunpowder, he would explode a small amount of gunpowder. Until then, not many people had made such experiments. Today, scientists are always experimenting; they have big laboratories where they perform their experiments. Roger Bacon is often called the Father of Modern Science.

The people of Europe learned about gunpowder from the Arabs. They did not know very much about using gunpowder, however. Roger Bacon said that it would be possible to make weapons which would use gunpowder. He said that these weapons could put holes in stone walls and destroy whole cities. It was not long after he died that cannons were being used in war. Bacon also said that someday it would be possible to run boats and carriages with explosives. These ideas sounded very strange in the thirteenth century. His words were proved true about six centuries later. Gasoline is used to run motor boats and automobiles, and gasoline is an explosive.

Roger Bacon studied the stars. While doing so, he learned that the calendar which Julius Caesar had made was not correct. People did not believe him when he said this. Years later, they discovered that he had been right.

Saint Thomas Aquinas Was a Great Scholar. Another of Saint Albert's students was Saint Thomas Aquinas. As a student, Saint Thomas was so humble and silent that his classmates called him the "dumb ox." Saint Albert, however, was sure that his pupil would do great things. "The dumb ox's bellowing," said Saint Albert, "will one day resound throughout the world."

Thomas became a Dominican. He taught at the universities of Cologne, Paris, Rome, Naples, and Bologna. Like Saint Albert and Roger Bacon, Saint Thomas was interested in many things. He is best known, however, for his work in theology—the science which studies religion and religious beliefs. Saint Thomas' greatest work in theology is the *Summa*, which means summary. In this book, Saint Thomas summed up all the truths of the Catholic Church.

1. How were the great universities started? Mention three thirteenth century cities that had a famous university. How were classes conducted in these early universities?
2. In what field did Roger Bacon become most famous? What method did he use to learn about the world around him?
3. What name do we give to the study of religion and religious beliefs? Mention a scholar of the thirteenth century who excelled in this field.

12 5

Great Artists and Writers

There Were Many Great Artists. We have read enough about the thirteenth century to know that many great artists, architects, and sculptors lived between the years 1200 and 1300. The architects planned the great cathedrals and churches. The artists and sculptors helped decorate them. It is not possible to name all the artists who beautified the cathedrals of the Middle Ages. There is one, however, who stands out above all others. His name is Giotto. Giotto lived in Italy. He decorated churches in every part of his country. Many of his pictures showed scenes from the life of Christ and from the life of Saint Francis.

Hymns and Poems. At the beginning of the thirteenth century, Saint Francis wrote some simple little hymns. Other men also wrote hymns during this century. Some, like Saint Francis, wrote in the language of

Dante's poem tells us his thoughts about life and death and how we can be saved by the mercy of God.

the people. Others wrote in Latin. Several hymns which we still sing come from the thirteenth century. Two of the best known are the *Stabat Mater* which we sing at the Stations of the Cross, and the *Pange Lingua*. The last two verses of the *Pange Lingua* are called the Tantum Ergo, and they are sung at Benediction. Saint Thomas Aquinas wrote this hymn to express his great devotion to Our Lord in the Blessed Sacrament.

One of the most famous poets of all time lived in Florence, Italy, at the end of the thirteenth century. His name was Dante. When Dante first started to write poems, he did not know whether to write in Latin or in Italian. He finally decided to use Italian, so that the ordinary people of Italy could understand what he wrote. Dante was the first really great poet of the Middle Ages to write in the language of the people. The most famous of all Dante's works is the *Divine Comedy*. In this great poem, Dante takes the reader on an imaginary trip through Hell, Purgatory, and Heaven.

1. Who is the author of the *Divine Comedy?* What is its subject matter?
2. In what language was the *Divine Comedy* written? Why was this language chosen?

12 6

The People of Europe Learn More About the Far East

Missionaries Go to the Far East. The eastern part of Asia is called the Far East, or the Orient. This part of the world contains China, Japan, India, and many other countries. Over the centuries, people who belonged to Western civilization sometimes came in contact with the Far East. Alexander the Great carried Greek civilization as far as the Indus River in India. When the Roman Empire was at its height, many ships sailed back and forth between the Empire and India. We know that Chinese silk was on sale in Rome, although few Romans had ever visited China, and fewer Chinese had visited Rome. After the fall of the Western Empire, the people of Western Europe almost forgot that there was such a place as the Far East. This situation lasted for about six hundred years. Crusaders went to the Near East and saw goods which came from the Orient. This started a trade between Western Europe and the Far East, but nobody from Europe went to the Orient. Western Europe and the Orient were like two different worlds.

Among other things for which it is famous, the thirteenth century is known as the time when travelers from Europe went to the Far East.

Some of the first men to travel to the Far East were missionaries. Many of them were Franciscans. Some were Dominicans. The Pope sent John of Caprini to visit the ruler of Mongolia. John was a Franciscan friar. It took him several years to make this long trip. When Friar John returned to Europe, he wrote a book about his travels. Other famous Franciscan friars who traveled to the Far East were Odoric and William of Rubruquis. These men came home and told amazing stories about the things they had seen.

Marco Polo Visits the Far East. The most famous thirteenth century traveler to the Far East was not a missionary. He was Marco Polo, the son of a merchant of Venice.

When Marco was a little boy, his father and uncle went to the land we now call China. They were gone fourteen years, and they came home with wonderful tales of the Far East. In 1271, Marco's father and uncle left for another trip to the Orient. This time, they took Marco along. He was seventeen years old.

The three Polos went by ship to the eastern shore of the Mediterranean Sea. Then they traveled across Asia on foot and by horseback. They crossed wide deserts and high mountains. People called Mongols had conquered a great part of Asia and also part of eastern Europe. Almost all the land through which the Polos traveled was ruled by the Mongols. The Polos carried a tablet from the Mongol ruler. This tablet said

Marco Polo tells his story in prison. His famous book made people realize that the world was twice as big as they had thought it was.

that the Polos should be allowed to travel through this land and that nobody should bother them.

After traveling for two years, the Polos reached the city where the Mongol ruler lived. This was the city we now call Peking. It is in the eastern part of China.

The Mongol ruler was always called the Khan, and the name of this Khan was Kublai. Therefore, he was called Kublai Khan.

Kublai Khan took a great liking to young Marco Polo. He taught Marco to read and write the language of the Mongols. He sent Marco on many trips throughout the Far East. Marco saw marvelous sights. He saw great cities which were larger than any cities in Europe. He marveled when he saw Chinese people burning coal. He saw princes in India riding richly decorated elephants. In Japan, he saw palaces with roofs made of gold. In the empire of the Kublai Khan, there was a palace where 6000 men could eat at one time. Marco Polo found the wealthy people of the Far East using beautiful carpets and silks, and wearing dazzling jewelry. He found that in the Far East these things cost much less than they did in Europe.

After about twenty years, the Polos decided to return to Venice. Kublai Khan did not want them to leave, but finally he gave them permission to do so. The journey back to Venice took a long time. When the Polos got back, they had been gone almost twenty-five years. They wore Chinese clothes, and they had changed so much that nobody knew them. Marco Polo was no longer a boy. His father and uncle were old.

The Polos gave a banquet. After the guests had eaten, the Polos brought out three old cloaks which they had worn on their travels. They ripped the lining out of the coats. A shower of sapphires, rubies, and diamonds fell on the floor. The guests could hardly believe their eyes. The Polos were now famous.

Marco Polo Writes a Book. Few people outside of Venice would have heard of Marco Polo's travels if it had not been for a war beween Venice and Genoa. Marco Polo commanded a ship that was going to fight Genoa. His ship was captured. He was taken to Genoa and put in prison for three years.

While he was in prison, Marco Polo told another prisoner about his travels in the Far East. The prisoner wrote down what Marco Polo said. This became known as the *Book of Marco Polo*.

Many people read Marco Polo's book and marveled at the things he had seen. Some people thought that perhaps he had exaggerated a little. He said, "On the contrary, I have not told half the amazing things I saw with my own eyes."

Years after Marco Polo died, the printing press was invented. Copies of his book were printed, and more people were able to read it than ever before. We shall see that the *Book of Marco Polo* helped lead to the discovery of America.

1. When did Europeans lose contact with the Far East? In what century did Europeans begin to renew contact with the Far East? Who were the first Europeans to visit the Far East in the Middle Ages?
2. How did the world learn of the travels of Marco Polo?

Chapter 12. REVIEW

Learning To Use New Words

Use each of the following terms in an original sentence expressing something you have learned in Chapter 12:

university	journeyman	festival
watchtower	apprentice	theology
craft	Gothic	
guild	experiment	

Knowing the Important Facts

1. What were the outstanding features of the towns of the Middle Ages?
2. What were the guilds? How did they operate?
3. What did a cathedral in the Gothic style look like? Who built the great cathedrals of the Middle Ages?
4. List three great scholars of the thirteenth century and describe their work.
5. What famous European visited the Far East during the thirteenth century? Who was the ruler of China at that time?

Thinking Through the Facts

1. How are modern labor unions like the guilds of the Middle Ages? How are they different?
2. Why did the people of the Middle Ages build such beautiful cathedrals?
3. How did life in a thirteenth century town differ from life today?
4. Why was the *Book of Marco Polo* important?
5. How have universities changed since the thirteenth century? How have they remained the same?

Unit FOUR *Summary*

I Should Know That...

1. The Eastern or Byzantine Empire outlived the Western Empire by about 1000 years. The culture of the Eastern Empire was more Greek than Roman.
2. Mohammed founded the Islamic religion. His followers soon conquered territory stretching from Central Asia to Spain.
3. Moslem culture contributed new ideas to art and science. Arabic numerals were an important achievement in mathematics.
4. Charlemagne united Western Europe and improved commerce and education. His empire broke up after his death.
5. Feudalism was a way of life based on self-sufficient manors and fixed classes of clergy, nobility, and serfs.
6. The Crusades did not succeed in driving the Moslems from the Holy Land. Europe began a rich trade with the East after the Crusades.
7. As towns grew up and a merchant class developed, feudalism became weaker. Guilds were formed to help to regulate price and insure good workmanship.
8. Gothic architecture developed during the Middle Ages. The people used this new architecture to build beautiful cathedrals.
9. Many people became interested in education during the late Middle Ages. By the thirteenth century, most large cities had cathedral schools and universities.

Dates I Should Remember...

622—Mohammed flees to Mecca
732—Battle of Tours
1095—Beginning of the Crusades
1453—Fall of Constantinople

Books I Should Read...

Hewes, A. D., *A Boy of the Lost Crusade.*
Scott, M. J., *A Boy Knight.*
Kent, Louise, *He Went with Marco Polo.*
Tappan, E. M., *When Knights Were Bold.*
Cottler and Jaffe, *Heroes of Civilization.*
Maritain, Raissa, *The Angel of the Schools.*

Some Interesting Things To Do...

1. Make a copy of your favorite poem. Try to make it beautiful by imitating the technique the monks used to illustrate manuscripts.
2. Pretend you are a reporter traveling with the First Crusade. Write a newspaper report describing the trip to the Holy Land, a battle, and the first sight of Jerusalem.
3. Make a collection of pictures of buildings having Gothic design.

FIVE The Rise of Nations in Europe

Chapter *13*

The Story of England

We Americans should be very much interested in the story of England. Our language comes from this country. So do many of our laws and customs. Even more important is the fact that we have inherited our English forefathers' great love of liberty.

We shall read the story of England from the time of Julius Caesar to the time of the Model Parliament in 1295. This is a period of more than thirteen hundred years. We shall see that people from many lands helped make England a nation, and that each group added something to the culture of the country.

13 1

Early England

The Romans in Britain. When Julius Caesar was conquering France, or Gaul as it was then called, he learned that the Gauls were receiving help. They were being helped by people who lived on a large island about twenty miles from the coast of Gaul. This was the island of Britain. The people who helped the Gauls lived on the southern part of the island. They were called Britons.

Caesar gathered together a large number of boats and took an army across the English Channel to Britain. He was not able to conquer the Britons. Later, other Romans did conquer the southern part of the island. They were not able to conquer the Picts and Scots in the north. We know that the Romans under Emperor Hadrian built a large wall across the island. The wall protected

Anglo-Saxon Era in England   *Hundred Years' War*

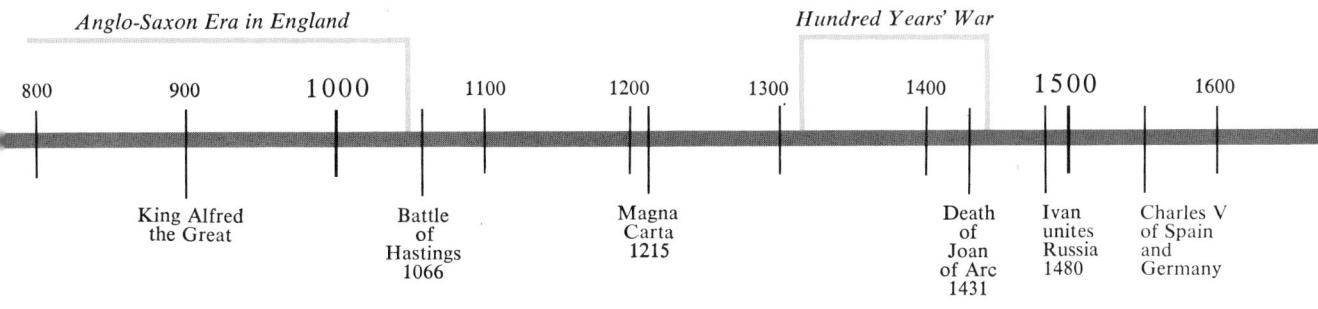

800	900	1000	1100	1200	1300	1400	1500	1600
	King Alfred the Great		Battle of Hastings 1066		Magna Carta 1215		Death of Joan of Arc 1431	Ivan unites Russia 1480	Charles V of Spain and Germany

the Roman province of Britain from the Picts and the Scots.

The Romans ruled Britain for about 350 years. They built towns, roads, and baths. Some of these can still be seen.

In 410, the city of Rome was captured by the Visigoths. The Roman soldiers in Britain were called back to aid their capital city. The Britons were left to rule themselves and to defend themselves.

The Germans Invade Britain. As soon as the Roman soldiers left Britain, the Picts and Scots came over Hadrian's Wall. The Britons were not able to defend themselves against the fierce invaders. They sent messages to Germans on the continent asking for help. The first Germans to come to

Julius Caesar described the early Britons as tall and strong, with blue eyes. Each tribe had its own leader.

177

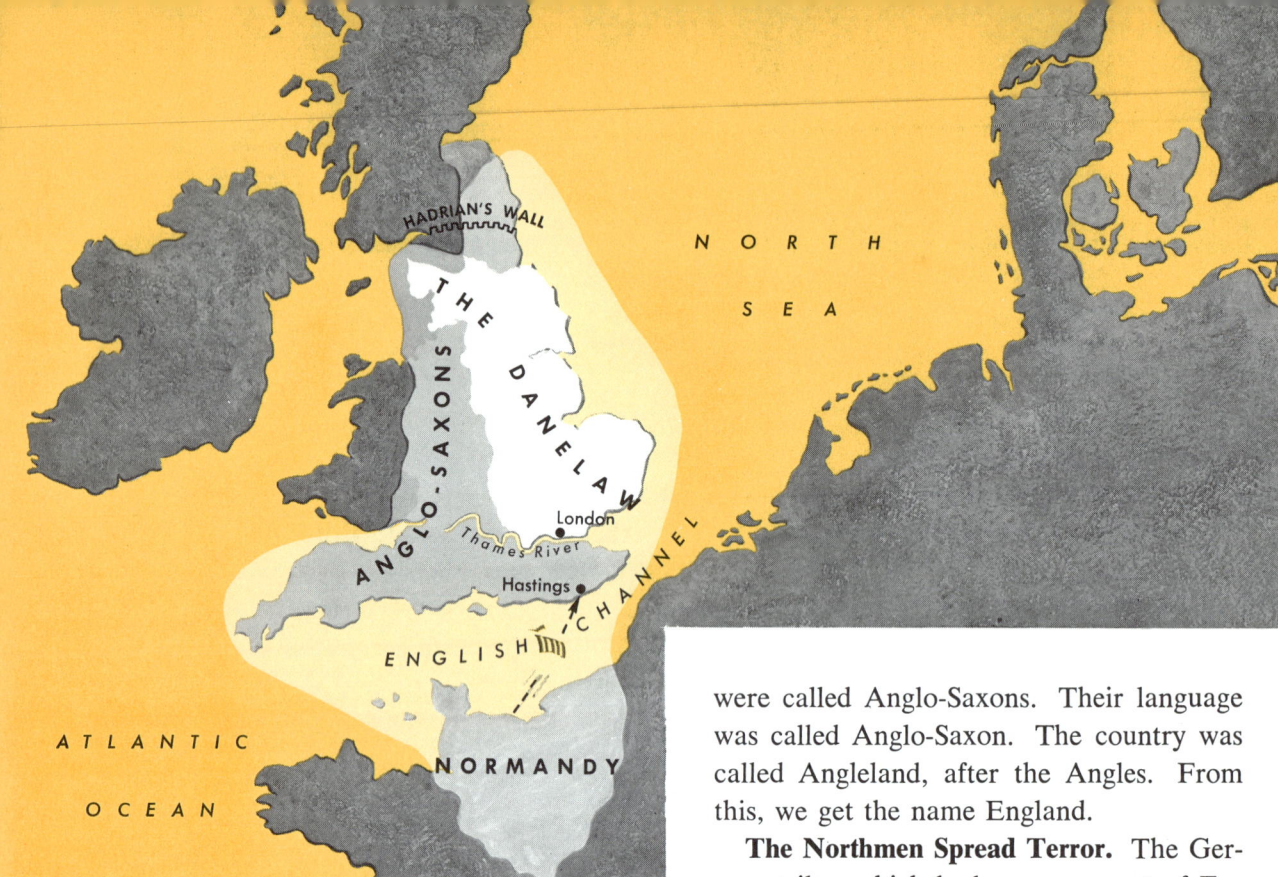

Britain were the Jutes from Jutland in western Denmark. They were followed by large numbers of Angles and Saxons, who lived along the northern seacoast of Germany. The Germans drove out the Picts and the Scots, but they did not give the land back to the Britons. They kept the land for themselves. The Britons tried to drive out the Germans, but they were defeated. Some of the Britons then crossed over into France. The French province of Brittany is named for them.

The Angles, Saxons, and Jutes now ruled most of Britain. They had seven kingdoms on the island. There were more Angles and Saxons than there were Jutes, so the people were called Anglo-Saxons. Their language was called Anglo-Saxon. The country was called Angleland, after the Angles. From this, we get the name England.

The Northmen Spread Terror. The German tribes which had overrun most of Europe in the last days of the Roman Empire had settled down. They had become converts to Christianity and its civilizing influence. Charlemagne, a German, became a great Christian emperor. In England, Saint Augustine and other missionaries had succeeded in bringing Christianity and civilization to the Germans.

The Germans who lived in Denmark, Norway, and Sweden, however, were not civilized. These were the Northmen. The Northmen were still pagans. They worshipped Odin and Thor and the other German gods. The Northmen were good sailors and fierce fighters. They sailed along the coasts of Europe in their swift, long boats. They also sailed up the large rivers of Europe. When they saw a town that was

St. Augustine

The Romans had brought Christianity and civilization to Britain. After the Jutes and Angles and Saxons invaded Britain, the Church had to bring the Christian religion and civilization back to England. One of the most famous of the missionaries was Saint Augustine of Canterbury.

One version of how Saint Augustine happened to be sent to England has become almost a legend. A monk named Gregory lived near Rome. Today we call him Saint Gregory. One day in the market place, Gregory noticed some boys who were being sold as slaves. They had a light complexion, fair hair, and blue eyes. Saint Gregory thought they were very handsome. He asked who the boys were. He was told that they were Angles from Britain. "Not Angles, but angels," Gregory said. He made up his mind that he would bring the Christian religion to England.

Gregory was not able to go to England himself because he was elected Pope. But he did not forget his beloved Angles, even after he became Pope. Pope Gregory sent a monk named Augustine to England in 596. Saint Augustine took forty monks to England with him. Within a few years, thousands of Angles were baptized.

---

not defended, they would capture it. They would kill most of the people, set the buildings on fire, and steal everything that was valuable. When an army arrived to defend the town, the Northmen would be gone. People who lived near the seacoasts or along the rivers were in constant terror of the Northmen.

Sometimes the Northmen did not destroy a town and run away. Sometimes they settled in an area that they liked. Many of them settled along the coast of France. This region became known as Normandy, or land of the Northmen. The people were called Normans. Other Northmen became the rulers of Russia. Still others started a kingdom in southern Italy.

Hundreds of years before Columbus, the Northmen sailed from Europe across treacherous seas and founded a colony in Greenland.

The Danes Invade England. Great numbers of Northmen invaded England. These Northmen were called Danes. They came from the same part of Europe where the Anglo-Saxons had lived hundreds of years before. Soon, the Danes had overrun much of England. Alfred was king of most of England at that time. For a while, Alfred was like a king without a country. He had to hide in the woods and swamps, while he was preparing to fight the Danes. One story tells us that Alfred went into a Danish camp dressed as a minstrel. He played the harp for the Danes and sang songs for them. While he was there, he learned their plans and so was able to defeat them.

Another story tells us that, while Alfred was hiding from the Danes, he stopped at a little cottage in the forest. The lady who lived in the cottage told him he might rest by the fire, if he watched the cakes baking on the hearth. Alfred was tired and worried. He forgot all about the cakes. When the woman came back, she scolded him for letting the cakes burn. She did not know that she was scolding the king!

Alfred Is Called the Great. Alfred gathered a large army and defeated the Danes. Then he made an agreement with the Danes. They were to stay in the northern and eastern section of the island. Here they would have their own laws. This section was called the Danelaw. The Anglo-Saxons were to have the rest of the island. They were also to have their own laws. Alfred was to be king of both sections.

Alfred then turned to other problems. Like Charlemagne, he wished to encourage education. Also, like Charlemagne, he earned the title "Great." Today, we call him Alfred the Great.

Alfred founded many schools. He did much for the churches and monasteries. He sent missionaries to the pagan Danes. He learned Latin, and he translated books from Latin into Anglo-Saxon. He began the *Anglo-Saxon Chronicle,* a history of early England. Alfred also built a strong army and navy, and worked to give England a good government.

Alfred the Great had a school at Court to which he invited, as professors, the great scholars of other lands.

Alfred died in 900. His work was carried on by his son and grandson. Little by little, the Danes who lived in the Danelaw became more like the Anglo-Saxons. They became Christians, and they adopted the Anglo-Saxon laws. The Danelaw disappeared. The English now had the beginnings of one religion, one language, and one government.

England Is Conquered by King Canute. About a hundred years after Alfred's death, England was again invaded by Danes. This invasion was different from the invasion of Alfred's time. When Alfred was king, the Danes had belonged to many different tribes and were not united under one ruler. This time, the Danes were united under King Canute. Canute defeated the Anglo-Saxons, and he made himself king of England.

Canute was a good king. He allowed the Anglo-Saxons to keep their own laws. He used many Anglo-Saxons in his government. He became a Christian and founded monasteries and churches.

There is a story about King Canute which tells us a great deal about his character. The people around the king were always flatter-

"The Danes are coming," was a cry that brought terror to the towns along the English seacoast, as the invading Danes captured all of England.

ing him. They told him that he was the mightiest king who ever lived. "Your every wish is law," these people said. "All you have to do is to give a command, and it will be carried out."

Canute then ordered that his throne be carried down to the seashore. The tide was coming in at this time. Canute held up his hand and ordered the tide to stop. The tide, of course, kept coming in. Then Canute turned to his advisers. "See how foolish you have been," he said. "Although I am a king, I am really very weak. Only God can control the sea. All men are weak, and only God is strong."

1. What was the Danelaw?
2. How did Roman rule of Britain come to an end?
3. How did King Canute treat the conquered English?

13 2

The Beginning of Modern England

William of Normandy Conquers Britain. Ethelred II was king of England when Canute and his Danes invaded Britain. Ethelred had married a Norman woman. They had two sons, Edmund and Edward. Edmund died in England after having tried to keep Canute from becoming king.

Ethelred, his queen, and his son Edward had fled to the court of William, Duke of Normandy. Ethelred died there soon after. His son Edward was raised in Normandy, and he spoke French better than he spoke the language of Britain.

When Canute died, his two sons reigned in England. The sons had no children. When Edward was forty years old, he returned to Britain and became the king. Edward was such a good and pious man that he is honored as a saint. We call him Saint Edward and also Edward the Confessor.

Edward the Confessor died without leaving any children. Who would be the next king? William, Duke of Normandy, thought that he should be king. He had two reasons for thinking this. One reason was that he was Edward's first cousin. He said this put him next in line for the throne. The other reason was that he thought that Edward had promised him the throne.

The Anglo-Saxons did not want a Norman for king. They chose a Saxon named Harold.

When Duke William of Normandy heard of this, he said that the throne had been stolen from him. He gathered a large army and built many ships. In October, 1066, Duke William took his army across the English Channel. Harold's army marched forth to meet William's. A great battle took place near the town of Hastings. Harold was

---

Normans Come to England

The ruler of Normandy, France, in 1066 was Duke William, who claimed a right to the throne of England after the death of Edward the Confessor. William's claim to the throne was disputed by Harold who was chosen king. William gathered an army and crossed the English Channel to fight for the throne.

The English defended themselves against the Norman invaders. The Norman soldiers were knights who fought on horseback and foot soldiers with bows and arrows. The English soldiers wore shields and fought on foot.

ENGLISH SOLDIER   NORMAN SOLDIER

killed in the battle. He was the last of the Anglo-Saxon kings.

The Normans won the battle. William the Conqueror was crowned king on Christmas Day in 1066 in Westminster Abbey.

The year 1066 is an important one in English history. It was the year the Normans conquered Britain. The island has never been conquered since then. In some ways, 1066 was the beginning of modern England.

1 Battle of Hastings. Harold, the English king, met the Norman forces under William in the Battle of Hastings. Harold was killed and William became King of England in 1066.

2 Norman Influence. The Normans brought to England new ways to dress and new manners. They left an enduring mark on the English language, customs, and government.

3 Bayeux Tapestry. This tapestry belongs to the time of the Norman Conquest. There are seventy-two scenes picturing various events in the history of the Norman Conquest.

The Normans Become the Ruling Class. William the Conqueror rewarded some of his followers by giving them land in England. He also gave most of the important government posts to Normans. Most of the nobles and the men in the highest positions, therefore, were Normans. The common people were Anglo-Saxons.

We have read that the first Normans were Northmen who settled in France. By the time of William the Conqueror, the Normans had forgotten most of their old ways. They spoke the French language and observed French customs. They brought their language and their customs to England. The Normans built many castles in England which looked like the castles in France. The most famous of these is the Tower of London which still stands.

In religion, there was no difference between the rulers and the common people. Both the Normans and the Anglo-Saxons were Christians.

The Domesday Book. William the Conqueror wanted to know all about the country he was to rule. He ordered the people to register their land. Each owner had to state how much money his land was worth, how many people lived on the land, and how much livestock was on the land. This register was called the *Domesday Book*. This book gave the tax collectors a great deal of information concerning the wealth of the people of the country.

The English Language Comes from French and Anglo-Saxon. Two languages were spoken in England after William conquered the island. The Normans, who were the rulers, spoke French. This was the language that was used in the court of the king and the castles of the nobles. The farmers, workers, and the other common people spoke Anglo-Saxon. At first, the members

People said that they wouldn't be examined more closely on the day of judgment, so they called the book registering their property the Domesday Book.

Saxon peasants tended the pigs and sheep so that Norman nobles could enjoy dinners of pork and mutton.

of the upper class and the members of the lower class could not understand each other.

In time, many of the nobles learned Anglo-Saxon, and many of the common people learned French. The two languages were combined. Our modern English language comes mostly from Anglo-Saxon, but it contains many words of French and Latin origin.

The words pig, cow, calf, and sheep are from Anglo-Saxon. The words pork, beef, veal, and mutton are from French. Do you know why this is? The Anglo-Saxons were the workers. They fed the farm animals. They gave them water. They did all the other things that had to be done for the animals when they were alive. The Normans did not know much about the animals when they were alive. They were more interested in the meat that was served at the table. When Anglo-Saxons talked about farm animals, they usually talked about the live animals. The Normans talked about the meat that came from the animals. So, we have the Anglo-Saxon names for the live animals and the French names for the meat.

We have kept both the French and the Anglo-Saxon names for certain things. This means that when we write or speak we can choose between the words. This makes English a rich and interesting language.

The People Call Themselves English. As the years passed, many Normans married Anglo-Saxons. The children from such marriages did not think of themselves as Normans or Anglo-Saxons. They just thought of themselves as English. All the people, therefore, eventually called themselves English instead of Normans or Anglo-Saxons.

1. How did the Normans become the ruling class in England?
2. What was the *Domesday Book?*
3. Who were the following men: Edward the Confessor, Ethelred, Harold, Canute, William of Normandy.

On Trial

1 The law of our country can be traced to practices, customs, and laws in the past ages. The ancient peoples, the Romans, and, particularly, the English contributed to our body of law. The ancients were the first to write down laws, the Romans made a list of laws for all to know their rights, and the English improved on them and gave us what is called "common law."

2 From the days of King Arthur, English law was based on the decisions of judges. The Magna Carta forced the kings to guarantee certain rights to the people and limited the power of kings. In time the decisions of judges were grouped into a set of laws, which became the common law of the land.

3 Henry IV gave us the idea of our modern trial by jury. In English law a person is innocent until proved guilty. In French law, a man is guilty until proved innocent. Except in Louisiana, English practice is followed in America.

13 3

The People of England Receive More Rights and Liberties

Henry II Weakens the Power of the Nobles. We have followed the story of England from its earliest days down through the rule of William the Conqueror.

William was a powerful king. While he ruled, there was peace in the land. His sons, however, were not such strong rulers. They were not able to keep peace, and there were many wars between powerful nobles.

In 1154, another strong ruler came to the throne. This was Henry II, William's great-grandson. Henry II took away some of the power of the nobles. He said that the nobles should pay money to the king instead of providing knights for his army. Since the nobles no longer had to employ large numbers of knights, their quarrels became less frequent. In this way, too, the nobles became less powerful.

Henry Improves the Law. When Henry became king, he set up royal courts to take the place of the courts established by the nobles. When a man was accused of a crime, a group of men from his neighborhood were selected as jurors. These men had to tell under oath what they knew about the crime which had been committed. The jurors were of equal rank with the accused man. This is called being tried by a jury of one's peers. The word *peers* means "equals."

Later, members of the jury were chosen not because they already knew about the case being tried, but because they did not know about it. In this way, they decided whether a man was guilty or not on the basis of what they heard in court. Our modern jury system has developed from this practice. Today, the guilt or innocence of the accused is decided by a group of local residents who judge only from what they hear in court.

Henry instructed his judges to keep a careful record of each case that was tried. When a man was convicted of a crime, the judge could look up earlier trials. He could see what punishment other men had been given for the same crime. In this way, the judges always gave the same punishments for the same crimes. This was the beginning of what the English called common law. Centuries later, this common law was brought to America by the English settlers. Many of the laws in our country today are based on English common law.

Thomas à Becket Is Murdered by the King's Men. King Henry II, like powerful rulers before and after him, wished to rule everything, including the Church. He tried to tell priests and bishops how to perform their duties, and he tried to interfere in many Church matters. Thomas à Becket was the Archbishop of Canterbury at that time. Thomas repeatedly told the king that he had no right to attempt to control Church affairs.

King Henry became more and more impatient with the archbishop and, in a burst of anger, expressed the wish that someone would rid him of "the insolent priest." Taking this as an order, a group of his followers entered the Cathedral of Canterbury and murdered Thomas at the foot of God's altar, where he knelt in prayer.

The people of England were shocked by this terrible murder. Thomas à Becket was canonized within three years. Many pilgrims went every year to his tomb at Canterbury. Two centuries later, an English poet named Geoffrey Chaucer wrote a series of stories about a group of pilgrims on their

Murder of the Archbishop. Thomas à Becket's loyal follower attempts to prevent the assassins from carrying out their evil plans.

The armed forces of the English Barons convinced King John it would be best to sign the Great Charter.

way to this shrine. These famous stories, called the *Canterbury Tales,* are still read widely.

King John Becomes Unpopular with His People. When Henry II died, his son Richard became king. Richard was such a brave fighter that he was known as the Lion-Heart. Richard loved adventure, and many stories have been written about him. However, Richard is not very important in the story of England. As you know, he left his country for a long time to take part in the Third Crusade. On his way home, he was captured and kept prisoner in Austria. The people of England had to pay a huge sum of money for his ransom. He died a few years after he returned to England.

After the death of Richard the Lion-Heart, his brother John became king. John was cruel and selfish. He had even tried to steal the throne while his brother Richard was fighting for the Holy Land.

Like his father, John tried to rule the Church. Pope Innocent III had appointed Stephen Langton Archbishop of Canterbury. King John would not let the Archbishop come into England. He claimed all the property that belonged to the Archbishopric of Canterbury. The Pope put England under an interdict. This meant that all the churches were closed. Mass could not be said anywhere in the kingdom, and the people could not receive the sacraments.

Almost all the people of England were Christians. They were unhappy when they could not attend Mass, and they blamed the king for this great misfortune. He became more and more unpopular.

For five years, King John refused to allow Stephen Langton to enter the country. During that time, the Pope excommunicated him. The Pope also said that John should no longer be king, and he asked Philip Augustus, the king of France, to invade England and carry out this sentence. Because John feared defeat by the French king, he made peace with the Church.

King John remained unpopular even after the interdict was lifted. He ruled as he pleased, without asking the advice of anyone. He was unfair and cruel. This kind of a ruler is called a tyrant.

One of the things that made King John unpopular was the fact that he made the people pay high taxes. He was often unreasonable, and he did not tell the people how their money was to be used.

King John Is Forced to Grant More Freedom. The people of England now faced a grave problem. In earlier days, the people had hoped that the king would become more powerful. They thought a powerful king would protect them from cruel and selfish nobles. But what could the people do when the king himself was cruel and selfish?

Stephen Langton, Archbishop of Canterbury, suggested that the bishops and nobles make a list of rights which the king could not take away from the people. This list was called the Magna Carta. This is Latin for Great Charter. On June 15, 1215, the bishops and nobles met King John in a meadow called Runnymede. They asked him to seal the Great Charter. The King sealed the Charter only because the nobles forced him to do so.

The first part of the Great Charter was concerned with the Church. It said that the king could not interfere in the affairs of the Church.

The Great Charter listed many other things that a king could not do. He could not keep a man in prison, for example, without giving the man a trial. The charter also said that the king could not ask for more taxes without the permission of the Great Council. This council was supposed to represent the people who were paying the taxes. In other words, the king could not levy taxes without the consent of the people who were being taxed. Englishmen have struggled to keep this right ever since.

The Englishmen who came to America brought this idea with them. More than 550 years after the Great Charter was signed, English colonists in America insisted that they could not be taxed without their consent. This was one of the causes of the American Revolution. The Charter was an important step toward democracy.

The important thing about the Great Charter is that it protected the people against the king. The king, as well as the people, had to obey the law.

The Great Charter

The Great Charter is an historic declaration of liberty. It is the cornerstone of justice under the law for Englishmen and for freedom-loving people everywhere. It proclaims basic human freedoms and civil rights for all men. It is the very seed and root of democracy.

1 In 1215 the English barons forced King John to affix his seal to the Great Charter. Their chief interest was to limit the king's power over them and to protect their own rights.

2 The Great Charter also affirmed the right of freemen, merchants, and townsmen to justice under the law. These freemen, merchants, and townsmen were to become the great body of the common people of England.

3 English settlers in the New World bore with them the spirit of the Great Charter. They forced another king to recognize their right to justice under the law. The Great Charter inspired the framers of the American Constitution.

4 The Great Charter is still a living force today. Its spirit and ideals form the core of the Charter of the United Nations.

191

The Great Charter gave important liberties only to "free men." Most of the English people were still serfs at that time and were not considered "free men." As feudalism came to an end, more and more people became free. As a result, the Great Charter applied to greater numbers of people. It later became even more important than it was when it was first published.

To this day, the people of England look back on the Great Charter and consider it the foundation of all their liberties. Since the United States got most of its laws and customs from England, the Great Charter is important to Americans also.

The Great Charter was sealed in the year 1215. This was in the thirteenth century. In the last chapter, we read about many great things that happened in that century. To this list, we can now add the granting of the Great Charter.

The Great Charter had said that the king could not ask for more taxes without consulting the Great Council. The name of the council was later changed to Parliament. This is from a French word which means "to speak." Why was a French name given to an English council? Only nobles belonged to the council at first, and most of the nobles were Normans at that time. The Normans, as you know, spoke French. It was the Normans who gave the Council its name.

Parliament Is Divided into Two Houses. In 1265, Parliament was divided. The nobles met by themselves and became known as the House of Lords. The members who were not nobles met by themselves. There were two knights from each county. They

A noble addresses the House of Lords while the king listens attentively. Parliament grew stronger as the power of the King lessened.

called themselves the House of Commons because they were supposedly the common people. The poor people actually had little voice in the government. Many years were to pass before they had anything to say about the laws.

King Edward I, who was King John's grandson, knew that the merchants and bankers of the towns had more money than many of the nobles. He thought they should also be asked about taxes, because they would be paying much higher taxes than the nobles. The Parliament which Edward I called in 1295 included merchants and bankers as well as nobles. This is sometimes called the Model Parliament, because later Parliaments used it as a model.

The King Loses His Power To Make the Laws. At first, the only thing that Parliament did was to levy taxes. This gave Parliament control over the king's source of money. Later, Parliament asked the king to change certain laws which it did not like. The king found that, if he did not do as Parliament asked, he would not get any money. Little by little, Parliament won control over the laws. After a time, Parliament passed the laws, and the king signed them. At one time, the members of Parliament did not like the reigning king. They forced him to give up his throne. Parliament was becoming more powerful, and the king was losing his power.

1. How did King Henry II reduce the power of the nobles?
2. What was the Magna Carta? What was the Model Parliament?
3. How did Parliament's power to levy taxes affect the king's power to make laws?

Chapter 13. REVIEW

Learning To Use New Words
Use each of the following terms in an original sentence, expressing something you have learned in Chapter 13:

Anglo-Saxon	juror
Normandy	interdict
Danes	tyrant
Hastings	Magna Carta
Domesday Book	Parliament

Knowing the Important Facts
1. Make a list of the invaders who conquered Britain from the time of the Romans to the Norman Conquest.
2. What did Henry II do to protect the liberties of the people? Describe the way the royal courts operated.
3. What famous document was sealed on June 15, 1215? Whose rights did it protect?
4. Describe how Parliament was divided into two houses.
5. From what languages does modern English come?

Thinking Through the Facts
1. Why were the Northmen successful in their conquests? How did they influence the Britains?
2. Why was the Magna Carta important to the English people? How did it affect American government?
3. How were Alfred the Great and Charlemagne alike? How were they different?
4. Why did William of Normandy think he had a right to the English throne? Why was the battle of Hastings important in English history?
5. Explain how King Henry II and King John each came into conflict with the Church.

Developing a Time Sense
Arrange the following events in the proper time order:
1. William the Conqueror wins the Battle of Hastings
2. Henry II improves the jury system
3. King Alfred rules England
4. The Magna Carta is approved

NORWAY
SWEDEN
SCOTLAND
IRELAND
DENMARK
RUSSIA
WALES
ENGLAND
London
Paris
NORMANDY
BRITTANY
GERMANY
POLAND
FRANCE
Tours
HOLY ROMAN EMPIRE
HUNGARY
LEON
NAVARRE
PORTUGAL
CASTILE
ARAGON
SPAIN
Cordova
Florence
Assisi
Rome
KINGDOM OF NAPLES AND SICILY
Constantinople
EASTERN ROMAN EMPIRE
ASIA MINOR
GREECE
Athens

Chapter 14 How Some Modern Nations Developed

In the early days of feudalism, there were no strong nations in Western Europe. How did the nations of today develop? We have already read how the nation of England developed. Now, we shall read the stories of France, Spain, and Portugal. The story of Russia is included, even though it is in Eastern, not Western, Europe. We shall also study two countries that did not become strong until the last century, Germany and Italy.

14 1

The King of France Becomes More Powerful

King Philip Augustus Makes Himself More Powerful Than the Nobles. After Charlemagne died, his empire was divided among his three grandsons. Charles the Bald became the ruler of what we now call France. Charles was not a very strong ruler. Many of his nobles had more power than he had.

For many years after Charles' reign, the nobles became stronger and stronger. They refused to obey the king. The nobles went to war against each other. They made their own laws. They even coined their own money. The king of France was a king in name only.

In 1180, a fifteen-year-old boy named Philip Augustus became king of France. He ruled for forty-three years. King Philip gained greater power with the help of the people who lived in the towns. He built up his army until it was greater than the armies of most of the nobles.

The most powerful noble who owned land in France was the king of England. How could a king also be a noble? This happened because Duke William of Normandy conquered England and made himself king. After that, the two titles went together. This meant that the king of England controlled more land in France than did the king of France. Through the years, and after a number of battles, King Philip brought this land under his control. About a century later, the English kings tried to win back this territory in the Hundred Years' War.

King Philip not only made himself more powerful than the nobles, but he gave France a good central government. As government officials, he usually selected people from the towns.

Louis IX, King and Saint. Louis IX was the grandson of Philip Augustus. He became king of France when he was twelve years old. His mother ruled for him until he was nineteen. He became one of the best loved of all kings. Even when he was alive,

Royal court. King Louis IX decides a lawsuit between a peasant and a knight. Both rich and poor had to accept the court's judgment.

people called him a saint. After his death, the Church declared him a saint. We have already read that Louis IX led two Crusades.

Louis made his government strong in many ways. He sent out officers to different parts of the kingdom to see that the laws were obeyed and that taxes were paid. He made changes in the courts, so that the poor would receive the same treatment as the rich. Sometimes, Louis himself acted as a judge. If a person did not think he had received a fair trial at a noble's court, he could come to the king's court and receive another hearing.

Louis said that the nobles would no longer be allowed to coin money. Only the king's government could do that. This made it easier for merchants to do business.

When Louis died, France was becoming a nation. France had a strong central government with the king at its head. The laws of the king were strictly enforced. Nobles were not quite so ready as they once were to defy the king.

1. How did King Philip gain more control of the French government?
2. Explain how the king of England could also be a French noble.

14 2
Feudalism Comes an End

France and England Fight for a Hundred Years. The English were not happy when Philip Augustus took Normandy away from their king. The French did not like the fact that the English king was still the feudal lord of some territory in France. The quarrel increased when a king of England said he was the rightful heir to the throne of

France. The French king sent help to the Scots, who at that time were fighting the English. The English king then sent an army across the English Channel to invade France. This marked the beginning of the Hundred Years' War.

Actually, the Hundred Years' War was a series of wars. The fighting lasted more than a hundred years. The English invaded France in 1337. They were not driven out until 1453.

Joan of Arc Saves France. By 1420, the English held two thirds of France. The French no longer seemed strong enough to fight. They had all but lost the war. Because of the fighting, their king, Charles VII, could not be crowned in the beautiful cathedral at Reims where the kings of France were always crowned.

Joan of Arc was a peasant girl who lived in Domremy in northeastern France. One day, when she was thirteen years old, she was startled to hear heavenly voices speaking to her. They told Joan that God had chosen her to save France. The voices also told her that she must see that Charles VII was to be crowned king of France.

When she was sixteen, Joan went to see Charles. At first, nobody would believe her story. The English continued to win more battles. It seemed that the war would soon be lost. At last, Charles allowed Joan to lead an army. This was in 1429.

Joan rode forth at the head of her army. She wore armor, and she was mounted on an armored horse. In one hand, she carried a sword; in the other, she carried the banner of France. The French soldiers took new heart from their leader. They rode with her to Orleans, a walled city which was being threatened by the English. After four days of brilliant fighting, Joan succeeded in routing the enemy. At the time, she was only seventeen years old. After this great victory, she was called the "Maid of Orleans."

Joan of Arc is inspired to save France. Her heavenly voices tell her she is chosen to lead the French army to victory.

At first, the people laughed at the "girl general," but soon they hailed the victorious "Maid of Orleans."

Joan went with Charles to Reims and watched him receive his crown. She felt that she had obeyed her "voices," and she begged permission to return home. The king, however, commanded her to lead more battles.

Joan of Arc Is Put to Death. The Duke of Burgundy, a French noble, was working with the English against his own king. Soldiers of the Duke of Burgundy captured Joan. She was sold to the English, who accused her of getting help from Satan. Abandoned by the ungrateful Charles VII, Joan defended herself at her trial. She was convicted and burned at the stake. An Englishman who watched her die, cried out, "God help us, for we have burned a saint!" Joan of Arc was canonized in 1920. She is one of the patron saints of France.

The French fought on, after Joan's death. By 1453, the English held only the town of Calais on the English Channel. The Hundred Years' War had come to an end. The English had failed in their attempt to rule France.

The Black Death and the Hundred Years' War Put an End to Feudalism. In the early part of the Hundred Years' War, a great plague swept across Europe. This was called the Black Death. Between one-fourth and one-half of all the people in Western Europe died during this plague.

So many serfs died in the plague that the

serfs fled when an enemy approached. Spears and arrows could do nothing against the thick, stone walls. But, during the last few years of the war, both sides used a new weapon—the cannon. This was the first time gunpowder had been used in European wars. The cannons could blow large holes in castle walls, and the walls were no longer much protection against the enemy.

The serfs had worked on the noble's land in return for the protection he gave them. Now, he could no longer give them protection. So, by the thousands, serfs left the manors.

The Black Death and the Hundred Years' War had put an end to feudalism in England and France. It was also coming to an end in the other countries of Western Europe.

1. Why was Joan of Arc called the "Maid of Orleans"?
2. On what charges was Joan of Arc tried by the English?
3. What was the Black Death? What were the results of the Black Death?

Payday. By the end of the Hundred Years' War, labor was scarce. Serfs demanded wages for their services. Feudalism was dying.

nobles did not have enough people to do the work on their estates. Fields were not plowed. They became overrun with weeds. Cows and sheep ate the crops, because there was no one to watch them. Roads went to ruin.

The serfs who did not die saw how badly the nobles needed workers. They refused to work unless they were paid. Many nobles agreed to pay wages to their workers. When a worker was paid, he was no longer a serf. By the time the Hundred Years' War came to an end, there was scarcely a serf left in either France or England. They were becoming fewer in other countries, also.

The old walled castle had been an important part of feudalism. Here, the noble lived with his family and his knights. Here, the

14 3

Spain and Portugal Become Strong Nations

Spain and Portugal Have a Similar History. When you look at a map of Europe, you will see that Spain and Portugal are on the same peninsula. It is called the Iberian Peninsula. The two countries have a similar history.

The Peninsula once belonged to Carthage. It was here that the great general of Carthage, Hannibal, gathered the huge army he led against Rome. The Romans later defeated Carthage, and the peninsula became a Roman colony. During the days of Roman rule, missionaries brought the Christian religion to the Iberian peninsula. Later, it was invaded by the Vandals. The Vandals were driven out by the Visigoths. The Visigoths became Christians.

In 711, Moslems from Africa conquered the peninsula. These Moslem were called Moors. Charlemagne, king of the Franks, drove the Moors from the northern part of the peninsula.

Those are the things we have already read about. Now we shall see how Spain and Portugal became strong nations at the end of the Middle Ages.

Portugal Becomes an Independent Kingdom. Several small, Christian kingdoms were started in the land Charlemagne had freed. The most important of the kingdoms were Leon, Castile, and Aragon. From these grew the nations of Spain and Portugal.

The Christians in the northern kingdoms said the whole peninsula belonged to them.

The fall of Granada. Ferdinand accepts the surrender of the Moslems. Spain is a united kingdom at last.

Little by little, the Moors were pushed back.

The Christians of Leon pushed down the west coast of the peninsula. In 1150, they took part of the land they had conquered, and started the independent kingdom of Portugal. Later, more territory was added, and Portugal reached the size it is today.

Much of the land in Portugal is very poor, and few people could make their living by farming. Portugal has a long seacoast, and many of the Portuguese turned to the sea for a livelihood.

Ferdinand and Isabella Unite Their Kingdoms. Most of the other Christian kingdoms on the peninsula united and formed the two kingdoms of Castile and Aragon. In 1469, Princess Isabella of Castile married Prince Ferdinand of Aragon. Later, Isabella became the Queen of Castile and Ferdinand became the King of Aragon. Ferdinand and Isabella united their two kingdoms. This is sometimes called the beginning of modern Spain.

As in most of Western Europe, there were many powerful nobles in Spain. Ferdinand and Isabella knew that Spain could never be a strong country while the nobles kept their power. Ferdinand and Isabella began to take certain powers away from the nobles. The people of the towns supported the king and queen against the nobles. Little by little, the nobles lost most of their power. Under King Ferdinand and Queen Isabella, Spain became a strong and united nation.

The Moors Are Driven From Spain. In 1212, knights from England, France, and other nations of Western Europe had come to help the Spaniards against the Moors. The Moors were pushed back to the little kingdom of Granada in southern Spain. They kept this tiny toe hold on the continent of Europe for another two hundred and eighty years.

After Ferdinand and Isabella had established a strong government and had weakened the power of the nobles, they decided it was time to drive the Moors completely off the peninsula. The fighting lasted for ten years. Finally, on January 2, 1492, the Moors surrendered the last bit of territory they held. This was the city of Granada. The Moors had first invaded Spain in 711. They were finally defeated in 1492. We see, then, that they held parts of Spain for almost eight hundred years.

When the victorious armies of Ferdinand and Isabella marched into Granada, an Italian who was visiting in Spain marched in with them. His name was Christopher Columbus. Columbus must have been very happy. He had asked Ferdinand and Isabella to send him on a voyage across the Atlantic Ocean. They would not do this while they were fighting the Moors. Now that the Moors were defeated, perhaps Columbus would have his chance.

1. Where are Spain and Portugal located?
2. How did Portugal become an independent kingdom?
3. What part did the Moslems play in the history of Spain?
4. What became of the kingdoms of Leon, Castile and Aragon?

14 4

Germany and Italy Fail To Unite

The Holy Roman Empire. We have read what happened to the western part of Charlemagne's old empire. It slowly developed into a strong, united nation, France. The story of the eastern part is somewhat different, as we shall see. This part contained Germany and northern Italy.

Germany had a king, but he was weak. The nobles fought each other, and they fought the king.

In the tenth century, the nobles elected one of their number to be king. This was Otto, later known as Otto the Great. Otto tried to weaken the power of the nobles and to make Germany a strong country. Perhaps he would have succeeded, but he also became King of Italy. This meant that he could not devote full time to ruling both countries.

Many people in Europe had never given up the idea of a large empire, such as the Roman Empire had been. In 962, Pope John XII placed on the head of Otto the same crown that had once been placed on

Ferdinand and Isabella did much to make Spain a strong nation. The parliament they set up gave the people some voice in government.

the head of Charlemagne. The Pope declared Otto Emperor of the Romans. The land ruled by Otto—Germany and northern Italy—became known as the Holy Roman Empire.

The Pope hoped that all the people of Europe would be united in the Holy Roman Empire. This plan did not work out. Other peoples of Europe did not join the Empire. Not even Germany and Italy were able to unite. Otto's successors had to spend much time crossing the Alps, which separated the two countries. This was a long, hard journey. There were no telegraphs or telephones in those days, so while the emperor was in one country, he could not tell what was going on in the other country. When he was in Italy, the German nobles often revolted against him. When he went back to Germany to settle things there, trouble would break out in Italy.

The Pope had hoped that the Emperor and the Pope would work together. Instead, later emperors caused trouble for the Popes.

An emperor does penance. Henry IV kneels in the snows of Canossa. He is begging the Pope's forgiveness for his disobedience.

The Empire was not ruled from Rome. In fact, the Emperor had little control over Rome. The city was the capital of the Papal States, which were ruled by the Pope.

The Empire was so weak and disunited that it could hardly be called an empire at all.

These facts caused someone to say of the Holy Roman Empire: "It was not holy, it was not Roman, and it was not an empire."

Struggle Between the Pope and the Emperor. In the Middle Ages, kings and emperors gave large sections of land to bishops and archbishops. This meant that the bishops and archbishops were nobles. It made them vassals of the king or emperor. The bishops ruled the manor, collected taxes, and furnished knights to the king in time of war. This situation was not good for the Church. A bishop should be able to devote all his time to the needs of the Church. When a bishop was also a noble, he had to give much of his time to governing his land. He also had to take sides in wars between nobles and the king, or in wars between different nobles.

When a bishop is consecrated, he receives the crozier, the miter, and the ring. In the Middle Ages, many kings insisted upon giving these symbols to the new bishop. In this way, the king showed that he expected the bishop to be a faithful vassal. Because the king was a layman—that is, not a bishop or a priest—this practice was called lay investiture.

In 1073, Gregory VII became Pope. He said that lay investiture was a great evil and must be stopped. The emperor of the Holy Roman Empire at that time was Henry IV. The emperor defied the Pope. He insisted that he had the right to appoint bishops. Pope Gregory excommunicated Henry. When this happened, the nobles and the people would not have anything to do with the emperor. Henry saw that he was in danger of losing his throne. He decided that he would have to make peace with the Pope. Henry crossed the Alps in the middle of winter. He went to Canossa, where the Pope was staying. For three days, Henry stood in the snow begging the Pope to forgive him. The Pope pardoned Henry and received him back into the Church.

This did not end the struggle. When Henry became more powerful, he marched into Italy and forced the Pope to leave Rome. Pope Gregory died soon after that.

A later pope and a later emperor made an agreement called the Concordat of Worms. It was given this name because it was drawn up in the city of Worms. In this agreement, the emperor gave up the practice of investing bishops. The emperor said he would merely give the bishop the power over his lands. This was the reform which Gregory wanted.

The Empire Becomes Weaker. The Holy Roman Empire had never been very strong, and it gradually became weaker. First, Italy broke away from the Empire. Then, parts of Germany broke away.

In the north of Italy there were four city-states: Milan, Florence, Genoa, and Venice. In the central part of Italy were the Papal States, ruled by the Pope. The southern part was held at different times by Northmen, Moslems, Frenchmen, and Spaniards. Italy did not become a united country until less than a hundreds years ago.

Northern Germany divided into about three hundred tiny countries and city-states. The emperor ruled only in southern Germany. This is the country we now call Austria. Like Italy, Germany did not become a united country for many years.

1. What lands were included in the Holy Roman Empire? Who was crowned Emperor of the Romans by Pope John XII?
2. What is lay investiture?
3. Why did Pope Gregory VII excommunicate Henry IV?
4. What were the terms of the Concordat of Worms?

14 5
Russia in the Middle Ages

The Slavs and the Northmen. Just as the Germans overran most of Western Europe, so the Slavs overran most of Eastern Europe. At first, they lived by fishing and hunting, and did not stay very long in one place. They worshiped pagan gods.

As the number of Slavs increased, the eastern Slavs settled in the valleys of the Volga and Dnieper Rivers. This was some time between the fifth and eighth centuries.

Groups of Northmen sailing along the coast of Europe came to Constantinople,

Slavic peasants tend their crops. Slavs were among the first peoples to make permanent homes in Russia.

the capital of the Byzantine Empire. They had never seen anything like this beautiful, wealthy city. They saw that they could not capture it, because the city was at the end of a long strait. So, they decided to carry on a trade with the Byzantines. Instead of sailing around the continent of Europe, they hauled their ships overland to the Dnieper River. From here, it was easy to reach the Black Sea and go on to Constantinople. As they went down the river, they passed many Slav villages. This was the first time the Slavs and the Northmen had seen each other.

The Northmen liked the beautiful, fertile land along the Dnieper. It was so much better than the land in the rugged Scandinavian countries. Some of them decided to move to this land. About 892, Rurick, a leader of the Northmen, started a trading settlement inland from the Gulf of Finland. His chief village was Novgorod. Rurick took the title Prince of Novgorod, and Novgorod became the first Russian state. Rurick was the founder of a dynasty that was to lead Russia for seven hundred years.

Rurick's successors gained control of more of the land on which the eastern Slavs lived. They made the village of Kiev their capital. This was far to the south of Novgorod and much closer to the Byzantine Empire.

The Northmen were outnumbered by the Slavs they ruled. The Northmen adopted the language of the Slavs. They dressed like the Slavs, in hides and homespun cloth. They lived in log cabins like the Slavs. The

Russia began at Novgorod, where Rurick's Rus tribe of Northmen settled among the Slavs in 862.

Northmen and the Slavs intermarried. Soon, they were one people. From this point, they will be called Russians.

The early Russians had no written language, so we know little about their history.

Russia and the Byzantine Empire. From the Northmen, the Russians had learned the value of trade with the Byzantine Empire. They continued this trade. They took boatloads of slaves, lumber, grain, fur, and pitch to Constantinople. They brought back cloth, perfumes, wine, jewelry, and other goods.

As the Russian traders walked about Constantinople, they were in awe of the things they saw. How different this city was from their little villages of log cabins and dirt streets. They marveled at the beautiful church of Hagia Sophia and its art treasures. They admired the devotion of the Christians praying in the church. They asked questions about the Christian religion. When they went home, they told their neighbors and friends what they had seen.

Russian traders return from Constantinople. That famous city seemed wonderful, indeed, to the simple Russians.

Near the end of the tenth century, Vladimir, the Grand Duke of Kiev, became a Christian. He invited Christian missionaries from the Byzantine Empire to enter his country. They did so. The missionaries brought not only the Christian religion, but also many other things. One of these was the Greek alphabet. The missionaries founded churches, schools, and monasteries. These were built in the Byzantine style of architecture, with its many domes and lofty spires.

When the bishops of the Byzantine Empire voted to separate from the Roman Catholic Church, the leaders of the Church in Russia also decided to separate. This new church was called the Orthodox Church. Most Russians remained members of the Orthodox Church until the Communists took over the country in our own century.

Tartars, fierce Mongol warriors, conquered Russia in the Thirteenth Century. Their rule lasted two and a half centuries.

The Rule of the Mongols and the Rise of Moscow. Other cities were being founded in various parts of Russia. In 1147, a new city, Moscow, appeared in the records for the first time. The city became more and more important. The Grand Duke of Moscow was a descendant of Rurick. He came to be looked upon as the leader of all Russians and the protector of their church.

In 1237, fierce Mongol warriors from Asia swept into southern Russia. Later, they extended their rule over most of Russia. They ruled for more than two hundred and fifty years, and most of that time Russia was separated from Western civilization. The Russians adopted Oriental customs and ways. This period of Mongol rule had a big effect on Russia. Even when the Mongols no longer ruled, the Russians seemed as much Oriental as European. They were often suspicious of people from Western Europe.

The Mongols allowed most of the Russian princes and nobles to rule their lands as long as they paid taxes. They did not attempt to stamp out the Orthodox Church. In 1453, the Turks captured Constantinople, and this was the end of the Byzantine Empire. This also meant that Constantinople was no longer the center of the Orthodox Church. The highest officer of the Orthodox Church moved to Moscow, and Moscow became a religious center.

The Mongols fought among themselves and gradually became weaker. Ivan the Great, Grand Duke of Moscow, refused to pay taxes to them. In 1480, the Mongols sent an army against him, but the army retreated when it met Ivan's army.

This left Ivan the most powerful man in Russia. In 1498, he declared that he wished to be known as Czar and "Autocrat of All Russia."

1. Why didn't the Northmen attack Constantinople?
2. How did Moscow become a religious center?
3. What Asian tribe conquered Russia?
4. Who was Ivan the Great?

Chapter 14. REVIEW

Learning To Use New Words

Use each of the following terms in an original sentence, expressing something you have learned in Chapter 14:

nation	Black Death
canonized	Holy Roman Empire
plague	lay investiture
peninsula	Hagia Sophia
Moors	Moscow

Knowing the Important Facts
1. What steps did King Louis IX take to improve the French government?
2. What role did Joan of Arc play in saving France?
3. What two events hastened the end of feudalism in England and France?
4. Who were the Slavs, Northmen, and Mongols? What is their place in Russian history?
5. What problems led to disunity in Germany and Italy?

Thinking Through the Facts
1. Why was the Hundred Years' War fought? What were the results of the war?
2. Why has it been said of the Holy Roman Empire that "It was not holy, it was not Roman, and it was not an empire"?
3. Explain the conflict between the Church and the emperor during the reign of Henry IV.
4. Why was contact with the Byzantine Empire important to Russia?
5. Explain how two of the nations you have studied in this chapter developed strong central governments.

Developing a Time Sense
Arrange the following events in the proper time order:
1. Ivan the Great declares himself Czar of Russia
2. Joan of Arc saves France
3. The Hundred Years' War comes to an end
4. Philip Augustus strengthens the government of France
5. The Moors are driven from Spain

Unit FIVE *Summary*

I Should Know That . . .
1. England has been ruled by many different peoples. Romans, Anglo-Saxons, and Danes all contributed to early English history.
2. The Norman Conquest in 1066 was the last successful invasion of England.
3. Modern English developed from Anglo-Saxon and Norman French.
4. King Henry II reduced the power of the nobles and worked to improve the court system.
5. The English nobles forced King John to sign the Magna Carta. This charter or agreement limited the king's power and insured the people certain liberties.
6. The English Parliament grew from the council of nobles formed to advise the king on matters of taxation.
7. The Hundred Years' War and the Black Plague weakened feudalism in England and France.
8. By 1492 Spain and Portugal ruled the Iberian Peninsula. Portugal was formed from the Kingdom of Leon and Spain from Aragon and Castile.
9. The Holy Roman Empire was founded in the tenth century. It failed to unite Germany and Italy under one ruler.
10. Russia has been influenced by many peoples. Slavic settlers, Northern invaders, and traders and missionaries from Constantinople all played a part in early Russian history.

Dates I Should Remember . . .
1066—Norman Conquest
1215—Magna Carta
1295—Model Parliament
1492—Moors driven from Spain

Books I Should Read
Mildred Criss, *Isabella, Young Queen of Spain*
Howard Pyle, *Merry Adventures of Robin Hood*
Sir Bertrand Windle, *Romans in Britain*

Some Interesting Things to Do
1. Do you know who the present monarch of England is? See if you can find pictures of the kings and queens who have ruled England during the twentieth century.
2. Pretend you were given the task of defending Joan of Arc at her trial. How would you have answered the charge of witchcraft?
3. Choose one of the countries you have studied in this unit. See how much information you can find about that country's literature, music, art, and architecture.

SIX Western Civilization Expands

Chapter 15
New Ideas Change the World

We say that the Middle Ages came to an end about 1500 and that modern times began about then. At the end of the Middle Ages America was discovered. At the beginning of modern times North and South America were settled, mostly by people from Western Europe. The people of Western Europe not only discovered, explored, and settled the two huge continents of North and South America, but they did many other amazing things as well. For example, they sailed around the continent of Africa to India. They discovered an ocean many thousands of miles from Europe. Then they sailed on across this ocean and around the world. All this was done without the many inventions we have today to help explorers and settlers. And we must remember that the number of people who did all this was small as compared with the number of people in Western Europe today.

As Americans, we are especially interested in the discovery and settlement of America. The people of Western Europe brought Western Civilization to our side of the Atlantic Ocean. Think how different life in America would be if our continents had been discovered by people from China or India.

15 1

People of Europe Become Interested in Ancient Greece and Rome

Many Things Reminded the Italians of Ancient Rome. The period of the "new learning," or the Renaissance, lasted from about 1350 to about 1600. The word Renaissance means "new birth" or "awakening." In many ways there was a new birth of knowledge at the time.

In the days of feudalism, as we have seen, most people of Western Europe were peasants. They had to work all day at farming to make a living. They had no time to go to school, and so they did not learn to read or write. They would have had little time for reading even if they had known how.

The Crusades, the Black Death, and the

1200	1300	1400	1500	1600	1700	

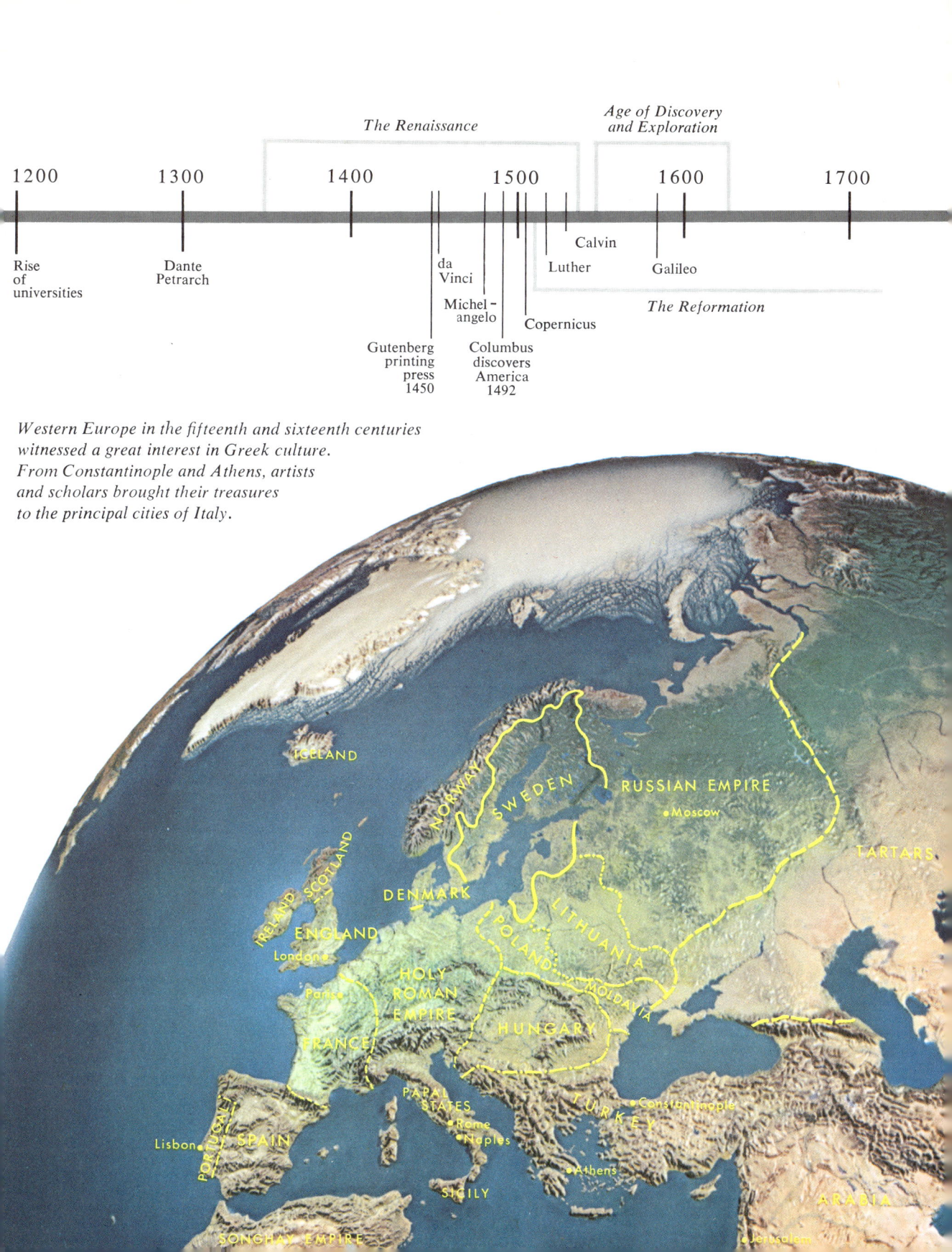

The Renaissance spans roughly 1400–1500s.

Age of Discovery and Exploration spans roughly late 1400s–1600s.

The Reformation spans roughly 1500s–1600s.

- 1200 — Rise of universities
- 1300 — Dante, Petrarch
- da Vinci
- Michelangelo
- Gutenberg printing press 1450
- Columbus discovers America 1492
- Copernicus
- Luther
- Calvin
- Galileo

Western Europe in the fifteenth and sixteenth centuries witnessed a great interest in Greek culture. From Constantinople and Athens, artists and scholars brought their treasures to the principal cities of Italy.

A Renaissance lad views the ruins of ancient Rome. He will soon be witnessing the rise of a new and beautiful city.

Hundred Years' War all helped to bring about an end to feudalism. The town began to replace the feudal manor. Towns grew in number and size, and the people who lived in the towns were freemen, not peasants. They had time to think and read and study. They had time to travel, too. Travel played an important role in the new birth of learning known as the Renaissance.

The Renaissance began in Italy. There, a freeman who traveled from town to town saw aqueducts erected centuries before by the Romans. He went over roads which had been built by the ancient Romans. All roads led to Rome. Once in the Eternal City, the traveler stood in awe amid the ruins of the Forum and the Colosseum. He walked beneath the splendid Arch of Titus. He saw buildings and temples dating back to the days when Rome was the heart of a mighty empire.

The fourteenth-century traveler was

ings were in Latin, but the monks were only too happy to teach interested freemen of the towns how to read Latin.

So it was that many Italians and other Europeans in the fourteenth century became very much interested in ancient Rome. This was the beginning of the "new learning."

Italians Become Interested in Ancient Greece. The Italians first became interested in ancient Rome because they had so many things to remind them of the days when Rome ruled the world. At first they did not know very much about ancient Greece. This situation changed as the Moslem Turks conquered more and more of the Eastern, or Byzantine, Empire. The Eastern Empire, as you know, had always been more Greek than Roman. As the Turks came closer and closer to Constantinople, the scholars and artists of that city fled. Many of them went to Venice, Genoa, Rome, and other cities of Italy. They brought ancient Greek writings with them. They brought Greek statues and other ancient treasures.

Many Italians had already become interested in the culture of ancient Rome. It was easy for them to become interested in the culture of ancient Greece.

It seems strange, in a way, that this interest in ancient cultures should be called the "new learning." The learning in which the Italians were interested was very, very old. Much of it went back to the days before the birth of Christ. But it was new to the Italians of the later Middle Ages.

The "New Learning" Spreads. The Popes helped the spread of this "new learning." There were many valuable old manuscripts in the Vatican. The Popes invited scholars

moved to admiration by what he beheld. His curiosity was aroused to know more about the ancient Romans. How did they live? What did they believe? What were their laws and government like? What kind of poems and plays did they enjoy?

A visit to one of the many monasteries in Italy would satisfy his curiosity and interest. All through the feudal period the monks in the monasteries had kept learning alive. They had collected many writings of the ancient Romans and stored the manuscripts in their libraries. These writ-

to study them. Pope Nicholas V gathered together most of the manuscripts and put them in one section of the Vatican. This was the beginning of the Vatican Library. The Vatican Library is still famous for its collection of ancient writings.

The spread of the "new learning" was also helped by wealthy merchants of Venice and Genoa and by wealthy bankers of Florence. These rich men sent messengers to search all over Europe and Asia for ancient manuscripts.

Men from other parts of Western Europe came to study in the Italian universities. They went back home and told other people about the "new learning" in Italy. In this way the Renaissance spread to all parts of Western Europe.

The Men of the "New Learning" Were Partly Right and Partly Wrong. Most men who were interested in the "new learning" thought like this: "The Greeks and Romans had the best civilization the world has ever known. They had the best writers, the best thinkers, the best sculptors, and the best architects. We can learn much from the ancient Greeks and Romans. We can learn nothing from the people who have lived since then."

People who felt this way were partly right and partly wrong. They were right when they said they could learn much from the Greeks and Romans. They were wrong when they said they could learn nothing from the people of the Middle Ages.

There were many good scholars, artists, architects, and writers in the Middle Ages. Cathedrals built in the Gothic style of the Middle Ages are still greatly admired today. These cathedrals contained beautiful stained glass windows and other works of art. St. Thomas Aquinas, one of the greatest scholars of all time, lived in the Middle Ages. The men of the "new learning" paid little attention to St. Thomas or the other learned men of the Middle Ages. This was a serious mistake.

1. Describe how Italians became interested in ancient Greece.
2. How was the new learning spread?
3. Who saved the writings of the ancient Romans?
4. What Bible stories are illustrated on the stained glass windows in your church?

15 2

Architects and Sculptors of the Renaissance

Architects Model Their Buildings After Those of Greece and Rome. In the twelfth and thirteenth centuries, as we know, architects built churches in a new style, known as Gothic. The men of the "new learning" did not like anything about the Middle Ages. Therefore, they did not like Gothic architecture.

The Renaissance architects modeled their buildings after those of ancient Greece and Rome. They used Greek columns and Roman domes. This was called classic architecture.

In 1506, work was begun on the new St. Peter's in Rome. This is the famous church that is still standing. It took the place of the old St. Peter's which had been built by Constantine.

Michelangelo supervises work on St. Peter's. Scaffolding around the dome enables masons and carpenters to complete their work.

St. Peter's is a good example of classic architecture. If you look at a picture of it, you will see the great dome and the many columns. The architect who first planned St. Peter's was named Bramante. When he died, other architects took his place. One of them was the famous Michelangelo. Michelangelo designed the dome for St. Peter's. This is the largest dome in the world and one of the most beautiful.

St. Peter's is still the largest church in the world. The main altar stands over the tomb of Saint Peter. This famous church is visited by hundreds of thousands of people every year.

Classic architecture was used not only for churches but also for palaces, public buildings, and even for homes.

Sculptors Learn from the Greeks and Romans. The scholars who fled from Constantinople brought to Italy many ancient Greek statues. In Italy there were already many ancient Roman statues. Italian sculptors studied these models and made statues like them. Indeed, many of the Italian statues were better than the Greek and Roman statues.

One of the most famous sculptors was Lorenzo Ghiberti. Among other things he carved the bronze doors of the baptistry at Florence. Michelangelo said these doors were so beautiful that they were "worthy of being placed at the entrance of Paradise."

Michelangelo himself was a great sculptor. One of his most famous statues is in St. Peter's. It shows the Blessed Mother holding the body of her dead Son after He had been

Pietà, the sorrowful mother receives her Son. In 1964 this famous statue left the Vatican on loan to the New York World's Fair.

taken down from the Cross. The statue is called the *Pietà*. As you look at this famous statue and study the face of Our Lady you feel some of the sorrow she felt. Only a great artist can make you feel this way. Michelangelo was only twenty-four years old when he carved this statue. Millions of Americans had an opportunity to see it at the World's Fair held in New York during 1964-1965. It was loaned to the Fair by the Pope.

Some of the other Renaissance sculptors admired Greece and Rome so much that they carved statues of ancient heroes. They also carved statues of the ancient gods.

1. Mention two architects who helped design St. Peter's.
2. What is the name of the architecture modeled after the buildings of ancient Greece and Rome?
3. What is Ghiberti's most famous work?
4. Describe the *Pietà*.

15　3

Some Painters of the Renaissance

Michelangelo Again. Some of the world's greatest painters lived during the Renaissance. One was Michelangelo.

Pope Julius II asked Michelangelo to paint the ceiling of his Sistine Chapel. Michelangelo said he was not a painter but a sculptor. Pope Julius insisted. The only way Michelangelo could paint the ceiling was to build a scaffold and lie on his back. He worked like this for four and a half years. The painting tells many stories from the Bible from the birth of Adam to the Flood. It contains more than 300 figures.

On the altar wall of the Sistine Chapel, Michelangelo painted *The Last Judgment*. This is one of the world's most famous pictures.

At the age of seventy, Michelangelo became the architect of St. Peter's. He served the Popes as sculptor, painter, and architect. He was one of the most gifted men who ever lived.

Leonardo da Vinci. Another remarkable man who lived in Italy at the same time as Michelangelo was Leonardo da Vinci. Like Michelangelo, he had many talents. He studied the flights of the birds and made drawings for a flying machine. He designed a canal in northern Italy. He planned the fortifications around the city of Milan. Leonardo was a good sculptor, scientist, architect, and also a good musician.

One day the king of France visited Milan. The king was amazed when he saw a huge mechanical lion that roared and stood up on its hind legs. On the lion's chest was the

Leonardo da Vinci puts the finishing brush strokes on a painting of one of his military machines.

Statue of Moses
Michelangelo Buonarroti

Las Meninas (Maids of Honor)
Velasquez

Assumption of the Madonna
Titian

Il Castiglioni
Raphael

Assumption of the Virgin
Bartolomé Murillo

Mona Lisa
Leonardo da Vinci

Peasants Dancing (detail)
Pieter Brueghel the Elder

The Art of the Renaissance

The Renaissance inspired a golden age in the fine arts. Paintings glow with beauty of color and line. Statues excel in lifelike grace, strength, and nobility. The masterpieces offer rich variety in religious subjects and in scenes drawn from court, town, and countryside.

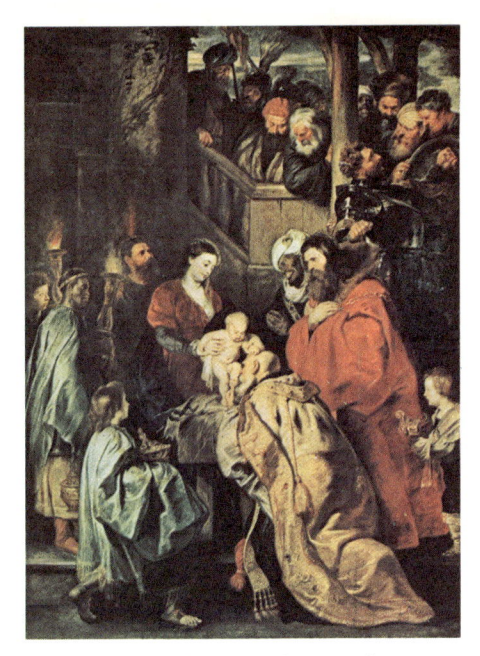

Adoration of the Magi
Peter Paul Rubens

Madonna of the Chair
Raphael

Four Negro Heads
Peter Paul Rubens

coat of arms of France. The lion had been built by Leonardo.

One of Leonardo's most famous paintings is **The Last Supper**. Our Lord has just announced to the Apostles that one of them will betray Him. You can see the guilt on the face of Judas. You can also see the sorrow and surprise on the faces of the others.

Raphael Worked for the Popes. Another famous painter of this period was Raphael. For most of his life Raphael lived in Rome. He worked for Pope Julius II and Pope Leo X. He decorated many parts of the Vatican. He and Michelangelo were working in the Vatican at the same time.

Raphael is known for his pictures of the Blessed Virgin. One of the most famous is called the *Sistine Madonna*.

There Were Many Other Renaissance Painters. Michelangelo, Leonardo da Vinci, and Raphael are probably the most famous of the Renaissance painters, but there were many others almost as famous. Not all of them lived in Italy. Some lived in Spain, France, the Netherlands, and Germany. There were more famous painters during the Renaissance than there were at any other period in all history. Among the most famous are: Rubens (Flemish), El Greco (Spanish), Rembrandt (Dutch), and Holbein (German).

1. Who painted the Sistine Chapel? How was the ceiling painted?
2. Mention three accomplishments of Leonardo da Vinci.
3. For what type of painting is Raphael famous?
4. Describe Leonardo da Vinci's most famous painting.

15　4

Books Came Into Wide Use

A New Way of Printing Is Discovered. One of the greatest inventions of all time was made during the Renaissance. This was the invention of a new way of printing.

In ancient times and during most of the Middle Ages there were few books. The reason for this was that each book had to be copied by hand. It took a long time to make just one copy of a book. Books were so scarce and so expensive that ordinary people could not own them; even the students at the universities did not own books.

Late in the Middle Ages the people of Western Europe learned about block printing. The printer carved all the pictures and all the words of a certain page on a block of wood. Then he put ink on this block of wood. Many pages could be printed from it. This was better than writing each book by hand, but it was still a slow process. It took a long time to carve all the letters of a page.

A German printer named Johann Gutenberg improved on this idea. Why not carve each letter separately instead of carving a whole page at a time? Then the letters could be put into their proper places. After one page was printed the letters could be arranged in a different way and used for another page. In this way, the same letters could be used over and over. Gutenberg's invention was called movable type. He worked on it for a long time. He found that wooden letters wore out quickly, therefore he decided to use metal letters. Then he had to invent a printing press which could print from the metal letters. He began printing in this new way about 1450. The first book he printed was the Bible.

In other parts of Europe other printers heard about Gutenberg's invention. Soon many new printing presses were built. These were small and did not look like the great presses of today, but they were a great improvement over block printing.

Paper Mills Are Started. Gutenberg would not have been able to use his printing press if the people of Europe had not learned how to make paper. The early Egyptians had written on papyrus, a plant which grew along the Nile. The monks of the Middle Ages had written on parchment. Parchment is made from the skins of animals. Both

A master printer studies the work turned out by his assistant. Soon he will hang this printed sheet up to dry.

papyrus and parchment were too stiff and too expensive to use for printing.

The Chinese had learned to make paper from rags. The Arabs had learned this from the Chinese, and the people of Europe had learned it from the Arabs. The Spaniards then learned how to make paper from hemp and flax. Both these plants grow in Spain.

After the printing press was invented, many new paper mills were built in Spain and in other parts of Europe. There was plenty of paper for the new presses.

Many Books Are Printed. Books were now printed in large numbers. By 1500, there were seven or eight million books in Western Europe. Many people were able to buy books now. Those who could not buy books could read them in the new libraries which were built in many places.

Many booklets and pamphlets were also printed. Later, magazines and newspapers were printed.

With so many things to read, people could learn about the world in which they lived. We have seen that the first book Gutenberg printed was the Bible. The book which Marco Polo had written almost two hundred years before was printed. Many people read about the Orient for the first time in Marco Polo's book.

Printing also helped to spread the "new learning." The writings of the ancient Greeks and Romans were printed so that everybody could read them.

1. How did Gutenberg's method of printing differ from block printing?
2. Why were many paper mills started after the invention of the printing press?
3. How did printing help the "new learning"?

15　5

New Discoveries in Science

Men Study the Stars. In ancient Greece many men had studied the stars and had made a record of their findings. During the Renaissance, when there was a great interest in ancient Greece, men read the records which the Greek scientists had kept. The scientists of the Renaissance became very much interested in the stars.

The Greeks believed that our Earth was the most important body in the universe. They thought we were in the center of everything. They were convinced that the sun and all the other stars revolved around the Earth. For many centuries, almost everybody believed this. A cleric named Copernicus lived in Poland during the Renaissance. Copernicus studied the stars for many years. He decided that the Earth and the other planets move around the sun. He wrote a book explaining his ideas, and dedicated it to the Pope.

Not very many people believed Copernicus. About fifty years later an Italian astronomer named Galileo made a telescope. With this telescope he studied the stars and the planets. He said that Copernicus had been right. He proved that the Earth really did move around the sun.

Even then, people did not want to change their ideas about the Earth. It was still some time before people were convinced that Copernicus and Galileo had been right.

Pope Gregory XIII Changes the Calendar. More telescopes were made, and astronomers carefully studied the stars. They discovered that the calendar which had been drawn up by Julius Caesar (the Julian calendar) was wrong. Pope Gregory XIII ordered that ten days be dropped. Millions of people went to bed on the night of October 4, 1582; when they woke up, it was October 15. The calendar year was now in agreement with the sun year.

Julius Caesar had said that there should be an extra day every four years. Pope Gregory said that this extra day should be omitted three times in every 400 years. This improved calendar is called the Gregorian calendar.

New Inventions Help Sailors. Until the time of the Renaissance most sailors had been afraid to sail too far from land. They were afraid that they would not be able to find their way back. This was true at night when they were unable to use the sun for directions.

The Chinese had known for a long time how to build a simple compass. They made a magnet out of a needle. Then they floated this needle on water. The needle pointed

Discoveries in Science

1 A new world of scientific discovery was opened up in the fifteenth and sixteenth centuries. Alchemists trying to turn other metals into gold gave way to scientists paving the way for modern chemistry and physics. Medicine and geography made notable progress. Copernicus, the father of modern astronomy, taught that the earth turns upon its own axis and, together with other planets in the solar system, revolves around the sun. The invention of the printing press was to help spread word of these and other discoveries far and wide.

2 Galileo made one of the first telescopes. Through it he saw the sun turning on its axis, studied the movements of the planets, and explored the Milky Way.

3 The compass is a magnetized needle which points to the north. It was probably invented by the Chinese. The compass gave explorers their bearings even in bad weather.

4 The astrolabe was widely used from the fifteenth century on. It enabled a captain to find his ship's latitude, or distance north or south of the equator.

north and south. This was not much help to sailors during storms. In stormy weather the water in which the needle floated splashed wildly. Then the needle would sink. During the Renaissance men discovered how to mount the needle in a box. The compass could then be used in all kinds of weather.

The astrolabe was invented about this time. With an astrolabe sailors could tell how far north or south of the equator they were.

Ships Are Improved. Ships themselves were improved during the Renaissance. In early times all ships had to be rowed. Later, a sail was added to the ships. The sail could be used only when the wind was blowing in the right direction. When the wind was blowing in the wrong direction, the men had to start rowing again.

Around 1400, a new kind of ship came into use. This ship had many sails which could be turned in various directions. With these movable sails it was possible to guide the ship in the right direction no matter which way the wind was blowing.

With the new kind of sails and the new inventions to tell them where they were, sailors were ready to go farther away from their homes. They were ready to make voyages which would lead to new discoveries and change the history of the world.

1. What did the ancient Greeks believe was the most important body in the universe?
2. Who first corrected this error of the ancient Greeks?
3. How was Galileo able to prove that the Earth revolved around the sun?
4. Why did Pope Gregory XIII change the Julian calendar?

Chapter **15. REVIEW**

Learning to Use New Words
Use each of the following terms in an original sentence, expressing something you have learned in Chapter 15:

Renaissance	compass
astronomer	astrolabe
manuscript	sculptor
telescope	classic architecture
Gothic architecture	

Knowing the Important Facts
1. List four ways in which the people of Europe showed interest in the cultures of ancient Rome and Greece.
2. List four Renaissance painters or sculptors, and the countries from which they came.
3. Describe how books were copied before and after the invention of the printing press.
4. Draw up a list of scientific accomplishments made during the Renaissance. Mention three men who contributed to scientific progress during the Renaissance.
5. Describe classic architecture. Give examples of this type of architecture.

Thinking Through the Facts
1. What do we mean when we say, "the Renaissance formed a bridge from the ancient to the modern world"?
2. Why did Italy become the center of the Renaissance?
3. Explain what is meant by the statement, "The Renaissance spirit stressed change."
4. How did each of these inventions change men's life: compass, printing press, and paper?
5. Why did many Greek scholars come to Italy during the fifteenth century?
6. What did Copernicus and Galileo believe about the solar system? Discuss their views.

Developing a Time Sense
Arrange the following events in the proper time order:
1. The Turks capture Constantinople
2. The printing press is invented by Gutenberg
3. The Gregorian calendar is adopted
4. Movable sails come into use

Chapter 16
Revolt, Reform, Rivalry

When Christopher Columbus discovered America in 1492, there was just one Christian religion in Europe. Just twenty-five years later, in 1517, a religious revolt broke out. Thousands of people broke away from the Catholic Church and joined the new Protestant religions. This breaking away from the Church is called the Protestant Reformation or the Protestant Revolt.

The Protestant Revolt is one of the most important events in history. It had an effect upon the way people worshipped, thought, and lived. It still has an effect upon our world today.

Among the nations of Europe at this time, rivalry for trade and new lands increased. The colonies in the New World were one result of this rivalry.

16 1
Background of Religious Revolt

Changing Times. One fact stands out about the thirteenth century in Western Europe. It was the Age of Faith. At that time almost everyone in Western Europe was Catholic, and most people were devout in their faith. All acknowledged that the Pope was their spiritual leader. By the end of the thirteenth century, however, conditions had begun to change. People were shaken out of many of their old ways of living and thinking. This upheaval weakened the influence of the Church from the outside.

The old feudal system was crumbling. A new class of merchants and tradesmen arose in cities and towns all over Europe. Men ran after the immense wealth and riches which poured into Europe as a result of geographic discoveries and explorations. The Renaissance, or the "new learning," brought about a new way of looking at life. Men thought more and more about themselves and this world, and less and less about God and the next world. Pagan ideas and practices were revived.

One outstanding sign of the changing times was the rise of *nationalism*. Nationalism is a deep and even exaggerated love of one's country. During most of the Middle Ages the people had not thought of themselves as belonging to one nation or another. But now, Englishmen were very proud of being Englishmen, and Frenchmen were very proud of being Frenchmen.

King Philip IV of France had a bitter political quarrel with Pope Boniface VIII. Most French people sided with their king. So did many of the priests in France. This dispute weakened the Pope's authority throughout the whole of Christian Europe.

The Popes were rulers of the Papal States as well as spiritual leaders. Some Popes gave more time to ruling the Papal States than they gave to the affairs of the Church.

Catholics in other countries sometimes found it hard to look up to the Pope as their spiritual leader.

A Weakened Church. There were weaknesses inside the Church also. The bishops of some dioceses lived and ruled like worldly princes instead of being spiritual leaders. Priests were often poorly educated and ill-trained for their sacred calling. Some monks, priests, bishops, and even Popes led lives of sin and scandal. Ignorance, superstition, and religious lukewarmness were widespread among the lay people. Many men and women tried to reform these conditions. Others openly criticized and attacked the abuses found in the Church. A new invention called the printing press enabled them to spread their attacks abroad.

This was the situation in Western Europe at the beginning of the sixteenth century. The Church had been weakened by forces from the outside as well as by abuses from the inside. Signs of change and unrest were everywhere. Then, in 1517 a religious revolt broke out in Germany.

1. Name some changes in Europe which weakened the Church from the outside.
2. How was the Church at this time weakened from the inside?

16 2

The Protestant Revolt Begins in Germany

Martin Luther, 1483-1546. Martin Luther was born in central Germany of fairly well-to-do peasant parents. After completing college, he became an Augustinian monk. Ordained a priest in 1507, he soon made a name for himself as professor of theology at the University of Wittenberg.

The changing times left their mark upon the lives of churchmen, courtiers, merchants, and peasants.

At Wittenberg Luther was long tormented by fear that he would lose his soul. From a study of the writings of St. Paul and St. Augustine he gradually arrived at an idea that seemed to calm his fears. He decided that a person could be saved by faith alone. In this Luther differed from the doctrine of the Church that man was saved by faith *and* good works.

Though not opposed to good works, Luther claimed that they did not help man to get to heaven. Man was saved only by faith. To Luther, faith meant trust in the merits of Christ.

Luther taught these views to his students at the University of Wittenberg. His teachings caused little stir at first. He considered himself a priest in good standing and referred to "Mother Church."

The Question of Indulgences. Pope Leo X, head of the Church at that time, was a great admirer of the Renaissance. He planned the new St. Peter's Church in Rome as a magnificent example of Renaissance architecture. To help raise the funds to build it, Pope Leo sent priests all over Europe to preach a special indulgence. An indulgence is a remission, in whole or in part, of the temporal punishment due to sins already forgiven. One of the conditions for gaining this special indulgence was to make an offering to help build the new St. Peter's.

In the region of Germany near Wittenberg, the preacher was a Dominican friar, John Tetzel. Though he did not come to Wittenberg, he did preach close by. People from Wittenberg went to hear him and made their contributions.

Many Germans were disturbed by John Tetzel. His methods were in bad taste and put the Church in a bad light. People said he used high-pressure means to get money. They accused him of "selling indulgences." They held that granting indulgences should have nothing to do with money raising. Among John Tetzel's bitterest opponents was Martin Luther.

Luther's New Religion. Inflamed by Tetzel's preaching, Luther attacked not only "money payments" for indulgences but the whole Catholic doctrine of good works. In 1517 he posted a document containing his views on the door of the Wittenberg cathedral. Written in Latin, it was meant to challenge scholars to debate. It was translated into German, however, and to Luther's surprise it caused great excitement throughout the country.

Luther did much preaching and writing after that. The printing press brought his writings to many readers. Each time he spoke or wrote, he got further away from the Church. He attacked the authority of the Pope. He said that religion was based only on the Bible. He taught that Baptism and the Lord's Supper were the only two sacraments. He also said there should be no Mass.

In 1520 the Pope excommunicated Luther. In 1521 at the Diet (assembly) at Worms the German emperor declared Luther an enemy of the state.

However, many powerful German nobles who did not like the emperor protected Luther. Other nobles sided with him because they saw a chance to take land belonging to the Church. Luther told them they were justified in taking the land. With these nobles on his side Luther went on preaching.

Wittenberg Cathedral. Martin Luther posts his ninety-five objections. Even he did not guess that his ideas could divide Germany.

He was afraid of neither Pope nor emperor.

People who followed Luther's teachings became known as Lutherans. After Luther was excommunicated, Lutherans were no longer members of the Catholic Church. They were followers of a new religion. In Germany people ruled by a Lutheran noble usually became Lutherans. People ruled by a Catholic noble remained Catholics.

The Peasants' Revolt. The German nobles lived in luxury on their estates. Some bishops and priests were wealthy nobles. Most German peasants, however, lived in dire poverty and misery. They paid high rents and taxes. Luther had encouraged the nobles to seize the Church's lands and wealth. The peasants decided that they, too, should have their share. Luther at first agreed with them.

So the peasants rose in revolt and sacked churches and monasteries. They plundered the homes of bishops. Next they turned against nobles who were not churchmen. Then Luther condemned the peasant uprising. The revolt was crushed with great cruelty. Over 50,000 people were killed before it was stopped.

Peasant uprising. The poor farmers of Germany tried to seize land and wealth from the nobles and churchmen.

The Peasants' Revolt kept Luther from gaining many new followers in Germany. The nobles blamed Luther for stirring up the peasants. The peasants accused him of turning against them. The spread of Luther's teachings against the Church was checked.

By this time, most of the people of northern Germany had become Lutherans. Most of the people of southern Germany remained Catholic.

1. Which doctrines of the Church did Luther deny?
2. How was Luther able to spread his teachings so rapidly?
3. Why did many nobles follow Luther rather than the Pope and the emperor?
4. How did the Peasants' Revolt hurt Martin Luther's cause?

16 3

The Revolt Spreads

The Scandinavian Countries Become Lutheran. Martin Luther's followers failed to make Germany completely Lutheran. They succeeded, however, in making the Scandinavian countries completely Lutheran. These countries are Norway, Sweden, and Denmark. The kings of these countries decided to make their nations Lutheran. They made laws to do away with the Catholic Church in their lands. They seized the Church's land and wealth. They brought Lutheran teachers from Germany to spread the new religion. People who insisted on remaining Catholic were severely punished. By 1600 few Catholics were to be found in these three countries.

John Calvin Starts a New Religion. John Calvin was born in France. He began to study to be a priest but changed to study law. Calvin taught that God has decided to send some men to heaven and other men to hell. Men could do nothing to save their souls, said Calvin, and they did not need the help of the Church. He said that Baptism is the only sacrament.

King Francis I of France, a Catholic, opposed Calvin's teachings. Calvin fled to Switzerland. There he gained many followers and became religious and political ruler of Geneva. Those who opposed his teachings were either imprisoned or put to death.

Calvin's religion spread to other countries. John Knox, his most famous disciple, brought it to Scotland. In Scotland and in England Calvin's followers were called Presbyterians. In France they were called Huguenots. The Huguenots suffered much for their beliefs in Catholic France.

Other Protestant Religions. Martin Luther had started a religious revolt that became hard to check. He had rejected many Catholic doctrines. He had attacked the authority of the Pope and the bishops. He had said that religion was based on the Bible alone.

Now other men followed Luther's example. The Bible, however, did not mean the same thing to them as it meant to Luther. These Protestants, as they called themselves, disagreed on many points. Some of them, like John Calvin, started their own new religions. Christian Europe was now split into many different churches and sects.

Religious Persecution. A king or a noble usually tried to make all his subjects join the church to which he belonged. Those who refused to do so were persecuted. A

A strict ruler. Calvin pronounces sentence in a Geneva court. He ruled both Church and State with a stern hand.

Lutheran king persecuted Catholics in his country. He also persecuted Protestants who were not Lutherans. Persecution meant loss of job or property. It often meant imprisonment and death.

Today, religious freedom exists in our country and in most other countries of the free world. People of many religions live and work side by side. The government does not force the people to belong to any church. It protects the right to freedom of worship. Such freedom was almost unknown in Europe in the sixteenth and seventeenth centuries.

1. What does the word "Protestant" mean?
2. What does Calvinism teach about salvation?
3. Why did Calvin leave his native country?
4. Was religious toleration an idea widely accepted in the sixteenth and seventeenth centuries?

16 4

The Revolt in England

King Henry VIII, 1509-1547. France had defeated England in the Hundred Years' War. After their defeat the English fought for thirty years among themselves in the War of the Roses. Two rival families struggled for the English throne. Thousands were killed. Finally, in 1485, Henry Tudor became King Henry VII.

King Henry VII was a powerful ruler. He had little opposition from the nobles. Most of them had been killed in the War of the Roses. Parliament was friendly and usually voted according to the king's wishes.

A disappointed king. Henry VIII is unhappy over the Pope's refusal to set aside his marriage to Catherine.

When Henry VII died, his son became King Henry VIII. He was England's ruler when Luther started his new religion. Answering Luther's attack on the sacraments of the Church, Henry VIII wrote a book, *In Defense of the Seven Sacraments*. For this book the Pope gave Henry a new title: Defender of the Faith. Kings and queens of England still use this title.

King Henry Versus the Pope. Catherine of Aragon, daughter of King Ferdinand and Queen Isabella of Spain, had married Henry's brother. Then the brother had died. In 1509 the Pope granted Henry a dispensation to marry his brother's widow. Henry and Catherine had six children, but only one child lived, Mary Tudor.

Henry wanted a son as heir to his crown. He said his marriage to Catherine bothered his conscience. He sent Cardinal Wolsey, his chief minister, to Rome to ask the Pope to annul the marriage. The Pope found no reason to do so. Other matters, however, delayed the Pope in making a final decision.

Henry VIII became impatient. He obtained Parliament's approval to appoint bishops in England. Henry chose Thomas Cranmer to be Archbishop of Canterbury. Cranmer said that Henry's marriage to Catherine was null and void. The King then married Anne Boleyn, a maid of honor at court. In 1534 Pope Clement VII declared that Henry's marriage to Catherine was valid and lawful. Henry refused to accept the Pope's decision and had Parliament declare him head of the Church of England. Thus Henry broke away completely from the authority of the Pope.

England Becomes Protestant. After Henry's death his only son became King Edward VI. Since Edward was very young, England was ruled by a council. This council was strongly Protestant. Laws against Catholics were passed. English Protestants were allowed to preach their doctrines freely.

In 1553 Mary Tudor, daughter of Henry and Catherine of Aragon, came to the throne. She tried to restore the Catholic religion. Bishops who had refused to submit to Henry came back to their sees. Laws against Catholics were repealed. Many Protestants were put to death, but their deaths only strengthened the Protestant cause. Moreover, Mary had married Philip II, Catholic king of Spain and staunch defender of the Catholic Church. She had made an alliance with Spain. Both marriage and alliance were unpopular in England.

Mary died after a reign of five years. She was succeeded by Elizabeth, her half-sister, daughter of Henry and Anne Boleyn. Queen Elizabeth I, a Protestant, called herself head of the Church of England. Under her the Church of England became the official religion. Everyone was forced to support it. It is still England's official religion, and its head is the king or queen of England. Often called the Anglican Church, its members are called Anglicans. The Protestant Episcopal Church in our country is very much like the Anglican Church. Its members are known as Episcopalians.

Persecutions in England. Under Elizabeth I and her successors, Catholics were severely persecuted. Soon other new religions arose in England. People called Puritans held that the Anglican Church was still too much like the Catholic Church. The Anglicans persecuted the Puritans, but the Puritans grew stronger under persecution. In a bloody civil war the Puritans gained control of England and ruled for about twenty years. They persecuted Anglicans.

A group known as Separatists wished to separate from the Church of England. Another group known as the Friends formed their own religion. They are better known as Quakers. Both Separatists and Quakers were also persecuted in England.

These persecutions were still going on when the English planted their colonies in North America. Many English people came to America to escape persecution. The Pilgrims were a group of Separatists who founded Plymouth Colony. The Puritans founded Massachusetts Bay Colony. When the Puritans ruled England, many Anglicans fled to Virginia to escape persecution. The Quakers founded the Pennsylvania colony.

Maryland was founded as a refuge for Catholics from England.

1. How did Henry VIII come to break with the Catholic Church?
2. How did Mary Tudor try to restore the Catholic Church in England?
3. Who made the Anglican Church the official religion of England?
4. Describe the religious persecutions which took place in England.
5. What effect did persecutions have on English colonies in North America?

16 5

The Catholic Reformation

Problems Within and Without. The Church faced many problems even before the Protestant Revolt. The Revolt added new problems. The weaknesses within the Church aided the spread of the Revolt. People wondered how the Church would survive. The tide turned, however, and the Church gained new strength. This strength came from the Catholic Reformation.

Pope Paul III Calls a Council. Paul III became Pope in 1534. He spurred the Catholic Reformation by calling a General Council of the bishops of the Church. It is called the Council of Trent after the city in which it met in 1545. Interrupted by wars and by a plague, it did not end until 1563. Here are some of the problems the Council sought to solve:

1. How could Catholics and non-Catholics learn just what the Church teaches?

Self-examination. The Council of Trent gave the Church a chance to make her doctrines clear and to reform abuses.

2. What could be done to prevent more people from leaving the Church?

3. What could be done to win back people who had left the Church?

4. How could Christ's word be brought to all peoples, including those in the New World of North and South America?

5. How could the administration of the Church be improved?

The Council Acts. The Council of Trent clearly stated the Church's teachings. Here are some doctrines that the Council proclaimed anew:

Man is saved by faith and good works. Martin Luther said man is saved by faith alone. John Calvin said that some men cannot be saved at all.

The Bible *and* Tradition are the bases of the Catholic religion. Martin Luther said religion is based on the Bible only.

The Church decides what the Bible means. Protestants said each man can decide for himself what the Bible means.

The Pope is the supreme head of the Church on earth. All Protestants rejected the authority of the Pope.

Christ instituted seven sacraments. Martin Luther said two. Other Protestants had various numbers. Some had no sacraments.

The doctrine of indulgences was upheld, but granting indulgences for payment of money was forbidden.

The Council also reformed many things within the Church. It set up seminaries to train men who wished to become priests. It forbade Church officials to favor their relatives when appointing men to office. It made strict rules in regard to the money matters of the Church.

1. How did Pope Paul III promote the Catholic Reformation?
2. What problems did the Council of Trent seek to solve?
3. Mention three abuses which the Council aimed to correct.

16 6
Rivalry for Trade, Treasure, and New Lands

A New Europe. By 1600 the Christian unity of Western Europe was shattered. The religious upheaval left Germany part Catholic and part Lutheran. Switzerland and the Netherlands were also divided into Catholic and Protestant. Norway, Sweden, and Denmark were Lutheran. England had adopted the Anglican form of Protestantism, and Scotland had become Presbyterian. France remained largely Catholic. The revolt had made no headway in Spain, Portugal, Ireland, and the Italian states. They clung to the Old Faith, now renewed and strengthened by the reforms brought about by the Council of Trent.

These religious divisions helped turn Europe into one big armed camp. Religion was usually one of the causes of wars among nations and of civil wars within nations. Christian fought against Christian. Persecutions were harsh, cruel, and bloody. Catholics were pitted against Protestants. Protestant groups sometimes fought among themselves. All Protestants were generally united, however, in their opposition to the Church of Rome.

Long before 1600 the feudal system had begun to collapse throughout Europe. The castle and manor were no longer the centers of the religious, social, and economic life of the people. There were fewer feudal serfs but more townsmen and peasant farmers. Tradesmen and craftsmen formed the core of the new middle class which sprung up in every country. The knight gave way to the foot soldier. The nobles were no longer so powerful as once they had been in the heyday of feudalism.

The number of towns and cities increased. Shops, schools, and places of amusement bustled with activity. Provinces were being welded into nations. Kings and queens grew more powerful. They were in reality the supreme rulers of their realms. A king had to strengthen his nation from within and protect it from attack from without. Nations often clashed over religious matters, over boundaries, or over succession to a throne. Countries sometimes formed alliances to keep any one nation from growing too powerful.

It took a lot of money to keep a nation strong and to try to increase its power at home and abroad. Royal taxes always fell far short of what a ruler needed to run his country. Kings were ever on the lookout for new sources of wealth. In the sixteenth century these sources lay in distant lands across the seas. The kings of Europe launched a thousand ships to bear the riches of the Far East and the treasures of the New World back to Europe. Their galleons and caravels carried explorers, soldiers, missionaries, and settlers to strange new worlds beyond the oceans. The seas were white with the sails of Europe's merchantmen and men-of-war.

In those days there was another fleet that roamed the Seven Seas. It was made up of ships owned and manned by the buccaneers. The buccaneers, also called freebooters or pirates, formed a kind of empire all their own. They were at once a powerful naval force and a seaborne army. They came from all nations. Some were adventurers and soldiers of fortune. Others were in trouble with the law or out of favor with their king. Many took to piracy to regain lost fortunes. Queen Elizabeth I of England commissioned sailors like Sir Walter Raleigh and Sir Francis Drake to seize Spain's merchantmen and attack Spanish colonies.

Struggle for Wealth and Power. The leading nations of Europe were Portugal, Holland, France, Spain, and England. They

Queen Elizabeth I makes Sir Francis Drake a knight for his plunder of Spanish settlements and galleons.

locked in a struggle to rule the seas and to extend their empires to faraway lands. Rivalry among them for treasure, trade, and new lands grew intense.

Portugal led the way. Portuguese navigators charted the great trade routes to the Far East. They set up a commercial empire in India, Malaya, the islands of the East, Africa, and South America. Portugal's only real settlement was Brazil. During the time that Portugal was united with Spain as one kingdom, Holland seized a large part of its overseas possessions.

Holland became a leader in overseas settlement after throwing off the yoke of Spanish rule. The Dutch then captured most of Portugal's rich empire in the Far East. The Dutch East India Company and the Dutch West India Company were organized to promote overseas commerce and settlement. Dutch ports were the most thriving in Europe. At one time there were Dutch settlements in Asia, Africa, and North and South America. Struggles with France and England forced Holland to yield in the race for power.

France also played a leading role in the struggle for the wealth and lands of the New World. It based its claim on the explorations of Jacques Cartier. Samuel de Champlain founded the first French settlements. Explorers and missionaries extended France's territory to the region drained by the Mississippi River. The French became firmly established in the New World. Their main sources of wealth were in furs, fishing, and farming.

Spain's colonial empire was once largest and best of all. It covered most of Latin America and a large part of North America, as well as the Caribbean Islands and the Philippines. Spain brought its language, culture, and religion to its colonies. Treasure and trade made Spain very wealthy. For a long time Spain was supreme. Then war and other troubles at home led to a decline. Besides, Spain could not always find leaders to rule its vast domains.

Spain's mightly arm was its fleet. In his war against Elizabeth of England, Philip II of Spain amassed his fleet into the Great Armada to invade and conquer England. The rout of the Armada by England's navy under Sir Francis Drake was a deadly blow to Spain. A terrible gale completed the overthrow of Armada and of Spain's supremacy.

England had contributed little to early discovery and exploration of the New World. Under Queen Elizabeth I, England made its bid for supremacy. Elizabeth's reign was a golden age in English history. The English language had come into its own. The Renaissance spirit lifted literature to glorious heights. It was the age of William Shakespeare and Francis Bacon.

The English people were proud of their nation and their Queen. She had made the Anglican Church the state religion. Harsh laws against Catholics and Dissenters had brought a certain unity and peace. Industry prospered, and trade was growing. English mastery of the seas was unchallenged. Now a first-rate power, England entered in earnest into the struggle for the wealth and lands of the New World.

It was from this nation at its peak that the first English settlers set forth for the New World. There they were to set up their

Thirteen Colonies along the Atlantic coast of North America.

1. State the effects of the religious revolt upon Christian unity in Europe.
2. To what new sources of wealth and power did European nations turn at this time?
3. What was the role of the buccaneers in the struggle for wealth and power?
4. Tell how (*a*) Portugal, (*b*) Holland, and (*c*) France became leaders in this struggle?
5. How did Spain lose its supremacy as a colonial power?
6. What events and conditions led to England's rise as a colonial power?

Chapter 16. REVIEW

Learning to Use New Words

Use each of the following terms in an original sentence, expressing something you have learned in Chapter 16:

Protestant	persecuted	trade
excommunicate	toleration	colony
nationalism	seminary	buccaneer
ordain	reformation	indulgence

Knowing the Important Facts

1. Who was Martin Luther? What doctrines did he teach?

In Shakespeare's plays and poems the English language reached new peaks of beauty, strength, and nobility.

2. Make a list of Protestant leaders, the countries they worked in, and the names of the groups they founded.
3. Describe the steps taken by the Church to solve the problems the Protestant Revolution had brought to light.
4. Describe the way in which England became separated from the Catholic Church.
5. Explain how rivalry began among the nations of Europe for trade, treasure, and new lands.

Thinking Through the Facts

1. Why did Martin Luther break away from the Church? Do you agree with any of the criticism he raised against the Church?
2. Why did growing nations oppose a strong international Church?
3. How did the work of John Tetzel lead to the religious revolution in Europe?
4. How did the Council of Trent strengthen the Church? Does the Church still call councils today? What work would a modern council perform?
5. Tell how each nation became a colonial power: Portugal, Holland, France, Spain, England.

Chapter 17 Europe Finds a New World

We have been studying cultures and civilizations. Mostly, we have been reading about Western Civilization, or the civilization of Western Europe. This civilization came largely from Greece, the Valley of the Two Rivers, and other civilizations.

Now, we jump from Western Europe across 4000 miles of ocean to the Western Hemisphere. The Western Hemisphere is where we live. It is half the world. It contains the great continents of North and South America and the islands that are near these continents.

17·1 Europeans Learn More About the World

Most of the World Was Unknown to the People of the Middle Ages. In 1460 the people of Europe did not know that the two great continents of North and South America lay across the Atlantic Ocean. Leif Ericson and a band of Northmen had landed on the coast of North America some time around the year 1000, but this discovery had made very little impression on the people of Europe. By 1460 they had almost forgotten that such a person as Leif Ericson had ever lived.

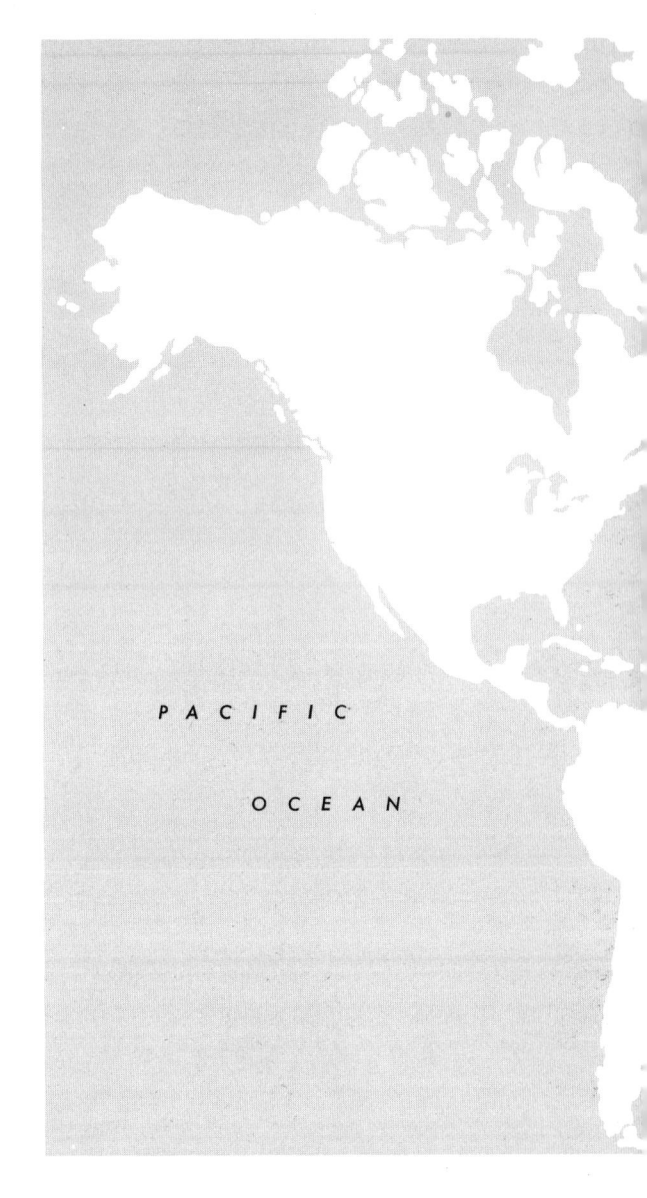

The people of Europe in 1460 knew very little about the Atlantic Ocean. They called it the Sea of Darkness. Sailors were afraid to sail very far out on this great ocean. They thought that terrible things might happen to them if they dared to sail out of sight of land.

Although the people of Europe had known

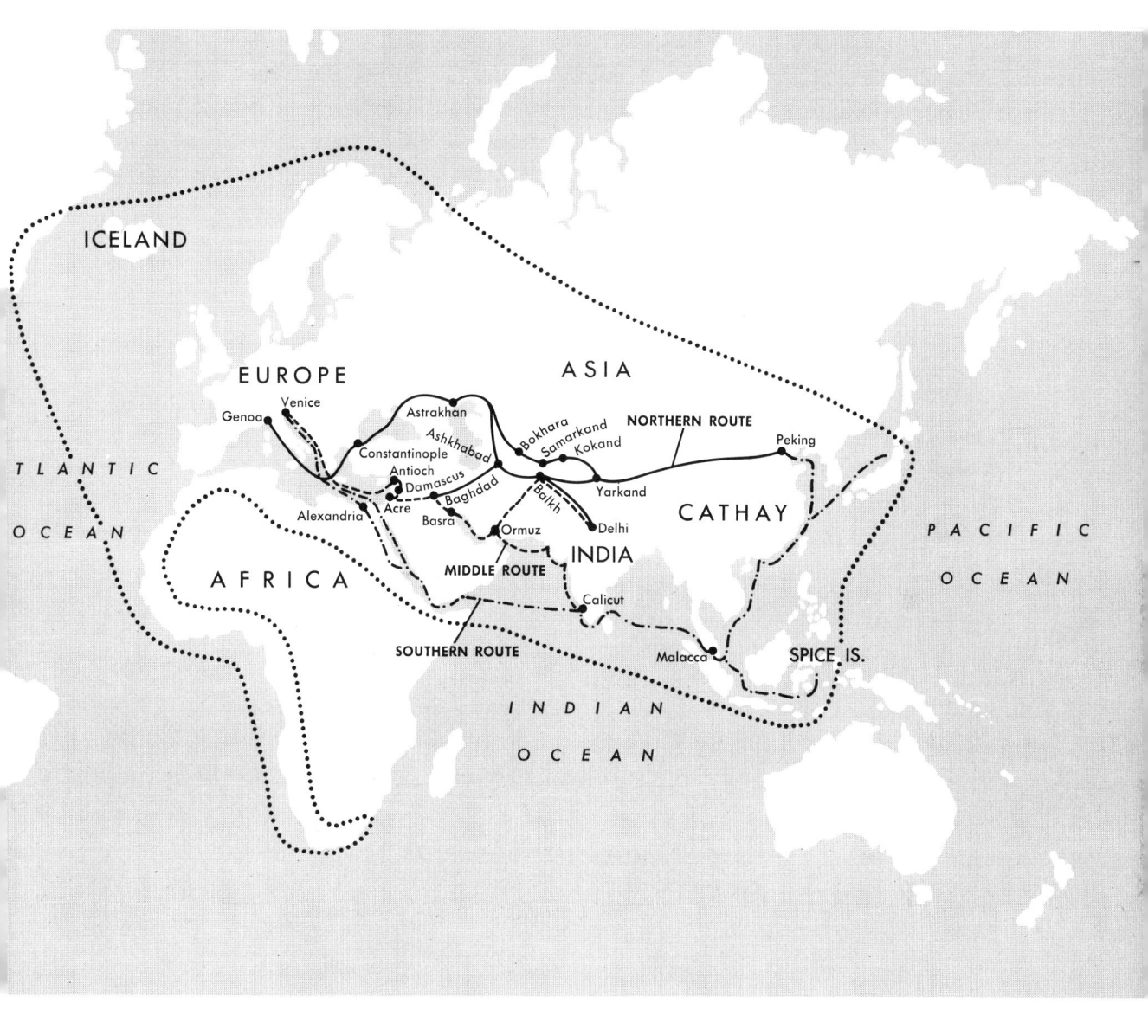

the northern part of Africa for many centuries, they knew very little about the rest of this great continent. By land, northern Africa was cut off from southern Africa by a great desert, the Sahara. By sea, the distance was very great. In 1460 Portuguese ships were sailing down the east coast of Africa. They had not yet reached the tip of the continent. How far did Africa extend? Was it possible for a ship to sail around the continent? No one knew.

Somewhere to the east of Europe lay the great lands of India, China, and Japan. Marco Polo and a few missionaries had visited these Oriental lands. The people of Europe received spices and other goods from these lands, but few Europeans had ever been there. The trip by land was too long and difficult. Besides, the Moslem Turks had conquered Constantinople and most of the other land at the eastern end of the Mediterranean Sea, and these Turks hated Christians. They made the land route even more difficult and dangerous than it was before. Nobody had yet discovered an all-sea route from Europe to the Far East.

In 1460 the Mediterranean Sea was the most important body of water to the people of Europe. Most of the land they knew centered around this sea. In this way Europe had changed little from the days of the Roman Empire, when the Mediterranean Sea had been called "a Roman lake."

Within a short time after 1460 a big change took place. The people of Europe learned much more about the world in which they lived. Sailors and explorers brought back wonderful tales of new lands and new seas.

People Became Interested in Finding a New Route to the Orient. In the days of ancient Rome there was much trade between Western Europe and the Orient. Then there were wars and revolutions in both the East and the West. Trade was broken off. The people of Western Europe almost forgot that there was such a place as the Orient. During the Crusades soldiers from Europe found many Oriental goods in the markets of the New East. The people of Europe became very much interested in securing these goods.

The Mediterranean Sea was important to the Europeans. After 1460 many new and important water routes were discovered.

The goods were expensive because they came a long way over deserts and mountains and changed hands many times on the way.

Marco Polo visited the Orient and wrote a book about what he saw. After the printing press was invented, many people in Europe read the book. They were very much interested in what Marco Polo had to say. He said that the spices and other goods cost much less in the Orient than they did in Europe. He also described a great ocean which he saw in the Orient.

When men in Western Europe read this, they said: "There is an ocean in the Orient, and there is an ocean here. These two oceans probably join. Perhaps it is possible for a ship to sail from here to the Orient."

The men also said: "If we can bring goods from the Orient by ship, they will cost less. It is cheaper to travel by water than by land. Also, the goods will be handled by fewer people."

Many men in Western Europe, therefore, became interested in finding a water route to the Orient. They were helped by the new inventions and discoveries which made it possible for sailors to go farther out on the ocean than they had ever gone before.

Portugal Leads the Way. Prince Henry was the oldest son of King John of Portugal. Prince Henry was so interested in sailing that he was called Prince Henry the Navigator. *Navigator* means "sailor." Prince Henry wished to find a water route to the Orient. He decided that the best way to do this was to sail around Africa.

Prince Henry knew that if sailors could read maps and use such instruments as the astrolabe, they would be able to guide their

Portugal's school for sailors. Prince Henry uses a scale model to demonstrate the advantages of movable sails.

ships more accurately. He started a school for this purpose. After he had trained a number of sailors, he sent them out to explore the west coast of Africa.

Prince Henry's men sailed farther and farther down the coast of this continent. When Henry died in 1460, Portuguese sailors had reached Cape Verde near the equator.

In 1487 Bartholomeu Dias, a Portu-

the curved surface of the Earth on a flat map. This is something that nobody can do perfectly even today. In addition to the errors that are always on a flat map of the world, Ptolemy made other errors. These were due to the fact that he knew very little about the world away from the Mediterranean, and he had to use his imagination.

Because the world is round, Ptolemy believed that it was possible to sail west from Europe and reach the Orient. This is true. But Ptolemy believed the world to be much smaller than it is, and he believed Europe to be much closer to Asia than it is. If you will look at a globe, you will see the immense distance between the west coast of Europe and the east coast of Asia. It is more than half the distance around the world. Ptolemy knew only that there was an Atlantic Ocean. He did not know that the continent of North America and the whole Pacific Ocean were also between Europe and Asia.

The men of the fifteenth century did know much more about the world than Ptolemy had known. Among those who accepted his teachings was Christopher Columbus, a mariner of the city-state of Genoa in Italy. Columbus dreamed of getting to the riches of the Orient by sailing west.

Columbus asked the king of Portugal to give him ships and money to carry out his plan. At that time, however, the King was more interested in Prince Henry's plan: finding a route to the East by sailing around Africa.

Columbus next approached Ferdinand and Isabella, the rulers of Spain. The rulers agreed to help Columbus.

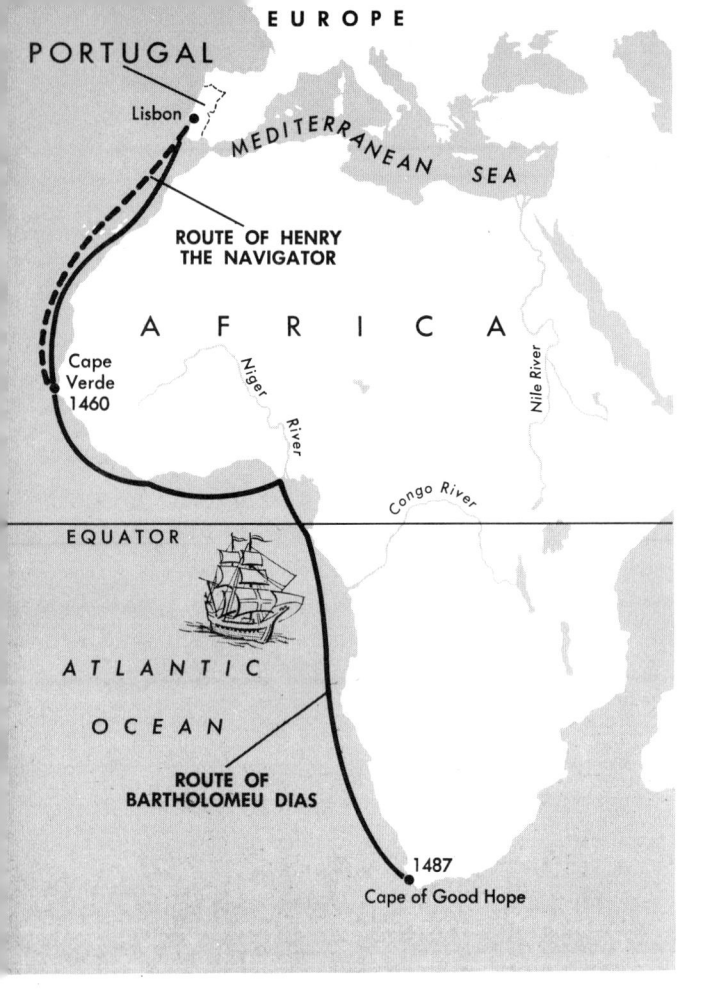

guese sailor, reached the southern tip of Africa. The Portuguese were now convinced that it would be possible to sail around Africa and on to India. The king of Portugal was so happy when he heard what Dias had done that he named the tip of Africa the Cape of Good Hope.

The Dream of Christopher Columbus. An important part of the Renaissance, as we know, was the re-discovery of the writings of ancient Greeks and Romans. Among those who were re-discovered was the Roman geographer, Ptolemy.

Ptolemy realized that the world is round. He made one of the first attempts to show

On to India. Columbus did not dream of discovering a new world. He hoped to find an all-water route to India.

Columbus Discovers America. On the morning of August 3, 1492, Columbus and his crew set sail from Spain on the *Nina, Pinta,* and *Santa Maria.*

After stopping at the Canary Islands for repairs, the small expedition sailed for days without seeing land. The sailors lost their courage and talked of forcing Columbus to turn back. Columbus, however, kept his faith and on the morning of October 12, 1492, the island of San Salvador was sighted. Columbus thought that he had reached the Orient. He did not know that he had discovered a new world, consisting of the two great continents of North and South America.

Columbus made three more voyages to the New World. He received many honors which were on one occasion taken away from him and then returned. He was even put in prison for a short time. Christopher Columbus will always be honored in American history, however, because our country's story begins with the landing of Columbus on San Salvador. Columbus died before anyone realized that he had discovered a great New World.

1. Why was Henry of Portugal called "Henry the Navigator"?
2. What part of the world was known to men of the fifteenth century?
3. Why was the tip of Africa called the "Cape of Good Hope"?
4. Did the King of Portugal support Columbus' voyage?
5. Who was the first European to reach North America? When do we say American history begins?

17 2

The Way is Opened

The Portuguese Reach India. For many years the Portuguese had been trying to sail to the Orient by going around Africa. Now, when they heard about Columbus' voyage, they thought the Spaniards had reached the Orient first. This made the Portuguese more determined than ever. They succeeded in 1498. This successful expedition was led by Vasco da Gama. The goods that da Gama brought back from the Orient were worth sixty times the cost of the voyage. Da Gama became a great hero. He was considered even greater than Columbus, because he had brought back more riches than Columbus had.

Wide, wide world. Balboa discovers the Pacific Ocean. Europeans now realized the world is larger than they had guessed.

Balboa Discovers the Pacific Ocean. Many Spaniards settled on the islands close to the shores of North and South America. They started plantations on these islands. When they started these plantations, they still thought they were in the Orient, but it was not the way Marco Polo had described it.

One of the plantation owners was Vasco Nuñez de Balboa. The Indians told Balboa that to the south there was a land rich in gold. This was probably Peru, because vast amounts of gold were later found in Peru. Balboa set out to find this gold-rich land. He led his men across the Isthmus of Panama. This is the narrow strip of land that connects North America and South America.

Balboa and his men came to a huge body of water. They were the first Europeans to see the Pacific Ocean from the American side. Balboa never found any gold, but he had made an important discovery.

Interrupted journey. Magellan dies battling Philippine natives. His men must complete the voyage around the world alone.

The people of Europe now realized that America was not in the Orient. Anyone wishing to sail west from Europe to Asia had to cross the Atlantic Ocean, then sail past North America and South America, and then cross the Pacific Ocean. The world was much larger than anyone had thought.

Magellan's Men Sail Around the World. The Spaniards had been the first to try to reach the Orient by sailing west. They were still interested in the idea. The King aided Ferdinand Magellan to make this voyage.

Magellan knew that Balboa had discovered an ocean on the other side of America. Magellan wondered whether he could find a water passage through the Americas. He left Spain in the fall of 1519 with 243 men. The five ships sailed along the coast of South America. They could find no way to get through this continent. A year after they left home they passed through the strait which now bears Magellan's name and came out on the Pacific Ocean. It took them three months to cross this huge ocean. Finally they came to a group of islands. Magellan claimed the islands and named them the Philippines in honor of King Philip of Spain. This was the beginning of Spanish control of the islands.

The Philippines are in the Orient. Magellan had done what Columbus had tried to do. He had reached the Orient by sailing west. The voyage took so long, that no ships would use this for a regular route.

Magellan was killed in the Philippines. One of his ships with eighteen men crossed

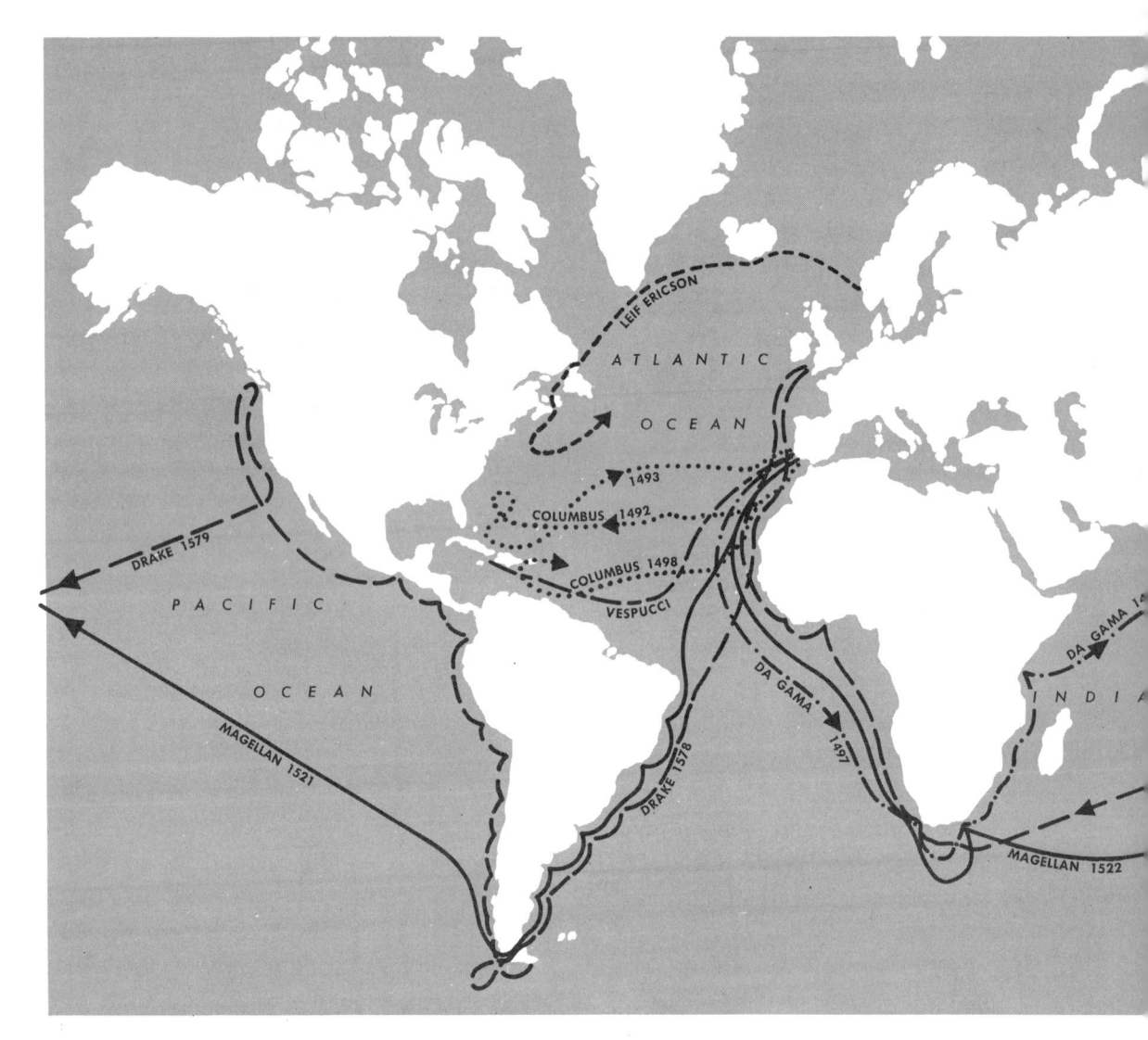

The Spirit of Discovery

In the year 1000 Leif Ericson and his Vikings discovered North America and settled Vinland. Their exploits caused no great stir in Europe. About 500 years later the quest for a route to the Indies aroused the spirit of exploration. Portuguese expeditions went down the African coast. The Azores and the Canaries were discovered. In 1488 Bartholomeu Dias reached the Cape of Good Hope.

Then in 1492, under the Spanish flag, Columbus set sail on the first of his epoch-making voyages, seeking a passage to India. By accident he made the momentous discovery of the New World. He never found a direct sea route to the Far East.

the Indian Ocean and rounded the Cape of Good Hope. The men arrived back in Spain in 1522. They had been gone for almost three years. These eighteen men had sailed all the way around the world. They were the first men to do so.

For the first time, the people of Europe realized what a big world they lived in. It opened up untold opportunities for adventurous men and women.

1. Why did the people of his time consider Vasco da Gama a greater hero than Columbus?
2. What made the people of Europe realize the world was much bigger than anyone had thought?
3. Name some of the things a school boy in the year 1522 would have known about the world.

17 3

The Nations of the Western Hemisphere

Western Civilization in the New World. The title of this book is *Before America*. It is the story of events that happened before the continents of North and South America were discovered and settled.

We have already read about the discovery of America, so we are almost at the end of the story.

There are twenty-two independent nations in the Western Hemisphere today. In eighteen of these nations most of the people speak Spanish. That is because these nations were founded by people from Spain. In one, they speak Portuguese, and in one they speak French. Those twenty countries

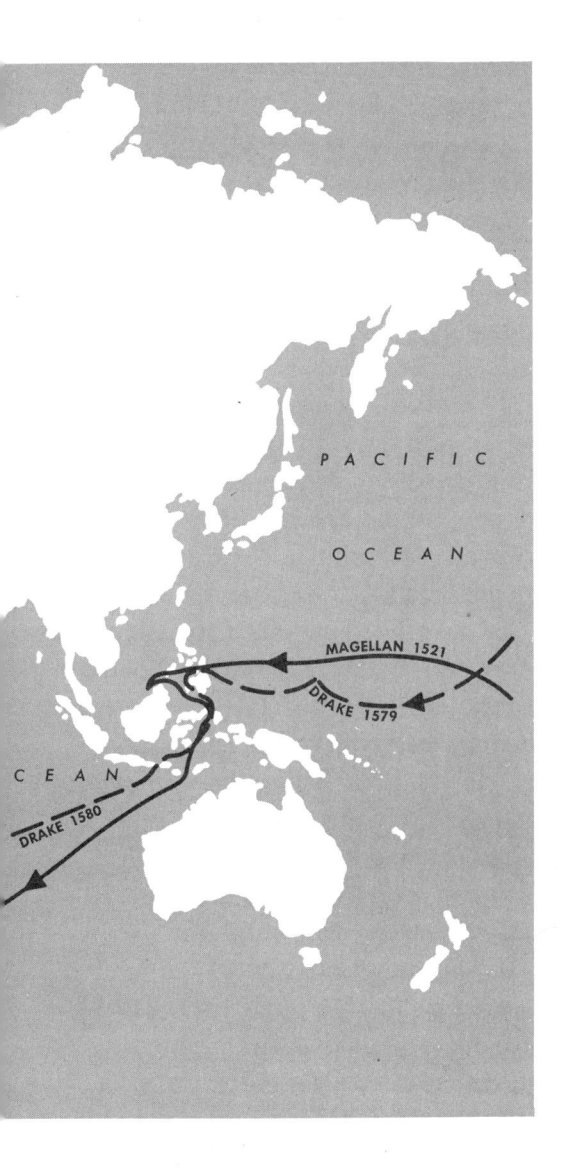

Vasco da Gama in 1497 rounded Good Hope and sailed on to India. In 1521 Magellan followed a westward course that took one of his ships around the world. Years later the *Golden Hind* under Sir Francis Drake circled the globe.

The Americas were named after Amerigo Vespucci, a Florentine.

are called Latin America, because all three of those languages developed from the Latin.

In the United States, of course, the principal language is English.

In Canada, our large neighbor to the north, two languages are spoken. About two-thirds of the people speak English, and about one-third speak French.

All twenty-two of these countries are considered part of Western Civilization. But Western Civilization changed somewhat when it crossed 4000 miles of Atlantic Ocean. Living conditions were not the same in the wilderness of the Western Hemisphere as they were in Europe, and so different ways of living developed. And people who were not from Western Europe added something to the civilizations of many of these countries. There were thousands of American Indians living here when the Western Europeans arrived. Each group of Indians had its own culture. Some had rather high states of civilization. In countries where the Indians were not driven off or where they did not die off, their cultures mixed with Western Civilization. Negroes who were brought here as slaves from Africa and later gained their freedom added something of their own. So did people from the Orient and from the islands of the Pacific.

But mainly the civilization that arose in America was Western Civilization, brought here from Western Europe.

The Spaniards and Portuguese in the New World. Christopher Columbus was sailing for Spain when he discovered the New World. He claimed for Spain all the land he discovered in the Western Hemisphere. The Spaniards thought their newly discovered land was in Asia. The Portuguese felt certain that soon they would be rounding Africa and also claiming land in Asia. The rulers of Spain and Portugal were afraid there would be confusion about their claims. They asked Pope Alexander VI to help them solve their problem. The Pope took a map of the world as it was known at that time and drew a line from the North Pole to the South Pole. All the land on one side was to belong to Spain and all the land on the other side was to belong to Portugal.

As more of the world was discovered and explored, it was found that Spain had been given all of the New World except the tip of South America. Portugal had the eastern tip of South America and all newly discovered lands in Asia and Africa. This line gave Spain a big start in settling the New World. She was not able to settle all the territory that the Pope had awarded her, because that was too much for one country.

Portugal later developed her tip of South America into the large colony of Brazil. That is why today Brazil is the one Portuguese-speaking country in South America.

Spanish explorers, settlers, and missionaries followed Columbus to the New World. The first settlements were made on the

Stockade. Pioneers build a log fortress around their settlement. Curious Indians watch from a distant vantage point.

islands that Columbus had discovered. From there, the Spaniards pushed on to nearby Mexico and to Central America. Then they went into Peru and other parts of South America. Settlements were also made on our continent of North America.

On the feast of St. Augustine in 1565, Pedro Menendez, Spanish governor of Florida, founded the oldest permanent white settlement in what is now the United States—St. Augustine. Among other Spanish settlements made in our country were Santa Fe, San Antonio, San Diego, Los Angeles, and San Francisco. But the greatest strength

The Spanish and the Portuguese in the New World

1 Spanish and Portuguese mariners led the way in discovery and exploration. The Spanish were the pioneer settlers in the New World. Spain built up a great world empire. It stretched across the Caribbean islands, most of Latin America, the Southwest of our country, and as far west as the Philippines. Portugal's efforts were divided between settling the New World and trading with India and the Far East. The one Portuguese colony was the vast, rich land of Brazil.

2 Pedro Cabral touched the shores of Brazil in 1500 and claimed it for Portugal. It was a Portuguese colony for 300 years. Portugal gave its language, culture, and Catholic faith to Brazil. Its treatment of the different races was the best in the New World. The people were Indian, white, and Negro, with the strains often mixed through intermarriage.

3 In Spain's colonies Spanish-born viceroys and other government officials formed the powerful ruling class. The *criollos,* those of Spanish descent born in the colonies, usually were wealthy landowners but were not of the ruling class. The *mestizos,* of mixed Spanish and Indian origin, in time became writers, artists, priests, and skilled craftsmen. Native Indians and Negro slaves were generally miners and farmers. On the whole Spain's policy in race relations was praiseworthy.

4 Spain's colonial system was one of the best the world has ever seen. Spanish missions form a glorious chapter in the spread of Christianity. Spain gave its language and religion to its colonial empire. It left its mark not only upon Latin America but upon our country as well. The Spanish influence is found in education, literature, architecture, music, folklore, dancing, costume, agriculture, and crafts.

VICEROYS

CRIOLLOS

MESTIZOS

NATIVES

of the Spaniards was in the land south of the United States.

The Spaniards and Portuguese Brought Many Gifts to the New World. Most of the Indians in North America and South America were living in a Stone Age when the first white men came. They had very simple weapons and tools. Most of them made their living by hunting and fishing. The Spaniards and Portuguese brought civilization to a large part of the New World. The Spaniards and Portuguese built cities with churches and schools. They taught some of the Indians to read and to raise crops. Before the sixteenth century came to an end, there were seven universities in Spanish America. This was before the English and French had made a single permanent settlement in the New World. In Mexico City the Spaniards set up the first printing press in the New World. It was used to print a catechism in 1534.

Mexico and the other Spanish colonies broke away from Spain in the nineteenth century. Brazil broke away from Portugal. They are now independent countries. But they still have the religion and the languages that were brought to them from the Spanish Peninsula.

The French Build and Lose an Empire in North America. In 1608, Samuel de Champlain, an explorer for France, built a fort on top of a great rock overlooking the St. Lawrence River. He called the fort Quebec. It was the first permanent French settlement in North America. It was the beginning of the French Empire in North America. This empire was to include the entire St. Lawrence Valley and the entire

Mississippi Valley. This was some of the most valuable territory on the continent.

While the French were claiming the St. Lawrence Valley and the Mississippi Valley, the English were planting colonies along the Atlantic Coast. There were thirteen of these English colonies. Many Englishmen came to North America and built homes. By 1750 there were 1,500,000 English colonists in North America. In the same year there were only about 80,000 Frenchmen in North America. The English colonists outnumbered the French about 18 to 1.

The French and the English were rivals in Europe. They fought four wars between 1680 and 1763. Whenever the French and English went to war in Europe, their colonists fought in America.

In North America the last of these four wars was called the French and Indian War. The French were defeated. When the treaty of peace was signed in 1763, the French were forced to give up their land in North America. They gave Canada and all the land east of the Mississippi except New Orleans to England. Spain had helped France in the war. Therefore, Spain had to give Florida to England. To make up for this loss, France gave Spain her land west of the Mississippi River and the city of New Orleans.

The map at the top of this page shows the territory owned by the various nations before the French and Indian War. The other map shows how North America was divided after the war. In the top map, notice how the French had explored eastern Canada, the Great Lakes, and the whole central section of the United States.

The French in the New World

1 Explorers and missionaries pioneered the great central region of our land. Father Marquette and Joliet explored the upper regions of the Mississippi River, and La Salle travelled the entire Mississippi to the Gulf of Mexico. He called the region Louisiana in honor of the French king.

2 French missionaries spread religion from Canada to Mexico.

3 Fur traders accompanied the expeditions and engaged in the profitable trade of buying furs.

4 The French language continues to be spoken in Louisiana and in parts of Canada.

5 French style in architecture is still noticeable in New Orleans.

6 In both the United States and Canada, many French customs are still followed. French cooking is very popular in this hemisphere.

251

You will see how the French lost most of their territory to the English after the French and Indian War (maps on page 250).

There Are Many Things to Remind Us that the French Were Here. Almost two hundred years have passed since the French lost their territory in North America. We still have many reminders of their empire, however. Many cities and towns in our country have French names. In New Orleans many houses which were built by the French are still standing. About one-third of the people of Canada speak French. These French Canadians are devout Catholics. As with the Spanish and the Portuguese, the greatest gift which the French brought to America was the Catholic faith.

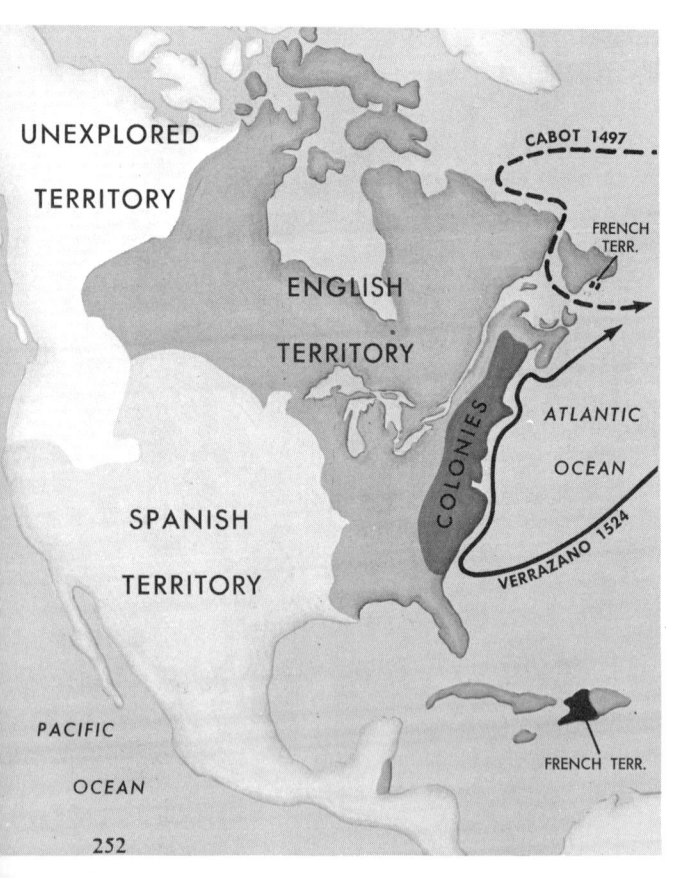

The English Colonies Become the United States of America. In 1607 a group of Englishmen built a tiny settlement on the shore of Chesapeake Bay. They called it Jamestown. This was the first permanent English settlement in the New World. Later, it grew into the colony of Virginia. In time there were thirteen English colonies. They later became the United States of America. In our country we have many things to remind us that the English were the first settlers.

One thing we have received from the English is our language. We also got our ideas of liberty and self-government from them. As early as 1215 the English had forced King John to sign the Great Charter which guaranteed the rights of the people. The English had insisted that the laws be made by Parliament which was elected by the people. The English settlers in America also insisted upon liberty and self-government. Americans have insisted upon these things ever since. No king or dictator tells us what to do. We make our own laws through the men we elect to Congress and the state legislatures.

The Spanish, French, and Portuguese who settled in the New World were Catholics. They brought the Catholic religion to the lands where they settled. Almost all the people in these lands are Catholics today.

The English, however, were mostly Protestants. The English settlers who came to America were Anglicans, Puritans, Separatists, Quakers, and members of various other sects. We still have many different religions in the United States, but each has learned to respect the belief of others.

The English in America

1 Many people came from England to America to find a better economic and social way of life. Others came seeking freedom from religious and political persecutions of the Old World. These early settlers planted the great English ideals of liberty and self-government in the New World. They brought the jury system, the beginnings of representative government, and a bill of rights. Their language was to become the mother tongue of our country.

2 The Virginia House of Burgesses (1619) was the first representative lawmaking body in North America. It was a giant step toward democratic government. The Mayflower Compact (1620) held that government gets its powers from the will of the people. This is a basic idea of American democracy. The Town Meeting had its beginnings in New England. Townsmen met to discuss and vote upon local issues. It was an example of pure democracy at work.

They Came from England

THE PURITAN    THE CAVALIER    THE DEBTOR    THE TRADESMAN

A Nation of Many People

The United States is a leading nation today because people from many nations brought a wide variety of talents and skills to make it great. Developing the land and its resources required much hard work. This work was done by immigrants. Immigrants helped clear the land, man the farms, and build huge industries. They became leaders in politics, religion, business, and the arts.

The Dutch were among the earliest settlers. To the New World they brought with them great skills and talents for trading, business, and farming. They are sturdy, thrifty, and industrious people with deep love and high esteem for family and home life.

Germans in Pennsylvania and the Middle West farmed our lands and worked in our factories. German interest in science, industry, and government has helped our nation prosper. German settlers were both Catholic and Lutheran.

The Swedes settled parts of Delaware, New York, and the north central region of our country. Many of them became prosperous farmers and dairymen. Their Nordic culture has enriched our nation.

The Poles planted their religious and political ideals in many cities and rural areas. They built roads and worked in mines. They supplied many leaders for government and other community activities.

Negroes were brought in large numbers to the New World as slaves. In our country they worked on the cotton plantations in the South. Theirs has been a long, uphill struggle to gain freedom and equality. Our country will be strengthened and enriched when our Negro citizens are truly free to use their talents, skills, and gifts in all walks of life.

People of Italian origin form a large part of our population. They are happy people, lovers of music and the arts. In business and industry they work hard to better themselves. They make themselves at home in both cities and in rural areas.

People of Irish descent cherish and guard our ideals of political and religious liberty. They readily fit into any community in which they settle. They make their living in many trades and professions. Their love of song and story add color to the American scene.

People From Many Countries Helped Build the United States. Even in colonial days there were many people here besides the English. Swedes established a colony in Delaware and continued to live there even after they were conquered by the Dutch. The Dutch established a colony in New Amsterdam and remained there after being conquered by the English. Many Germans settled in the colony of Pennsylvania. People from Ireland and other countries of Europe settled in various colonies.

After the United States became an independent country millions of people from Western Europe came to the United States. Many of these people lived in lands that were ruled by kings. These people wanted to get away from the kings and come to the United States where people ruled themselves. Some came from lands where the people were divided into the "ruling class" and the "lower class." These people wanted to come to a country which said that "all men are created equal." People also came from Asia, Africa, and the Pacific islands.

Among your friends and classmates there are probably boys and girls whose ancestors came from many different lands. All these people have helped to build the United States of America. They have all helped to make our country great.

1. Who helped build the United States?
2. What was the result of the French and Indian war?
3. How many nations are there in Latin America? Why are they called Latin American?
4. Where did the early Spanish settlers build their farms and plantations?
5. What does the phrase "all men are created equal" mean?

Chapter 17. REVIEW

Learning to Use New Words

Use each of the following terms in an original sentence, expressing something you have learned in Chapter 17:

Orient
navigator
equator
continent
expedition
plantations
descendant
legislature
ancestor

Knowing the Important Facts

1. Why did the people of Western Europe become interested in the Orient toward the end of the Middle Ages?
2. Briefly outline Christopher Columbus' story—his dream, voyage, and later years.
3. What role did the Spanish and Portuguese play in settling the New World?
4. Describe the French exploration and colonization of the New World.
5. In what ways did England contribute to the future of North America?

Thinking Through the Facts

1. How was Columbus influenced by the Roman geographer, Ptolemy?
2. Why was news of Magellan's voyage received with such enthusiasm by the people of Europe?
3. How did Spain and Portugal contribute to the growth of the New World? List some benefits the New World received from these two countries.
4. Why was the English colonization the greatest single contribution to the present United States?
5. Is the culture of the New World Western? Give reasons for your answer.

Developing a Time Sense

Arrange the following events in the proper time order?
1. Jamestown is founded
2. Columbus opens up a new period of history
3. Magellan's crew sails around the world
4. France is defeated in North America
5. The first printing press in the New World

Unit SIX *Summary*

I Should Know That . . .

1. The Renaissance period stressed change. The new learning was spread throughout Europe from Italy.
2. Renaissance artists contributed much to architecture, painting, and sculpture.
3. The effects of religious revolution of the sixteenth century can be seen today. Protestantism, begun by Martin Luther, gained many followers. Christianity became divided into different religions.
4. The Council of Trent acted to make clear the Church's teachings and to make necessary reforms within the Church.
5. The period of exploration gave the people of Western Europe an idea of the real size and appearance of the earth. Exploration was spurred by a desire for increased trade.

Dates I Should Remember . . .

1300–1600—Renaissance Period
1450—Gutenberg invents the printing press
1492–1600—Period of exploration
1517—Martin Luther's proclamation

Some Interesting Things to Do . . .

1. Organize a debate to consider whether it was better that the English settled America than the French.
2. Start a collection of examples of the art work of these famous Renaissance painters and sculptors: Michelangelo, Raphael, da Vinci, Rubens, El Greco, Rembrandt, Holbein.
3. On a map of the world locate the following: Genoa, Naples, Venice, Geneva, Wittenberg, Cape of Good Hope, Philippines, Strait of Magellan.

Books I Should Read . . .

Butterfield, *The Young Peoples Story of Architecture*
Walter C. Hodges, *Columbus Sails*
Louise Kent, *He Went with Vasco da Gama*
Patricia Lauber, *The Quest of Galileo*

Yesterday, Today and Tomorrow

We have read the story of man from the time of the Stone Age to the discovery of America. We have read about the religious beliefs of various peoples, about the way they lived, about their inventions and discoveries. Almost everything we have today we owe to people who lived in the past. Some of these things are good, and others are not so good. On the whole, we Americans can be thankful to the people who lived in our *past*.

Just as we owe much to the people who lived in the past, so the people who will live in the future will owe much to us. Will this be good or bad? Will we leave this a better world than we found it or a worse one? Will the people of the future be thankful to us?

Yesterday, today, and tomorrow—they are all tied together. "Today" soon becomes "yesterday," and "tomorrow" soon becomes "today."

Art and Architecture

From the very beginning people needed shelter. They needed places where they could eat and sleep. They needed places where they would be protected from wind, rain, snow, and wild animals. Early people often made their homes in caves. Later, people learned to make simple huts from sticks, leaves, clay, and animal skins. When men drew plans for their buildings and tried to make them beautiful as well as useful, this was the beginning of architecture. Some of the best of the early architecture was in temples and public buildings. Some was in the homes of the wealthy people.

The Egyptians built beautiful temples. They also built the pyramids, which were tombs for their kings. The Greeks developed three styles of columns, which supported the roofs of large buildings. The Romans learned about columns from the Greeks, and they learned about the arch from the Etruscans. The Romans developed the dome. They were among the best builders of all times. The Gothic style was developed during the Middle Ages.

Men painted pictures before they could write. In Chapter 1 we read that there are paintings on the walls of caves that are at least 15,000 years old and perhaps much older. Different people developed different ways and different styles of painting. The Chinese paintings were quite different from the European ones. The Egyptians had their own kinds of paintings.

Sculpture is also older than writing. In many parts of the world archaeologists have found statues that date back to the Stone Age. In many cases the statues represent the gods whom the people worshipped. The Egyptians were carving giant statues 5,000 years ago. The largest of all Egyptian statues was the Sphinx.

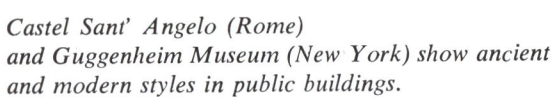

Castel Sant' Angelo (Rome) and Guggenheim Museum (New York) show ancient and modern styles in public buildings.

The ancient Greeks carved statues which are among the best the world has ever known. The ancient Romans learned sculpture from the Greeks.

Sculpture reached a great height in its development during the Renaissance, especially in Italy. Some of the great painters of that time were Michelangelo, Raphael, and Leonardo da Vinci. Michelangelo was a sculptor as well as a painter. One of his greatest works was his *Pieta,* a portrait of Our Lady and the Crucified Christ.

Today's artists, sculptors, and architects study the works of long ago and learn much from them. We find columns and domes, for example, in many of our public buildings of today. But today's artists, sculptors, and architects do not just copy the masters of the past. They learn from these men of long ago, but they also develop their own way of doing things. They also have many new kinds of tools and many new kinds of material to work with.

1. In what need of ancient man did architecture have its beginning?
2. Are there any proofs in your town that modern man is still satisfying this need?
3. How did some of the ancient men express their feelings or tell what they thought about something before they could write?
4. What was the first thing some of the ancient men did as soon as they had **permanent** places to live?

Crafts and Manufacturing

When a man, after long careful training, learns to do a special kind of work with his hands, we say he has a craft. We call him a craftsman. A craftsman is something like an artist or a sculptor. These men also work with their hands.

We have read much about crafts in this book. In very early times men knew how to make weapons and tools by chipping and polishing stones. There were pottery makers in every civilization we have read about, and even uncivilized people made pottery. Thousands of years ago weavers made cloth from linen, cotton, and wool. The Chinese wove beautiful silk cloth. The Arabs wove beautiful rugs.

Early metal workers made tools, weapons, jewelry, and many other things. The metal workers used gold, silver, tin, and lead. When they learned to use bronze and, later, iron, then mankind entered first the Bronze Age, then the Iron Age.

Glass was made by the ancient Egyptians and Phoenicians. The Chinese learned how to make paper, and the Arabs took this knowledge to the Europeans. Woodworkers made all sorts of things, from ships to tiny statues.

Craftsmanship probably reached its height in Western Europe in the Thirteenth Century. We have read about the great pride that the craftsmen of that time took in their work. We know that the craftsmen organized into guilds, each with its own guildhall. The beautiful cathedrals and churches of the Middle Ages were built and decorated by craftsmen. We still admire these today.

The age of the craftsman lasted for many centuries. When George Washington became the first President of the United States, most work was still done by hand. If a man wished a pair of shoes, he went to the shoemaker. The shoemaker would make a special pair of shoes, just for him. If the man wished a hat, he went to a hatter who made hats by hand. Most women of the time were "craftsmen" because they spun thread and wove cloth in their own homes.

Cotton mills were started first in England and were introduced into the United States when Washington was President. These mills used power from waterfalls to spin thread by machinery, instead of by hand. A little later, machinery was used to make cloth from the thread. After that, more and more things were made by machinery. New kinds of power were found to run the machines, and a mill no longer had to be by a waterfall.

This machine stamps and presses steel into automobile bumpers at a Ford Motor Company plant in Michigan.

259

When there is a great change, we say a revolution has taken place. The change from handwork to machine work was called the Industrial Revolution. The Industrial Revolution brought many benefits to the people of the world, and it also brought some problems.

Today, almost everything we use was manufactured. This means it was made in a factory. We use very few things that were made by hand. The factories produce these goods more quickly at less expense than craftsmen could do. Also, the factories produce many things that the craftsmen never made. Imagine somebody trying to make a television set if he had to make every part, including the tubes, by hand! And, if he did finally build such a set, imagine what it would cost if you wished to buy it!

You can see some of the benefits of manufacturing if you just look about you. How many of the things you use every day were made in a factory? It would be hard to count them all.

The Industrial Revolution would never have come about, however, if it had not been for the work of the people who lived before the new machines were built. The inventors studied the work of the craftsmen very carefully before they were able to build machines that would do the same kind of work.

1. What does the artist have in common with the craftsman with regard to how they produce their work?
2. Which one produces more work in modern times? Why?
3. What are the benefits the machine brought that the craftsmen could never give?

Language and Literature

Spoken language is probably as old as man himself. We may be sure that when a number of people were living together they agreed on names for certain things and were able to talk to each other. It was the first of what we call today the "communication arts." But they had no written language and could not write down their thoughts. The people who spoke but did not write left few records of themselves. That is why we say these people lived in pre-historic times. They lived before history was written.

The Egyptians worked out a system of picture writing, or hieroglyphics. The Sumerians had wedge-shaped characters; this is called cuneiform writing. The Chinese had thousands of characters in their written language, and they still do. The Japanese borrowed their written language from the Chinese, and it, too, has many characters.

The Phoenicians either invented the alphabet or learned it from someone else. The Phoenicians were a nation of sailors. They took the alphabet everywhere they went. The Greeks and Romans changed the alphabet to suit their needs. The alphabet of the Greeks and Romans spread throughout Europe. We use it in our English language. The same alphabet is used in German, Spanish, French, and other languages of Western Europe.

It is only natural that people who lived in different places developed various languages. There was little travel, and people who lived in one region seldom saw the people from another region. Over hundreds of years they developed new words and new ways of spelling and pronouncing old words. They also developed new rules for grammar. Not only did entirely new languages develop, but many dialects developed within the same language. There came to be a High German and a Low German, for example. People who spoke the one dialect could hardly understand people who spoke the other dialect, but they were speaking the same language.

There are certain great families of languages. We have read that the languages which developed largely from Latin are called the Latin languages. These are Italian, Spanish, Portuguese, French, and Romanian. English came largely from Anglo-Saxon, so it is a Teutonic, or Germanic language. It belongs to the same family as German, Dutch, and the languages of the Scandinavian countries.

Often, a language takes words from other languages. This is the case with English. It is mostly based on Anglo-Saxon, but the Romans introduced a few Latin words while they were in England. The Normans introduced many French words when they ruled England. When English settlers came to North America, they added some words which they learned from the American Indians.

Even before they had written languages, many peoples expressed their ideas and feelings in poems, songs, and stories. These were passed on from parents to children for many centuries. Those famous stories, the *Iliad* and *Odyssey,* were kept alive in this way. After there were written languages, these old poems, songs, and stories were written down. Many new ones were also written. After the printing press was invented, many copies could be made.

UN delegates speak in nearly every tongue known to man. Language experts are kept busy translating debates and speeches.

People today read the writings of people who lived in the past. Some people read these things to learn more about the past.

Some people read them just for enjoyment. Many people read them for both reasons.

One of the greatest writers in the English language was William Shakespeare. He lived in England at the time of the Renaissance. Shakespeare wrote stirring plays. He wrote them in the form of poetry. Thus, he was both a poet and a playwright. Shakespeare used many old stories from the past for some of his stories, but he put them in a new form. In the same way, writers of today study the way Shakespeare wrote and learn much from him. But they write in their own way.

When you go into a library and look around at all the hundreds of books, think of the great knowledge they contain. Think of the ideas and feelings the authors have expressed in them. Think of the enjoyment they can provide. All those books are there for us to use. They are the result of years and years of work by many writers. Some of these writers are living now, but others lived far in the past. Because we have a written language and because we have printing presses, we can still read these books by people who lived in the past. We can still gain knowledge from these writers of the past. We can still learn of their thoughts and feelings. We can still gain great enjoyment from what they wrote.

1. Name some means of communication other than spoken language that modern man uses.
2. How did it come about that people speak different languages?
3. What are two great language families?
4. What books have you read which tell about people who lived before the Twentieth Century?

Science, Invention, Discoveries

Man has always studied himself and the world around him. He noticed that there was order in the way things happened. If one event took place, another event followed. Parents passed this information along to their children. As the children grew older, they gained new knowledge of their own. They passed this information along to *their* children. Thus, man's total knowledge continued to grow.

In the Stone Age, men learned how to raise certain crops. The people who lived along the Nile River and the people of the Valley of the Two Rivers lived on land where there was little rain. They found that crops would grow if they brought water to the land. They built the world's first irrigation systems.

Men found ways to count. The system we use is based on tens and was worked out in India. Arabs carried the system to Europe, and so we call it Arabic.

Egyptians and other peoples worked out a system of measuring land and finding the proper boundaries. This system was based on geometry.

Various ancient peoples studied the **sun**, the moon, and the stars. Men steered ships by the sun and the stars before the compass was invented. A calendar was worked out.

Men learned to measure the time of the day. The kind of clock we use today was invented in the Middle Ages. Men also worked out systems of weights and measurements. Hippocrates, the Greek, is called the Father of Medicine.

One of the greatest discoveries of man was the use of fire. The wheel was one of the greatest inventions of all time. The plow was also a very important invention. Two inventions that aided sailing in the Middle Ages were the compass and the astrolabe. Gunpowder was invented by the Chinese, and later Europeans learned about it. The Lydians, the wealthy traders of the Near East, made trading easier when they worked out a system of coins.

Today, the discoveries and inventions of the past are being put to use in a way that would amaze our ancestors. During the Renaissance, Leonardo da Vinci drew plans for a flying machine; few people thought man would ever really fly. Today, jet planes streak across oceans and continents, some of them faster than the speed of sound. Man has split the atom and has unleashed tremendous nuclear power. This power can be used to destroy, or it can be used to accomplish great wonders. Man has put satellites into space, each satellite following its own path in circling the Earth. Some of these satellites have carried men. Others carry equipment which sends valuable information back to Earth. A rocket has been landed on the moon. Another rocket has taken pictures of the moon and has sent them back to Earth. In a few years a man will probably land on the moon and then return to Earth.

1. How are we still profiting from man's greatest discovery and man's greatest invention?
2. How are the geniuses of today still working out the thoughts of one of the geniuses of the past?
3. Which do you think are the greatest modern scientific developments?

Launching a United States satellite at Cape Kennedy is an impressive display of tremendous nuclear power.

Education

The education of a human being begins the day he is born. It continues all his life. Education is the passing on of learning from one generation to another. In most cases the child receives his first education from his parents. This was true in the Stone Age, and it is true today. The parents teach him how to eat and drink. They teach him how to dress, walk, and talk. From the parents the child first learns religious attitudes, and from them he learns his first prayers. They teach him to share with others, to love his fellow man, and to have respect for law.

Stone Age fathers taught their sons how to make weapons and tools from stone. They taught their sons how to hunt and trap and fish. Stone Age mothers taught their daughters how to cook the meat and fish that was brought home by the men and boys. They taught their daughters how to make clothes out of animal skins.

As men became food producers instead of food gatherers, the boys and girls had more to learn. They had to learn how to plow the fields, plant the seeds, care for the crops, and gather the harvest.

As civilization developed, there were more things to learn. Boys had to learn how to build houses and dig irrigation ditches. Some boys learned crafts such as glass blowing, pottery working, or metal working. Girls learned to take care of houses instead of simple huts. They learned how to spin thread and weave cloth. They learned how to make clothes out of this cloth.

In Athens and in other cities of ancient Greece there was a well-developed civilization. There were many things to learn besides how to work with the hands. Fathers of wealthy families wished their sons to learn to read and write. They wished their sons to learn philosophy, history, geography, and science. These fathers had slaves called

In high school and colleges all over the nation, young Americans receive thorough training in all fields of science.

pedagogues who taught their sons. Most families could not afford to have pedagogues, so the boys learned only what their fathers could teach them. It was not considered proper for girls to receive a good education. Their mothers taught them how to sew, cook, and take care of the house.

In Sparta the government took charge of the boys when they were quite young. The boys were trained to be good soldiers. They were trained to obey without question, to endure great hardships, to be brave fighters. They learned little about subjects that wealthy boys in Athens studied.

In the Middle Ages most monasteries had schools, and most cathedrals had universities. Only a small percentage of the boys were able to attend schools and universities, and no girls attended them.

The English colonists who settled in North America thought that schools were very important. This was especially true of the New England colonists. In 1642 Massachusetts passed a law saying that every town of fifty families must have someone to teach reading and writing, and that each town of a hundred or more families must have a grammar school.

About 1840 the present system of public schools was started in the United States. These schools are supported by money from taxes. Young people attend them without having to pay tuition. Today, most states have laws saying that young people must attend school until they reach a certain age. In most cases this age is sixteen. The laws apply to girls as well as boys. Americans think it very important that everyone in the country receives an education. Boys and girls who want a really good education do not stop going to school when they are sixteen. They go on to graduate from high school. Many go on to college, and some receive further schooling after they have graduated from college.

Boys and girls who are going to school today are acquiring much knowledge from the people of the past. When they are out of school, they will use their knowledge to build a better world for future people.

1. In what way does the progress of our civilization force you to use your mind?
2. What are some important changes made in education from the time your parents went to school until the present?

Growth of National Spirit

We live in a world that is composed of many nations. When we think of a modern nation, we usually think of a large group of people united under an independent government. Our nation is the United States of America. Our neighboring nations are Canada and Mexico. There are many other nations in the world.

Most people love the nation of which they are citizens. They have *national spirit*.

Sometimes, we are likely to think that nations and national spirit have always existed in the world. This is not true. The earliest people lived in clans or tribes. These groups were not large enough to be called nations. The city-states of ancient Greece and other places were also too small to be called nations.

Most people who lived in the ancient empires had little national spirit. The Roman Empire covered a large section of the world. It included most of the civilized people known to the Romans at that time. In many ways it was well governed. Most of the people who lived in it were reasonably happy. But the people of the provinces, such as Egypt and Syria, had no great love for Rome. They were not like the Romans, they were kept in the Empire by force, and Rome seemed far away. If there was any national spirit in the Roman Empire, it was probably only in the city of Rome.

When the Roman Empire fell apart, the system of feudalism developed in Western Europe. There were kings, but the kings had little power. Most of the power belonged to the nobles. If you could have asked a French peasant of the Middle Ages what he was, he would not have said that he was a Frenchman. He would have said that he came from such-and-such village and that Lord So-and-So was his master.

Toward the end of the Middle Ages nobles had lost much of their power, and central governments had become stronger. Men began to develop great love for their various countries. They developed a national spirit.

Spaniards united in a long war against the Moors. When the Moors were finally defeated in 1492, the Spaniards felt a great love for the country for which they had fought. Englishmen learned to love their country while fighting in the Hundred Years' War. Frenchmen learned to love their country while defending it in the same war.

National spirit can be a good thing, or it can be a bad thing. Patriotism is a good

Visitors tour the UN buildings in New York City. Flags of member nations are displayed on the Plaza.

thing. It is loyalty to one's country and the desire to serve the country. Under nationalism the people of one country try to get ahead of the peoples of all other countries. They do this by any means possible. This results in bitter rivalries and wars.

Ever since the end of the Middle Ages, there has been too much nationalism. This has led to one war after another. Both great world wars of our own century were due to nationalism.

After World War I, some world leaders persuaded various nations to join an organization called the League of Nations. The United States did not join. It was hoped that the nations would work together in the League and that future wars would be avoided. But the rulers of some nations refused to abide by the wishes of the League of Nations. World War II started, and the League of Nations was dead. It had been killed by nationalism.

After World War II, another attempt was made to have the nations work together. This time the organization is called the United Nations. The United States was one of the first members. The headquarters of the UN is in New York City. The UN has been successful to some extent. It has helped settle disputes among various nations and has helped to keep law and order in various parts of the world. But the UN has been facing more and more opposition from various nations. Many people fear it is losing its strength. Will nationalism win again?

There can be no true world peace until the people of all countries understand the difference between patriotism and nationalism. The people must love their own countries, but they must be ready to work with the people of all other countries.

1. How are national spirit, patriotism, and nationalism different?
2. What happened when the nobles began to lose much of their power?
3. What is the United Nations fighting against?

Law and Government

Whenever people live together, some sort of government is necessary. This is true of a family, of a village, of a big city, of a nation. The government performs many services for its people. It also makes certain rules, and tries to see that the rules are obeyed. If it is good government, these rules are for the people's own good and makes life easier for them.

In a family the parents are the "government," although we seldom think of them in that way. Parents have great love for their children and try to do what is best for them. As we have read, the parents give children their first education. This includes religious instruction. Parents provide the children with a home, food, clothing, and many other things. To keep the house running smoothly parents must make certain rules. These include the time to go to bed, the time to get up, the time for meals, and the time for study. Certain household tasks are assigned to each child. If there are older children, the parents decide who is permitted to use the family automobile at certain times. If the parents did not make rules, there would be a breakdown in family life and even in the community.

The United States Supreme Court, the highest court in our nation, meets in this stately building in Washington, D.C.

The family is as old as man himself. We may be sure that Stone Age parents also served their children and made rules for them. When several tribes lived together, they formed a clan. Clans often joined into tribes. The clans and tribes were governed in different ways. Sometimes, all the men would gather together to make laws and to solve problems. Sometimes, just one man would be the ruler. But there was always some kind of government.

When tribes united into nations, new and more complicated kinds of government were needed. The Egyptians had a king, court, and laws. They collected taxes to support the government. Hammurabi, King of Babylon, had the laws of his kingdom carved on a great block of stone so everybody would know what they were.

Athens and other Greek city-states gave us the idea of democracy, or self-government. The freemen of the city gathered together and made laws and elected government officials. This was not perfect democracy, because the freemen were only a small portion of the population, but it was an important beginning.

Rome, too, had self-government until the people showed that they were no longer capable of ruling themselves. Then the power was given to an emperor. Rome ruled a vast empire, and on the whole did so justly and wisely. Roman laws were later written down. They form the basis for many laws in Western Civilization.

After the fall of the Roman Empire, the system of feudalism arose in Europe. The various nations had kings, but the kings had little power. Most of the power belonged to the nobles. The nobles were supposed to be under the rule of the king, but many of them paid little attention to the king.

Most people did not like the rule of the nobles. When the kings tried to take power away from the nobles, many people came to the support of the kings. Little by little, the kings became strong rulers.

Some kings were wise and just rulers. Some kings have even been declared saints. But some kings were unjust and cruel. The people who lived under such kings found that conditions were just as bad as they had been under the nobles.

The English were the first people in any of the modern nations who were able to limit the power of their king. In 1215 King John was forced to sign the Great Charter. This listed many things which the king was not allowed to do. It guaranteed that the nobles would retain the rights that the king had been taking from them. After that, the power of the English kings had many ups and downs. Some kings became powerful in spite of the Great Charter. In general, however, the kings lost more power as time went on. Later, the common people as well as the nobles gained more power. A Parliament, which was supposed to represent the people, had the power to levy taxes and make laws.

The English settlers who came to North America brought along their ideas of self-government. Each colony had an assembly which made the laws for that colony. The colonies were still under the government in London, however. After a century and a half, the colonists thought the British government was treating them unfairly. The colonists disliked the fact that Parliament was taxing them although they had no representatives in Parliament. This was against the principles of the Great Charter, they said. Their motto was, "No taxation without representation." The dispute led to a long, bitter war, the American Revolution. The colonists won the war and became an independent country, the United States of America.

When American leaders met to write a Constitution for the new nation, they followed English ideas to a certain extent. But they also added ideas of their own. The Constitution was changed, or amended, a number of times, but we are still governed by it today. The Constitution stressed the importance of the individual citizen, safeguarded us against tyranny, and provided a certain amount of self-government. The Amendments have further guaranteed the rights of the people and given the people an even larger voice in the government.

Today, we Americans are a nation of free, self-governing people. Our government makes mistakes because it is run by human beings, and no human being is perfect. But we think we have the best *form* of government in the world, and we think that it works better than any other government in the world.

For this we owe a great debt to thousands of people who lived in the past.

What about the people of the future? Will they thank us for keeping and improving our self-government? They will, if we are good citizens, take a strong interest in public affairs, and vote intelligently when we are old enough to do so. We must not forget the example of the Romans. They had self-government, and they lost it because they became greedy and lazy. We must not let that happen to us.

1. What did the Great Charter do with regard to the rights of the nobles and the powers of the king?
2. Why were the early settlers and, later, the early colonists dissatisfied with their government?
3. What was the important thing that the Constitution stressed?
4. What are some of the things that indicate good citizenship?

Religion

Why does the sun rise and set? Why does the rain fall from the sky? Why do plants grow? Why do people get sick and die? Early people asked themselves these questions. They knew that there was some power stronger than themselves. What was this power? Through the ages different peoples have given different answers to this question. Most people who did not know about the one God worshipped many gods. This was no doubt true of the Stone Age people. It was certainly true of the ancient Egyptians, Sumerians, Babylonians, Greeks, Romans, and all the other ancient people we have read about. In the writings of these early people we can read about their gods. Many statues of the gods are still in existence. Many temples built to the gods are still standing.

Most of the early people also believed in life after death. We know the Egyptians did. That is why they built such lavish burial places for their kings.

There are about 387 million Hindus in the world. This religion started in India, and most Hindus are in India. Buddhism also started in India. It spread over southern and eastern Asia, but it died out almost completely in India. There are about 159 million Buddhists today. In China, Buddhism mixed with Confucianism and Taoism, which are much alike. There are about 380 million Confucianists and Taoists in China. It is impossible to tell how many practice their religion, because China is ruled by Communists, who oppose all religion. In Japan, Buddhism blended with Shintoism. In 1867 Japan made Shintoism the state religion. According to this religion, the emperor was a god. After Japan was defeated in World War II, the American general, Douglas MacArthur, ruled Japan for a time. He said that there would be no state religion. On January 1, 1946, Emperor Hirohito told the people of his country that he was not a god.

The first people to believe in one God were the Hebrews, or Jews. This truth was revealed to the Jews by God Himself. To them God also gave the Ten Commandments. The Jews were surrounded by pagans who believed in many gods. They were conquered a number of times, and once they were carried away to captivity to Babylon. Through all their troubles and persecutions, the Jews clung to their belief in God. In Bethlehem, Jesus Christ was born to a Jewish family and lived His life among the Jews. After He founded His Church, many of the first converts to Christianity were Jews. Other Jews did not accept Christ and clung to their old religion. There are about

13 million members of the Jewish religion today, and about half of these live in the United States.

The Christian religion spread across Europe. By the year 1000 almost everybody who lived on that continent was a Christian. This means that almost everybody was a Catholic, because almost all Christians belonged to the Catholic Church in those days.

An Arab named Mohammed learned about God from Jews and Christians. He said that God had told him to found a new religion. This religion is known as Islam. Its members are called Moslems. The Moslems believed that God wished them to spread their religion by warfare. They also thought that they were assured of saving their souls if they died while fighting to spread their religion. They conquered much of eastern Asia and North Africa and held Spain for about seven centuries. Today, there are about 446 million Moslems. Christians, Jews, and Moslems all believe in the one God, but only Christians profess to be followers of Jesus Christ.

In time the Christians split into three large groups. First, a split grew between the Church in the East and the Church in the West. In 1054 the break became complete. Many Christians in the East no longer acknowledged the Pope as their head. This new Church became known as the Orthodox Church. The Orthodox Church has about 144 million members. They are found mostly in the Balkan peninsula, Asia Minor, Syria, and Russia. The Catholic Church, which remained loyal to the Pope, has about 558 million members.

Protestants take part in the Lord's Supper.

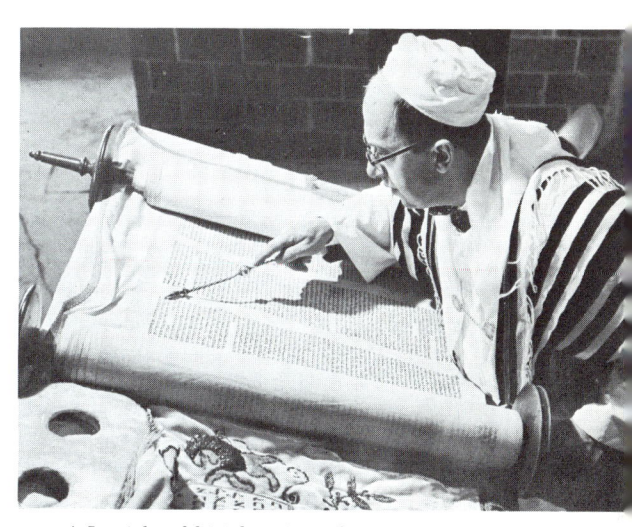

A Jewish rabbi (above) reads from the Torah, or sacred book of the law. A Catholic priest (below) celebrates the Liturgy of the Eucharist.

About 1517 Martin Luther disputed certain Catholic doctrines, and this led to the Protestant Revolt. The first Protestants were followers of Martin Luther, and were called Lutherans. Soon, there were many different Protestant churches. Some of the largest Protestant religions are the Anglican (Episcopalian in the United States), the Baptist, the Methodist, and the Presbyterian. There are about 220 million Protestants.

In some countries most of the people belong to one certain religion. Eighty-five percent of the people of India are Hindus. Most of the people in the Scandinavian countries are Lutherans. In Latin America most of the people are Catholics.

In the United States, on the other hand, we have people of many different religions. Most of the English people who settled in North America were Protestants of various kinds. England at that time had severe laws which forbade Catholics to practice their religion. Most of the English colonies had similar laws. At the time of the American Revolution, only one American out of every one hundred was a Catholic. The anti-religious laws were repealed by the end of the American Revolution. The United States Constitution guaranteed freedom of religion. Catholics came to the United States in large numbers. They came from Ireland, Germany, and other countries. Today, about one in five Americans is a Catholic. Of those Americans who claim church membership about 55.5 percent are Protestant, 37 percent are Catholic, 4.5 percent are Jewish, and the remaining 3 percent belong to other religions, such as Orthodox and Buddhist. The Protestants are divided into a great many churches. There are 80 religious bodies in the United States with 50,000 or more members each.

Americans of the various religions have learned to respect the beliefs of others. They have learned to live, work, and play side by side. On certain occasions they even pray side by side. Together, these people of various beliefs have worked to make the United States the great nation it is.

Today, it is important that, throughout the world, people of all religions understand each other and respect each other. That was one reason—but not the only reason—why Pope John XXIII called the Second Vatican Council. This was a general meeting of Catholic bishops. The council was continued under Pope John's successor, Paul VI. Leaders of other religions were invited to the meeting, and returned encouraged by what they had seen. The day seems far off when all Christians will be united in one church, but with the guidance of the Holy Spirit that day will no doubt come. In the meantime it is important that we stop quarreling among ourselves, and work together to overcome the problems that face all of us.

In his encyclical, *Pacem in Terris* (Peace on Earth), Pope John asked not only Catholics but also "all men of good will" to cooperate in "establishing universal peace in truth, justice, charity, and freedom."

1. What is the one thing most people agree on, no matter what their religion, or where or by whom it was founded?
2. How was the Hebrew religion different from all the other religions in the world?
3. On what do most Christians agree? On what do Christians and Jews agree?

Historical Glossary

The following glossary, or list of words, contains all the difficult or unusual words that have been used in this book. The meanings that are given explain the words as they are used when you first read them in your book.

The following key shows you the meaning of the diacritical (dī′*a*·krĭt′ĭ·kăl) marks that are used to help you pronounce the words:

āte	Afric*a*	īce	cŏntain	ûnite
alwåys	ēve	ĭll	sŏft	hut
câre	h*e*re	char*i*ty	mo͞on	circ*u*s
hăt	ĕvent	ōld	fo͝ot	fûr
ănother	ĕnd	ōbey	out	t͟hen
ärm	bush*e*l	ôr	*o*il	*th*in
åsk	mak*e*r	hŏt	ūse	pict*u*re

A

abbot (ăb′*u*t), head of a monastery

Acropolis (*a*·krŏp′ô·lĭs), a steep hill in Athens

A.D., abbreviation for *anno Domini* which means "in the year of the Lord." Sometimes used with dates which fall after the birth of Our Lord

Allah (ăl′*a*), the god worshiped by the Mohammedans

alphabet (ăl′f*a*·bĕt), the letters of a language arranged in their regular order

altar (ôl′tēr) **stone,** the center part of the altar which contains the relics of martyrs

amphitheater (ăm′fĭ·thē′*a*·tēr), a round or oval building with seats arranged in rounded rows around an open space on which games, plays, etc., take place

ancient (ān′shĕnt) **history,** events that happened in times long past down through the time the Roman Empire in the West came to an end

Anglican (ăng′glĭ·kăn), name by which members of the Church of England are called

apprentice (*a*·prĕn′tĭs), a person who is learning a new trade from a master workman

aqueduct (ăk′wĭ·dŭkt), a structure that looks like a bridge and carries water across a river or hollow

Arabic (ăr′*a*·bĭk) **numerals,** numbers coming from the Arabs: 1,2,3,4,5,6, 7,8,9,0

arch (ärch), the part of a structure that is rounded to a peak

archeologist (är·kê·ŏl′ô·jĭst), a specialist in the scientific study of material remains of past human life and activities

architect (är′kĭ·tĕkt), a person who plans buildings. **architecture** (är′kĭ·tĕk·tûr), the style or styles of building

armada (är·mä′d*a*), a large fleet of armed ships; as, the Spanish Armada

armor (är′mēr), a covering of metal and leather worn to protect the body in battle

artisan (är′tĭ·zăn), a person who works at a trade needing skill with the hands

assembly (*a*·sĕm′blĭ), a lawmaking body

astrolabe (ăs′trô·lāb), an instrument used to watch heavenly bodies

astronomy (ăs·trŏn′ô·mĭ), the science which gathers, studies, and explains facts about the stars, etc. **astronomer** (ăs·trŏn′ô·mēr), the person who does these things

B

barbarian (bär·bâr′ĭ·ăn), 1. a stranger; a foreigner. 2. an uncivilized person.

barter (bär′tēr), to trade one thing for another without using money

basilica (b*a*·sĭl′ĭ·k*a*), 1. an early Christian church. 2. the title given to churches with certain privileges

Black Death, a plague that killed many people in thirteenth-century Europe

block printing, printing from a block of wood on which is carved all the letters of a certain page

botany (bŏt′*a*·nĭ), the science which gathers, studies, and explains facts about plants and plant life

buttress (bŭt′rĕs), a support built out against a wall or building to steady it

C

calendar (kăl′ĕn·dēr), an arrangement of time into days, weeks, months, and years

Calvinism (kăl′vĭn·ĭz′m), the religion of John Calvin and his followers

canticle (kăn′tĭ·k′l), a hymn of praise

caste (kåst), one of the classes into which the people of India have been divided from the earliest times

273

castle (kàs′′l), a large building or group of buildings with thick walls, towers, and other defenses against attack

catacomb (kăt′*a*·kōm), an underground place of burial with passages and with spaces in the side for tombs

catechism (kăt′ē·kĭz′m), a book of questions and answers summarizing religious teachings

cathedral (k*a*·thē′drăl), the principal church of a diocese over which a bishop presides

cathedral school, the school connected with a cathedral in which certain courses were taught

Catholic Reformation (rĕf′ôr·mā′shŭn), the reform movement within the Church ordered by the Council of Trent in the 16th Century

census (sĕn′sŭs), in early Rome, the numbering of people so that they could be taxed

chariot (chăr′ĭ·ŭt), in ancient times a vehicle with two wheels used in war and racing

charter (chăr′tēr), a written guarantee of rights

chemical (kĕm′ĭ·kăl), anything that is used in chemistry. **chemistry** (kĕm′ĭs·trĭ), a science which deals with different substances

chivalry (shĭv′ăl·rĭ), the ideals of knighthood

city-state (sĭt′ĭ-stāt), a city and the region around it not subject to any higher state

civilization (sĭv′ĭ·lĭ·zā′shŭn), the total of everything that a people have learned about better ways to live

clan (klăn), a group made up of a number of households

classic (klăs′ĭk) **architecture,** the buildings that follow the style of ancient Greece and Rome

coin (koin), a piece of metal money

colony (kŏl′ô·nĭ), any distant territory belonging to a country

Colosseum (kŏl′ŏ·sē′ŭm), an amphitheater in Rome in which gladiators fought

column (kŏl′ŭm), a pillar supporting a roof. Columns are usually placed in rows and are often ornamental as well as useful.

compass (kŭm′pȧs), an instrument for finding directions on the earth's surface by means of a magnetic needle

congress (kŏng′grĕs), a gathering; usually a lawmaking body

conquest (kŏng′kwĕst), 1. the act of conquering. 2. a conquered territory or people.

consul (kŏn′sŭl), either of the two officials at the head of ancient Rome when Rome was a republic

convent (kŏn′vĕnt), the house or houses occupied by a group of nuns devoted to a religious life under a superior

council (koun′sĭl), a group of persons who are called together to give advice, and make decisions

courtyard (kōrt′yärd), a place surrounded with walls and attached to a castle

craftsman (kråfts′măn), one who works at a trade with much skill

crozier (krō′zhēr), the staff which is the symbol of the bishop's office

Crusade (krōō·sād′), the military expeditions undertaken in the 11th, 12th, and 13th centuries to recover the Holy Land from the Moslem Turks. **Crusader** (krōō·sād′ēr), one who takes part in a Crusade

culture (kŭl′chûr), anything and everything that man makes, does, or thinks

cuneiform (kū·nē′ĭ·fôrm), wedge-shaped characters used in writing in ancient Persia and Assyria

D

Danelaw (dān′lô′), the law in the part of England held by the Danes

Defender of the Faith, title given to King Henry VIII by the Pope and since used by rulers of Great Britain

democracy (dē·mŏk′r*a*·sĭ), government by the people

descendant (dē·sĕn′dănt), a person who is born of a certain family or group

dialect (dī′*a*·lĕkt), a form of language which belongs to a certain region, differing from the standard form in its local expressions and pronunciations

dictator (dĭk·tā′tēr), a person who has the highest authority with complete power over the people he rules

diocese (dī′ô·sēs), a section of a country and its people governed by a bishop

discus (dĭs′kŭs), a heavy round plate thrown by an athlete to test his strength and skill

Doctor of the Church, title given to certain saints because of their great knowledge and holiness

dome (dōm), a large roof shaped like a half circle

Domesday Book (dōmz′dā′), the record which William the Conqueror made of all the lands of England

Dominican (dô·mĭn′ĭ·kăn), a member of the Order of Preachers founded by St. Dominic

Donation (dô·nā′shŭn) **of Pepin,** the Frankish king's gift of terrritory to the Pope. This was the beginning of the Papal States.

donjon (dŭn′jŭn), the main tower in a castle

drawbridge (drô′brĭj′), a bridge which can be let down or drawn up. Used in medieval castles to cross the moat

dynasty (dī′năs·tĭ), a race or succession of kings of the same line or family

E

edict (ē′dĭkt), a notice made to the public

emperor (′em·pĕr·ẽr), the supreme monarch of an empire, such as the Roman emperor

empire (ĕm′pīr), a country with large territories and different peoples under the one government; as, the Roman Empire

Episcopalian (ē·pĭs′kŏ·pā′lĭ·ăn), the name by which members of the Church of England are known in this country

estate (ĕs·tāt′), 1. a class of people; a rank. 2. property owned by a person.

Eternal City, the, Rome

excommunicate (eks′kŏ·mū′nĭ·kat), to cut off officially from communion with the Church

experiment (ĕks·pĕr′ĭ·mĕnt), to test something out

F

fair (fâr), a gathering of people at a certain time to buy and sell goods

falcon (fôl′kŭn), a long-winged, swift-flying small hawk

Father of the Church, the title given to early Christian writers who are the witnesses of the true Faith as taught by the Apostles

festival (fĕs′tĭ·văl), a time of feasting and celebration

feudalism (fū′dăl·ĭz′m), a plan of living found in most European countries between the 9th and 15th Centuries by which men gave service to their lord in return for protection and the use of land

fief (fēf), an estate given to a vassal by a feudal lord

Flemish (flĕm′ĭsh), having to do with Flanders or the Flemings

float (flōt), a platform on wheels

forum (fō′rŭm), 1. in ancient Roman cities, the market place or public meeting place. 2. today, a public meeting for open discussion.

Franciscan (frăn·sĭs′kăn), member of the order founded by St. Francis of Assisi

friar (frī′ẽr), the name by which members of certain religious orders are called

G

geometry (jē·ŏm′ē·trĭ), the study of surfaces, lines, and angles

gladiator (glăd′ĭ·ā′tẽr), a man who fought with a weapon to entertain the people at celebrations in ancient Rome

Gothic (gŏth′ĭk) **architecture,** a style of building churches and other public buildings using pointed arches and high roofs

governor (gŭv′ẽr·nẽr), a person appointed to govern a town, a province, a colony, etc.

Great Charter, the MAGNA CARTA

guild (gĭld), a group of men in the one trade or business joined together in a sort of club

guildhall (gĭld′hôl′), the hall where a guild regularly meet

gunpowder (gŭn′pou′dẽr), an explosive used in guns, blasting, etc.

H

Hastings place in England where the battle between the English and Normans took place in 1066

hegira (hē·jī′rá), the flight of Mohammed from Mecca

heresy (hĕr′ĕ·sĭ), a teaching opposed to the doctrines of the Church. **heretic** (hĕr′ĕ·tĭk), one who teaches heresy

hermit (hûr′mĭt), a person who lives apart from others, usually for religious reasons

hieroglyphics (hī′ẽr·ō·glĭf′ĭks), the writing used by the ancient Egyptians

Holy Land, the, Palestine

Holy Roman Empire, the group of European countries which became united when the Pope crowned Charlemagne Roman emperor

holy war, name given to the Crusades

homage (hŏm′ĭj), the cermony in which the vassal promised his loyalty to his lord

homespun (hōm′spŭn′), a rough loosely-woven woolen cloth of plain color

hospice (hŏs′pĭs), an inn belonging to a religious order

House of Commons, the lower house of the British Parliament

House of Lords, the upper house of the British Parliament

Huguenot (hū′gē·nŏt), the name by which Calvin's followers were known in France

I

interdict (ĭn′tẽr·dĭkt), an order which forbids members of the Church to take part in certain ceremonies or to receive certain sacraments

invader (ĭn·vād′ẽr), a hostile person who enters another's town or city or country in order to conquer or destroy it

irrigation (ĭr′ĭ·gā·shŭn), bringing water to dry land and crops by means of a canal, pipe, etc.

Islam (ĭs′lȧm), the religion of the Moslems

J

Jesuit (jĕz′ū·ĭt), the order founded by St. Ignatius Loyola

journeyman (jûr′nĭ·măn), a worker who has learned a trade and works for a master worker

joust (joost), a contest on horseback between two knights with lances

juror (joor′ēr), a member of a jury

jury (joor′ĭ), a body of men chosen to decide someone's guilt or innocence. ... **of one's peers** (perz), a jury of one's equals

K

Khan (kän), the name by which a ruler in the East was known

keep (kēp), a stronghold or fortress, part of a medieval castle

knight (nīt), in feudal times, a mounted warrior serving a king or some lesser noble

Koran (kô·rän′), the scripture of the Mohammedans

L

laboratory (lăb′ô·rȧ·tō′rĭ), a room or building in which experiments are carried on

lance (lȧns), a long-handled weapon with a sharp steel head

Latin (lăt′ĭn), 1. the language of the ancient Romans. 2. having to do with peoples or countries whose language and civilization are from the ancient Romans.

Latin Vulgate (vŭl′gȧt), a translation of the Bible by St. Jerome

lay investiture (ĭn·vĕs′tĭ·tûr), the practice by nobles of raising bishops to their office

legislature (lĕj′ĭs·lā′tûr), a law making body

liberty (lĭb′ēr·tĭ), freedom

literature (lĭt′ēr·ȧ tûr), all the written and printed works of a people, country, or language

litter (lĭt′ēr), a couch with handles for carrying passengers

lord (lôrd), 1. in feudal times, the king or nobleman from whom a vassal received land. 2. a nobleman, a ruler.

lot (lŏt), the use of an object such as a piece of paper, a pebble, etc. to decide something by chance

Lutheran (lū′thēr·ăn), a follower of Martin Luther

M

Magna Carta (măg′nȧ kär′tȧ), the Great Charter which the English nobles forced King John to sign

manor (măn′ēr), an amount of land

manuscript (măn′ū·skrĭpt), a book or paper written by hand or, today, with a typewriter

martyr (mär′tēr), a person who dies rather than deny his religion

master (mȧs′tēr), 1. a person who is skilled at his trade. 2 a person who controls the actions of other people.

medieval (mē′dĭ·ē′văl), belonging to the Middle Ages

merchant (mûr′chȧnt), a person who carries on trade

Middle Ages (mĭd′l āj′ĕz), the period of time between ancient and modern times, from about 500 to 1500

minstrel (mĭn′strĕl), a singer of the Middle Ages who went from castle to castle entertaining the lord's guests

miracle (mĭr′ȧ·k'l) **play,** a medieval play about the life of a saint or a martyr

miter (mī′tēr), the headdress of a bishop

moat (mōt), a ditch filled with water

modern (mŏd′ērn) **times,** the time after the Middle Ages

monarchy (mŏn′ēr·kĭ), a country ruled by a king

monastery (mŏn′ăs·tēr′ĭ), the building or buildings in which a band of monks live

monk (mŭngk), a man who joins a religious group and lives with other men in a monastery

Moor (moor), one of the Saracens who invaded Spain

morality (mô·răl′ĭ·tĭ), **play,** a medieval play in which the characters took the parts of vices or virtues

Moslem (mŏz′lĕm), a follower of the religion of Mohammed

movable type, separately carved letters that can be moved around, used in printing

mummy (mŭm′ĭ), a dead body which is treated so that it will always remain as it was when buried

mystery (mĭs′tēr·ĭ), **play,** a medieval play about the life of Christ or the Bible

mythology (mĭ·thŏl′ô·jĭ), the stories and legends of gods and other imaginary people

N

nationalism (năsh′ŭn·ăl·ĭz′m), the abuse of patriotism by which the people of one country try to get ahead of the people of all countries

navigation (năv·ĭ·gā′shŭn), act of operating or controlling the course of an airplane or ship through the use of calculations as to position and directions, etc.

"new learning," the new interest in the ancient civilization of Greece and Rome; also called the Renaissance

New World, the Western Hemisphere including North America and South America

Nicene (nī·sēn′) **Creed,** the list of Catholic beliefs which was first drawn up at the Council of Nicaea. This creed is read at Sunday Mass and on certain feasts.

noble (nō′b'l, a person whose rank or station is above that of other persons

O

Old Law, the law preached to the Jews by Moses

oracle (ŏr′à·k'l), in ancient Greece, the person through whom the gods spoke

orator (ŏr′à·tēr), a public speaker

order (ôr′dēr), 1. a type of column together with the section of the wall resting on the top part of the column. 2. **religious order,** a group of persons who unite for religious reasons and are bound by vows under a superior.

Order of Preachers, the Order founded by St. Dominic

Orient (ō′rĭ·ĕnt), the East, especially those countries east of the Mediterranean Sea

P

pagan (pā′găn), a person who does not worship the One True God

page (pāj), a boy in training for knighthood

painting (pān′tĭng), a picture made by an artist with brushes and paint

paper (pā′pēr), writing material made in thin sheets from rags, wood, straw, bark, etc.

papyrus (pà·pī′rŭs), writing material made from the water plant found in Egypt and used by the ancient Egyptians, Greeks, and Romans

parchment (pärch′mĕnt), writing material made from the skin of sheep, goats, etc.

Parliament (pär′lĭ·mĕnt), the lawmaking body of many countries, such as Great Britain. **Model Parliament,** the Parliament called in 1295 which later Parliaments used as a model.

Parthenon (pär′thē·nŏn), famous marble temple built on the Acropolis

patrician (pà·trĭsh′ăn), a noble by right of birth or privilege; especially in ancient Rome

patriotism (pā′trĭ·ŭt·ĭz'm), love of one's own country

pavilion (pà·vĭl′yŭn), the place from which medieval lords and ladies watched the tournaments

Pax Romana (păks rō·mä′nà), Roman Peace

Peace of God, a rule of the Church which forbade knights to fight in certain places

peasant (pĕz′ănt), a farmer who works a small piece of ground

peer (pēr), a person of the same rank an equal

penitent (pĕn′ĭ·tĕnt), a person who is sorry for a sin or some other offense

Pentecost (pĕn′tĕ·kŏst), the feast which commemorates the descent of the Holy Ghost on the Apostles

persecution (pûr′sē·kū′shŭn), the cruel treatment of any group of people, especially for religious reasons

Pharaoh (fâr′ō), a king of ancient Egypt

Pharisees (făr′ĭ·sēz), the party among the Jews of Our Lord's day who became very proud and self-righteous

philosopher (fĭ·lŏs′ô·fēr), a lover of wisdom

Pieta (pyā·tä′), a statue by Michelangelo of the Blessed Virgin mourning over the dead body of Christ

pilgrim (pĭl′grĭm), 1. a person who travels to a holy place or shrine as an act of devotion. 2. **Pilgrims,** the religious group who broke away from the Church of England

pilgrimage (pĭl′grĭ·mĭj), a journey made to a religious shrine

plague (plāg), a contagious disease that strikes large numbers of people

plebeian (plē·bē′yăn), the lower class people of ancient Rome

Pope (pōp), the Bishop of Rome, the head of the Roman Catholic Church

prehistoric (prē·ĭs·tor′ĭk), relating or existing in the time before written history

Presbyterian (prĕz′bĭ·tēr·ĭ·ăn), the name given to Calvin's followers in Scotland

printing press, a machine which prints from type

prophet (prŏf′ĕt), a person inspired by God to speak for Him and to announce future events

Protestant (prŏt′ĕs·tănt), a Christian who is not a member of the Roman Catholic Church

Protestant Revolt, the revolt against the Church in the 16th Century, sometimes called the Protestant Reformation

province (prŏv′ĭns), a conquered territory outside the boundary of Rome

Psalm (säm), one of the hymns in the Book of Psalms in the Old Testament

Puritan (pū′rĭ·tăn), an Englishman of the 17th Century who tried to purify the Church of England by ridding it of ceremony

pyramid (pĭr′a·mĭd), a stone building with a square base and four sides that come together in a point at the top

R

ransom (răn′sŭm), the money asked for the freedom of a captive

reason (rē′z'n), the power to think

Redeemer (rĕ·dēm′ēr), Jesus Christ, the Saviour of mankind

Renaissance (rĕn′ĕ·säns′), the name meaning "new birth" given to the years between 1300 and 1600; so called because the people thought there had been a new birth of knowledge

republic (rē·pŭb′lĭk), a country in which the people who vote also hold the greatest power

Resurrection, the, (rĕz′ŭ·rĕk′shŭn), the rising of Christ from the dead

revelation (rĕv′ĕ·lā′shŭn), truths told to man by God

right of sanctuary (săngk′tṹ·ĕr′ĭ), the right to refuge or safety

Romance languages (rô·măns), the languages that developed from the Latin language spoken by the Romans

Romanesque (rō′măn·ĕsk) **architecture,** a medieval style of building marked by the round arch

Roman numerals, letters used as numbers: I, II, III, i, ii, iii, etc.

Rosetta (rô·zĕt′a) **stone,** the stone found in Egypt which gave man the first clue toward reading Egyptian hieroglyphics

S

sacrifice (săk′rĭ·fīs), the act of making an offering to God or to a god, usually on an altar

Sanskrit (săn′skrĭt), an ancient language that is the classical language of India

schism, (sĭz′m), a break, a split or a division

scholar (skŏl′ēr), 1. a student in a school. 2. one who knows much about one or more subjects.

Scribes (skrībz), the Jews of Our Lord's day who studied the law

sculptor (skŭlp′tēr), a person who carves, cuts, or chisels marble, stone, etc. into statues

self-government (sĕlf′gŭv′ērn·mĕnt), the governing of a people by themselves

Senate (sĕn′ĭt), in ancient Rome, the highest body of the State. **senator** (sĕn′a·tēr), a member of the Senate

Separatist (sĕp′a·rā′tĭst), a member of the regilious group which separated from the Church of England

serf (sûrf), member of the feudal system who was bound to the soil he worked

shield (shēld), a plate of metal, wood, or leather carried on the arm to protect oneself in battle

silt (sĭlt), a deposit of fine soil

slave (slāv), a person who is owned by another person and can be sold

Society of Jesus, the order founded by St. Ignatius Loyola

spear (spēr), a weapon with a long handle and a sharp head or point

spice (spīs), a plant used, usually as a powder, to season food.

squire (skwīr), a young man who was learning to be a knight

stained glass, colored glass

steed (stēd), a horse

surveying (sēr·vā′ĭng), finding out and recording the shape, size, position, etc. of a piece of land

sword (sōrd), a weapon with a long sharp blade and a cutting edge

T

telescope (tĕl′ē·skōp), a long instrument shaped like a tube and used for looking at faraway objects, such as the stars

thatched (thăch'd′) **roof,** a roof made of hay or straw

theology (thē·ŏl′ô·jĭ), study of religion and religious knowledge

tournament (tōor′na·mĕnt), a contest in which many kinghts showed their skill and courage by fighting each other for a prize

town (toun), a large center of population that is not a city

town hall, a public building where meetings are held

trade (trād), 1. a person's regular work. 2. buying and selling.

transmigration (trans·mĭ·grā′shĕn), to pass at death from one body or being to another

tribe (trīb), a group of people with a central head, or chief

tribune (trĭb′ūn), a Roman official who protected the common people from unfair treatment

troubadour (trōō′ba·dōor), a poet-musician who wrote and composed songs usually about love

Truce of God, a rule of the Church which forbade knights to fight at certain times

twelve tablets, the tablets on which the Roman laws were carved

tyrant (tīr′ănt), a ruler who has the final say and is unjust

U

universe (ū′nĭ·vûrs), all created things, the world

university (ū′nĭ·vûr′sĭ·tī), a school where higher branches of learning are taught

V

vassal (văs′ăl), a man who held land from a lord in return for protection

veto (vē′tō), the power or right to forbid something

W

watchtower (wŏch′tou′ēr), a tower on which a lookout is placed

Western Hemisphere (hĕm′ĭ·sfēr), the half of the earth which includes North and South America

IMPORTANT DATES

B.C.

5000
Beginning of Mesopotamian civilization

3500
Beginning of Sumerian civilization

c3000
Earliest written records kept by the Egyptians

2500
Pyramids Built

2200
Indus River civilization

2100
Code of Hammurabi

1600-1100
Aegean civilization

1500
First Chinese civilization

753
Rome founded

672
Assyrians conquer Egypt

586
Hebrews enter Babylonian captivity

551-479
Confucius lived in China

550-330
Persia rules the Middle East

509
Roman Republic founded

490
Battle of Marathon

480
Salamis

461-429
Age of Pericles

B.C.

431
Peloponnesian War

338
Philip of Macedon conquers Greeks

330-323
Alexander's Empire

264-146
Punic Wars

250
Rome unifies Italy

146
Destruction of Carthage

44
Death of Caesar

c4
Birth of Christ

A.D.

70
Capture of Jerusalem

313
Edict of Milan
Constantine accepts Christianity

325
Council of Nicea

410
Sack of Rome by Alaric

476
End of the Western Roman Empire

732
Battle of Tours

800
Charlemagne crowned by Pope

871-901
England under Alfred the Great

A.D.

1066
Battle of Hastings

1096
Beginning of the Crusades

1215
Magna Carta

1271-1295
Travels of Marco Polo

1295
Model Parliament

c1300-1600
Renaissance Period

1337-1453
Hundred Years' War

1450
Gutenberg invented the printing press

1453
Constantinople captured by Turks

1486
Cape of Good Hope rounded by Diaz

1492
Columbus discovered America

1492
Moors driven from Spain

1492-1600
Period of exploration

1498
da Gama reached India by rounding Africa

1517
Luther—the Protestant Revolt

1545-1563
Council of Trent

1519-1522
Magellan's trip around the world

1588
Defeat of Spanish Armada

Index

In this index you will find in parentheses an explanation of how certain words are pronounced. Certain symbols and diacritical markings are used to show the pronunciation of these words. Here is a list of key sounds to help you use the pronunciation guides.

āte	Afric*a*	īce	cŏntain	ûnite
alwåys	ēve	ĭll	sôft	hut
câre	hēre	charĭty	mo͞on	circ*u*s
hăt	ĕvent	ōld	fo͝ot	fûr
*a*nother	ĕnd	ôbey	*ou*t	*th*en
ärm	bush*e*l	ôr	*oi*l	*th*in
åsk	makēr	hŏt	ūse	pict*u*re

A

Aachen (ä′kĕn), 130
Abraham, 37
Acropolis, 62
A.D., defined, 8
Adrianople (ādrĭ·*an*·ō′p'l), **Battle of,** 110
Adriatic Sea, 74
Aegean civilization, 51
Aegean (ējē′ăn), **Sea,** *52*
Aeneas, 91
Aeneid, (ē·nē′ĭd), **the,** 91
Aix-la-Chapelle (ĕks·là·shà·pĕl′), 130
Alaric (ăl′*a*·rĭk), 110
Albert the Great, St., 169-171
Alcuin, 130
Alexander the Great, Emperor, 67-69
Alexander VI, Pope, 246-247
Alexandria, 68, 69, 92
Alfred the Great, King, 180-181
Allah, 125
alphabet, 4
    adaptation to Sanskrit, 40
    Greek, 207
    Greek use of, 53-54
    Phoenician, 35
    Slavic, 124
America
    discovery of, 8, *15*, 241
    English in North, 233, 250, 252, 253
    French in North, 249-252
    See also New World
American Indians, 16-17, 246, 249
American Revolution, 269

amphitheaters, Roman, 80
Angles (ăng′g'l), 111, 178, *179*
Anglicans (ăng′glĭ·kăn), 232
Anglo-Saxon Chronicle, 180
Anglo-Saxons, 178-185
    See also Saxons
Anne Boleyn, 231
Antigonids, the, 69
Antonine line, the, 100
Apennines (ăp′ĕ·nīnz), 74
Aphrodite (ăfrō·dī′tē), 54
Apollo, 54, 60
Aquinas, St. Thomas, 171-172
Arabia, 124
Arabian Nights, 127
Arabian Sea, 28
Arabic Numerals, 127
Aragon (ăr′*a*·gŏn)
    Catharine of, 231
    King Ferdinand of, 201-202
    Kingdom of, 200-201
Archaelaus, King, 94
archaeologists, *6*, 7, 9, 16
Aristotle (ăr′ĭs·tŏt′l), 64, 67, 170
Arius (a·′rī·es), 105-106
Aryans (ĕr′ĭ·ĕns), **in India,** 40-42
Asia, 172-174
    early civilization in, *15*
    Seleucids of, 69
Asia Minor, 33, 51, *52*, 53
Asoka (ă′·s(h)ōke), **King,** 44
Assyria (å·sĭr′ĭ·à), 31
    conquers Israel, 37-38
astrolabe, invented, 223
Athena (à·thē′nà), 54, 62

Athens, as a city-state, 55, 57-61, 66, 69, 72
Athenians, defeat Persians, 60
Atlantic Ocean, 35, 76
Attila, 111
Augustus Caesar, Emperor, 84-85, 90, 91, 94, 97, 100
Aurelius, Marcus, 101, 102
Aurelius, Commodus, 102
Australia, 9
Austria, 129, 188

B

Babylon, *34*
    Hanging Gardens of, *29*
    King of, 30, 31, 37, 38
Babylonia (băb′ĭ·lō′nĭ·à), 37-38
Babylonian Captivity, 38
Babylonian Empire, second, 31-32
Bacon, Roger, 170-171
Baghdad, 127
Balboa, Vasco Nunez de, 242
barbarians, 108
Barbarossa, Emperor Frederick I, 149-150
Basil the Great, St., 106
B.C., defined, 8
Becket (bĕkĕt), **Thomas à,** 187
Belgium, 129
Bethlehem, 97
Bible
    Gutenberg, 220-221
    Old Testament, 36-37, 93
Black Death, 198-199, 210, 212
Black Sea, 40
Boleyn, Anne, 231
Boniface VIII, Pope, 224
Boniface, St., 123-124, 128
Book of Marco Polo, 174, 239
Brahma (brä′m*a*), 42
Bramante (bra′·mänt·ē), 215
Brazil, 90, 248
Britain, 100, 111
    Roman invasion of, 176-177
    German invasion of, 177-178
    See also Anglo-Saxons, England
Brittany (brĭt′à·nĭ), **naming of,** 178
Bronze Age, 16
Buddha (bo͝od′à), 43, 47
Buddhism, 43-44
Bulgaria (bŭl·gâr′ĭ·à), 66
Burgundy, Duke of, 198
Byzantine (bĭ·zăn′tĭn), **Empire,** 114, 116, 117, 145, 146, 148, 150-152, 206-207, 208
Byzantium (bĭ·zăn′shĭ·*u*m), 104

C

Caesar, Augustus, 84-85
Caesar, Julius, 81-83
Caesar, Octavius, 84
Caiaphas, 95
Calais, 198
calendar
    Egyptian, 24, 82
    Gregorian, 222
    Julian, 171, 222
Caligula, Emperor, 94, 100
Calvin, John, 229, 230, 234
Canada, foundation of, *115*
Canossa, 204
Canterbury
    archbishops of, 187, 188, 190
    Cathedral, 187
Canterbury Tales, 187-188
Canute, King, 181-182
Cape of Good Hope, 240
capitals, Greek, 62, *63*
Carthage (kär′thĭj), 35, 68, 75-76, 77, 200
Castile
    Kingdom of, 200-201
    Queen Isabella of, 201-202, 231, 240
castles, feudal, 134, 136, 141
cathedral schools, 169
Catherine of Aragon, 241
Catholic Church, 118-119, 171, 207
    See also church building, Popes, Protestants, Rome
Catholic Reformation, 233-234
Ceylon, 44
Chaldeans (kal′dē·an), 31-32
    King of the, 32
Champlain, Samuel de, 249-250
Chapter Reviews, 19, 27, 38, 48-49, 69, 82-83, 96, 112-113, 132, 144, 156, 175, 193, 208-209, 223, 235, 256
    See also Summary
Charlemagne, 129-131
Charles VII, King, 196-198
Chartres (′shärt), **Cathedral,** 167
Chaucer (chô′sēr), **Geoffrey,** 187-188
Cheops (kē′ŏps), 23
Chesapeake Bay, settlement, 252
Ch'in dynasty, 45, 48
China, 12, 39, 44, 68, 76-77, 172, 174
    feudalism in, 45, 47-48
    first civilization of, 44-45
    Great Wall of, 48
    kings' power in, 58
Chinese
    characters, 35, 47-48
    dynasties, 44-45, 47, 48
    language, 4, 47-48
    picture-writing, 45
    See also culture

chivalry, laws of, 140
Chou (′jō), **dynasty,** 45-47, 48
Christ, 97-98
Church of England, 231-232
churches, building in Europe, 165, *166,* 171
Cincinnatus, *72*
Cicero (sĭs′ĕ·ro), 91
City of God, the, 111
civilization, defined, 12-13
    Aegean, 51
    Chinese, 44-48
    Christian, 14, *15*
    Cretan, 50
    early, *10-11, 15*
    Egyptian, 20-27
    Etruscan, 70-71
    Greek, 6, 61-66
    Indian, 39-44
    Latin, 77, 92
    Roman, *15*, 77, 92
    Sumerian, 28-30
    Western, 14, 76
Claudius, Emperor, 100
Clement VII, Pope, 231
Clermont, 146
Clotilda, Queen, 120
Clovis, King, 119, 126, 128
coins, Lydians introduce, 34
colonus, 103, 104
Colosseum (kŏl′ŏ·sē′ŭm), **Roman,** 88
Columbus, Christopher, 8, *15*, 17, 114, 202, 240-241, 246-247
columns, Greek, 62, *63*
Commodus (Aurelius), 102
Commons, House of, 192-193
Confucianism, 270
Confucius (kŏn·fū′shĭ·*us*), 47
Constantine, Emperor, 98-99, 104-105, 107
Constantinople, 104-105, 112, 114, 116, 117, 126, 127, 128, 146, 148, 150, 152, 205-206, 207, 208
    Archibishop of, 115
    See also Alexander the Great, Byzantine Empire, Crusades
Copernicus (kō·pŭr′nĭ·kŭs), 221
Corinth, Gulf of, *52*
Corinthian capitals, 62, *63*
Corsica, *74,* 75
Cranmer, Thomas, Archbishop, 231
Cretan civilization, 50
Crete (krēt), 50-51
Croesus (krē′sŭs), **King,** 33, 59
Crusades, the, 147-152, 210, 212
culture, defined, 9, 13
    See also civilization
Cuneiform (kyu′nēĭ·form), **writing,** 29
Cyrus, King of Persia, 38, 59, 92

D

Danelaw, 180-181
Danes, invade England, 180-181, 182
Dante, 172
Darius, King of Persia, 59-60
Darius III, King, 67
David, King, 37, 96, 97
Delphi, oracle at, 55
democracy, defined, 58
Denmark, 178
    See also Canute, Danes
Días, Bartholomeu, 239-240
Diocletian, Emperor, 103-104
Divine Comedy, the, 172
Dnieper (nē′pēr), **River,** 205-206
Doctors of the Church, 106-107
Domesday (doomz′dā′), **Book,** 184
Donation of Pepin, 128-129
Doric capitals, 62, *63*

E

Earth, age of, 16
Eastern culture, 9, 12
Eastern Empire, 105, 112, 114, 116-117
Eastern Schism, 116
Edward I, King, 193
Edward VI, King, 231
Edward the Confessor, King, 182
Egypt, 20-27
    Assyrians conquer, 31
    Lower, 22
    Pharaohs of, 22, 23, 24, 27
    Ptolemies of, 69
    Upper, 22
Egyptian
    calendar, 24
    glass making, 22
    gods, 26
    hieroglyphics, 25
    mummies, 27
    shadow clock, 24
    pyramids, 23, 27, 50, 63
Egyptians, 7, 21, 28
Eightfold Plan, the, 43
Elizabeth I, Queen, 232
England, 176
    Church of, 231-232
    Danes invade, 180-181
    in Hundred Years' War, 196-199
    Norman conquest of, 182-183
    Normans in, 184-185, 186
    See also Angles, Anglo-Saxons, Britain, feudal system
English
    Channel, 176, 182, 197
    colonists in North America, 250, 252, *253*

common law, 187
language, 4, 184-185
Parliament, 192-193
writing, 4
Episcopal Church, 232
Ericson (ĕr′ĭk·sŭn), **Leif,** 236
Ethelred, King, 182
Etruscans (ê·trŭs′kăn), 70-71, 74, 88
Euclid (ū′klĭd), 65
Euphrates (û·frā′tēz), **River,** 28, *34*, 44
Valley of the, *15*
See also Valley of the Two Rivers
Eurasia (ūr·ā′zhȧ), 10-11
Europe
from 6-10th Century, *115*
from 12th-15th Century, *194*
in 15th Century, *211*

F

Far East, 173-174
defined, *172*
feudal system, 133-144
effect of Crusades on, 152-156
fief, feudal, 134
Finland, Gulf of, 205
fire, discovery of, 17, *18*
Flavian (flā′vĭ·ăn), **dynasty,** 100
Flavius Vespasius, 100
Florence, baptistry at, 215
Forum, Roman, 73, 88
Fox, George, 232
France, *52*
becomes a nation, 195-196
See also Gaul, Norman conquest, William the Conqueror
Francis of Assisi, St., 171-172
Francis I, King, 229
Franks, 119-120, 126-128
freemen, 141
French and Indian War, 250
French in North America, 249-252
Friends, the, 232

G

Galilee (găl′ĭ·lē), 94-95
Galileo (găl′·ĭ·lēō), 221
Gama, Vasco da, 242
Gaul, 81, 111, 119, 131-132
See also France
Genoa, 154, 174
Germans, 108-112
invade Britain, 177-178
Germany, 202-205
See also Holy Roman Empire
Ghiberti, Lorenzo, 215

Gibraltar, Strait of, 35
Giotto, 171
Giza, 23
glass making, Egyptian, 22
Godfrey of Bouillon, 148-149
Good Hope, Cape of, 240
Gordian Knot, *67*
Gothic architecture, 165, 214
Gracchus, Gaius, 81
Gracchus, Tiberius, 81, 95, 100
Granada, 202
Great Charter, *186*, 190, *191*, 192, 252
Great Wall of China, 48
Greco, El, 219
Greece, 14, *15*, 50-69
as city-states, 53, 55-59, 66-67
democracy in, 58
Golden Age of, 61-66
Roman conquest of, 76
See also Alexander the Great, Roman Empire
Greek
ancient, *25*
belief in gods, 54-55
Doctors, 106-107
Schism, 116
use of alphabet, 53-54
See also Orthodox Church
Greeks in Italy, 70-71
Gregorian calendar, 222
Gregory XIII, Pope, 222
Gregory the Great, St., 106, *179*
Guatama, Prince, 43
guilds, 162, *163*, 164
gunpowder, 170, 263
Gutenberg, Johann, 220-221
Gutenberg Bible, 220-221

H

Hadrian, Emperor, 100, *176*
Hadrian's Wall, 100-101, 176-177
Hagia Sophi, church of, 116
Hammurabi, King of Babylon, 30
laws of, 31
Hannibal, 75, 110, 200
Harold II, King, 182-183
Hastings, Battle of, 182-183
Hebrews, 34, 36-38
hegira, the, 125
Henry II, King, 186-188
Henry IV, King, 204-205
Henry VII, King, 230
Henry VIII, King, 230-231
Henry the Navigator, Prince, 239-240
Herod the Great, King, 94
Herodotus (hê·rŏd′ô·tŭs), *63*
hieroglyphics (hī′ēr·ô·glĭf′ĭk), Egyptian, *25*

Hindu region of India, 42
Hinduism (hĭn′dōō·ĭz′m), 42-44
Hippo, St. Augustine, Bishop of, 111
Hippocrates (hĭ·pok′ra·tēs), 65
Hirohito, Emperor, 270
history, dating events in, *8*
History, the Stream of, *2-3*
Holbein (hōl·bīn), 219
Holland, 129
Holy Land, conquest of the, 145-152
Holy Roman Empire, 130, 203-205, 227-228
Homer, 51
House of Commons, 192-193
House of Lords, 192
Huguenots (hū′gē·nŏt), 229
Hundred Years' War, 195, 197-199, 210, 212
Hungary, 129
Huns, 109, 111
Hwang Ho River, 44

I

Iberia, 81
Iberian Peninsula, 200
Iliad, the, 51-52, 67, 91
India, 39-44, 76-77, *172*
Aryan invasion of, 40-42
caste system in, 40-41, 42
governing of ancient, 41
kings' power in, 58
Macedonian conquest of, 41, 68
religions of, 42-44
Indus
civilization, 39
River, 39, 44, 68, 76, *172*
Valley, 40, 41
Industrial Revolution, 260
Innocent III, Pope, 150, 151, 169, 188-189
Ionian cities, 59
Ionic (ī·ŏn′ĭk), **capitals,** 62, *63*
Iran, 28
Iraq, 28
Ireland, 119
Iron Age, 16, *18*
irrigation, Egyptian method of, 21
Islam, 125
Isle of Saints and Scholars, 119
Israel, 28
conquest of, 37-38
Kingdom of, 37
Ten Lost Tribes of, 38
See also Hebrews, Jews
Issus, Battle of, 67
Istanbul (ē′stän·bōōl), 105

Italy, 70-92
  See also Holy Roman Empire, Roman Empire, Rome
Ivan the Great, 208

J

Jacob, 37
Jamestown, 252
Japan, 12, 44, 172, 174
Jerusalem, 37, 38, 92, 145, 148, 151
Jesus Christ, see Christ
Jesus, Society of, 235
Jews, the Roman Empire and, 92-96, 145
  See also Hebrews, Holy Land, Israel, Palestine
Joan of Arc, St., 197-198
John, King of England, 188-190
John XII, Pope, 202-203
John XXIII, Pope, 272
Jordan, 28
Joseph (son of Jacob), 37
Judah (jōō′dȧ), kingdom of, 37-38
Julian calendar, 222
Julio-Claudians, 100
Jupiter (jōō′pĭ·tēr), 71
Justinian (jŭs·tĭn′ĭ·ăn), Emperor, 91
  Code of, 91-92, 114
Jutes (jōōts), 111, 178, 179
Jutland (jŭt′lănd), 178

K

Khyber Pass, 40
Kiev, Vladimir, Grand Duke of, 207
knighthood, the Church and, 140-141
knights, 138, 139, 140
  See also Crusades
Knossos, 50-51
Knox (nŏks), John, 229
Koran, the, 125
Korea, 44
Kublai Khan, 174

L

Langton, Stephen, Archbishop, 188-190
Last Judgment, The, 217
Last Supper, The, 219
Latin Doctors, 106-107
Latin language, influence of, 90-91
Latin Vulgate, the, 107
Latins, the, 70, 74
League of Nations, 266
Leo I, Pope, 111

Leonidas, King of Sparta, 61
Lepanto, Battle of, 152
Liu Chi, 48
Livy, 91
Lombards, 111
Lombardy, 111, 117, 128, 129
lords, feudal, 134
  See also feudal system, Crusades
Lords, House of, 192
Lorraine, 131
Lothaire, 131
Louis IX, King, 151-152, 195
Louis the German, 131
Louis the Pious, 131
Loyola, Ignatius, St., 235
Luther, Martin, 225-232
Lutherans (lū′thēr·ăn), 228
Lydia, King of, 33
Lydians, introduce coins, 33

M

Macedon (ma′sēdŏn), 66
Macedonia (mă·sē·don′ēā), 66-67, 76
  Antigonids dynasty of, 69
  See also Alexander the Great
Macedonian Empire, 41, 68
Magellan, Ferdinand, 243
Magna Carta, 186, 190, 191, 192, 252
Maid of Orleans, the, 197
man, early, 16-17
Man
  Great Discoveries of, 18
  March of, 14-15
manors, feudal, 134, 136, 141
Marathon (măr′ȧ·thŏn), Battle of, 60
Marco Polo, 173-174
Marcus Aurelius, 101-102
Martel, Charles, 126-127
Martel, Pepin (King of the Franks), 128
Mary Tudor, 231-232
Maryland, founding of, 233
Massachusetts Bay Colony, 233
Mecca (měk′ȧ), 124-125
Menendez, Pedro, 247
Mediterranean Sea, 15
Memphis, 22, 67
Menes, 22
Mexico City, 249
Michelangelo, 215-217, 219
Middle Ages, the, 114-175
Milan, Edict of, 99, 105, 106
Mississippi Valley, 250
Model Parliament, 193
Mohammed, 124-125
monasteries, 120-121, 168-169
Mongolia, 173

Mongols, 173-174
  rule in Russia, 208
Monte Cassino, 121
Moors, 201-202
Moscow
  founding of, 208
  Grand Duke of, 208
Moses, 37
Moslem Arabs, 117
  See also Turks
Moslems
  conquests of, 124-125
  defeat of, 126-127, 129
movable type, 220
Mycenae (mī′sė̇·nā), 50-51, 52

N

Nazareth, 97
Near East, defined, 28
Nebuchadnezzar (něb′ů·kăd·něz′ěr), King, 32, 38
Nero, Emperor 98, 100
Netherlands, the, 120
New Amsterdam (New York), colony, 255
New World
  discovery of, 15, 241-243, 244
  Portuguese in the, 246-249
  Spanish in the, 246-249
  See also America
Nicea, Council of, 106
Nicholas V, Pope, 214
Nile River, 15, 20, 21-22, 24, 25, 26, 28, 44
  god of the, 26
  Valley, 27
Nineveh, 29, 31
nobles, feudal, 134, 136-138, 139, 140
  See also lords, feudal system
Normans, 182-186
Normandy, 179, 182
  William, Duke of, 182-183
Northmen, 133-134, 178-180, 184, 205-207, 236
Norway, 178
Novgorod, 206
  Prince of, 206
numerals
  Arabic, 127
  Roman, 71

O

Octavius Caesar, 84
Odin, 178
Odoacer, 112

Odoric, 173
Odysseus (ô·dĭs′ūs), 51
Odyssey (ŏd′ĭ·sĭ), **the,** 51-52, 67, 91
Olympia, 54
Olympic Games, 54
Olympus, Mt., 54
Oriental culture, 9-10
Orthodox (ôr′thŏ·dŏks), **Church,** 116, 207, 208
Osiris, 26
Ostrogoths (ŏs′trŏ·gŏths), 111
Otto the Great, 202-203
Ovid, 91
Oxford, University, 169, 170

P

Pacem in Terris, 272
Pacific Ocean, discovery of, 242
Palestine, 93-95
Panama, Isthmus of, 242
Pantheon (păn·thē′ŏn), **the,** 89
Papal States, 128-129
paper mills, introduced, 220-221
papyrus scrolls, 25
Parliament, Houses of, 192-193
    Model, 193
Parthenon, the, 62
patricians, Roman, 72-73
Pax Romana, 85-86, 118, 130, 133, 134, 136
Peace of God, 140-141
Peasants' Revolt, the, 228
Peking, 45, 74
Pennsylvania, foundation of, 232
Pepin, King of the Franks, 128-129
    Donation of, 128-129
Pericles, 61-63
Persia, 33-34
    defeat by Athens, 60
    kings of, 38, 59, 60, 92
Persian Gulf, 28, *29*
Peru, discovery of, 242
Pharaohs, *see* Egypt
Pharisees, 93, 95-96, 97
Pheidippides, 60
Phidias, 62
Philip Augustus, 149-150
Philip, King of Macedonia, 66-67
Philip II, King of Spain, 231-232
Philip IV, King of France, 224
Philippines, discovery of, 243
Phoenicia, 50, *52*
Phoenicians (fē·nĭsh′ăns), 34-35, 36, 37, 53, 75, 76
Picts, 176-177, 178
Pieta, the, 216
pilgrims, 145-146

Pilgrims, the, 232-233
Pinta, 241
Plato, 64-65
plebeians, Roman, 72-73
Plymouth Colony, 232
Poland, 124, 129
Polo, Marco, 173-174, 221, 239
Pompeii (pŏm·pā′yē), 7
Pompey, 93
Pontius Pilate, 94-95, 98
Popes, *see under individual names*
Portugal, 132, 200-201
Portuguese in the New World, 246-249
prehistoric times, defined, 16
Presbyterians, 228-231
printing press, invention of, 220-221
Promised Land, 37
Protestant Reformation, 224-232
Protestant Revolt, 224-232
Ptolemies (tŏl′ĕ·mĭs), **the,** 69
Ptolemy (tŏl′ĕ·mĭ), 240
Punic wars, 75
Puritans, 232-233
pyramids, Egyptian, 23, 50, 63

Q

Quakers, 232-233
Quebec, naming of, 249

R

Raphael, 219
Ravenna, 105, 111
Re (rā′), 26
Red Sea, *20*, 28
Reims (rē′ĭms), **Cathedral,** 197, 198
Rembrandt, 219
Renaissance, the, 210-223
Rhine River, 119
Richard the Lion-Heart, King, 150, 188
Roderick, King, 126
Roland, 137
Roman Catholic Church, 118-119, 171, 207
Roman Empire, 84-96, 113, 114, 134-135, 172
    See also Eastern *and* Western Empire
Roman numerals, 7
Roman Peace, 85, 86, 118, 130, 133, 134, 136
Romance languages, 90
Romania (rō·mān′ĭä), 129
Romans, 14, *15*
    in Britain, 176-177
    See also Roman Empire, Rome

Rome, 14, 68
    as a city-state, 74
    as a Papal State, 128
    conquers Greece, 76
    conquers Macedonia, 76
    conquests, various, 110-111
    destroys Carthage, 75-76
    early, 70-71
    early Christians in, *98-99*
    early Republic of, 71-73
    emperors of, *101*
    laws of, 73
    saved from Lombards, 128-129
    trade with China and India, 76-77
    under Julius Caesar, 80-83
    unites Italy, 74
    wars with Gauls, 81

S

Sadducees (săd′ŭ-sē), 93, 95-96
Sahara Desert, 237
Saints
    Augustine of Canterbury, *179*
    Basil the Great, 106
    Benedict, 120-121
    Bernard, 149
    Boniface (bän′·ĭ-fis), 123-124, 128
    Francis of Assisi, 171-172
    Ignatius Loyola, *235*
    Jerome, 106-107
    Joan of Arc, 197-198
    John Chrysostom, 106
St. Augustine settlement, 247
St. Lawrence River, 249
    Valley, 250
St. Peter's, Rome, 214-216, 226
Saladin, 149-150
Salamis (salāmis), **Battle of,** 61
San Salvador, discovery of, 241
sanctuary (săŋk′tŭ·å·rĭ), **right of,** 140-141
Sanhedrin (săn′hĕ·drĭn), **the,** 95, 98
Sanskrit, 40
Santa Maria, 241
Sardinia, *74*, 75
Sardis, 33-34
Saul (Hebrew King), 37
Saxons, 111, 129, 131, 178, *179*
    See also Anglo-Saxons
Saxony, 129
Scandinavia, 229
Scots, 176-177, 178
Sea of Darkness, 236
Seleucids (sĕ·lū′sĭd), **the,** 69
Senate, Roman, 71-72
serfs, feudal, 134, 135-136, 141-144
Seven Wonders of the Ancient World, 23, 32

Severus, Septimius, 102
shadoof, 21
Shakespeare, William, 262
Shang dynasty, 44-45, 47
Shintoism (shĭn′tō·ĭz′m), 271
Sicily, *52*, 53, 70, *74*, *75*, 114
silt, 21
Sistine Chapel, 217
Sistine Madonna, 219
Slavic alphabet, 124
Slavs, 11, 112, 117
Socrates, 59, 63-65
Solomon, King, 37, 96
Spain, 200-201
Spanish in the New World, 246-249
Sparta, 55-57
    King Leonidas of, 61
Sphinx (sfĭnks), **the,** 23-24
Stephen II, Pope, 128
Stone Age, 17, *18*
    New, 16, 17, 19
    Old, 16
Sulla, 81
Sumer (sŭm′ēr), 28-30
Sumerian civilization, 28-30
Summa, **the,** 71
sun god, Egyptian, 26
surveying land, Egyptian method, 24
Susa, 33-34
    fall of, 68
Sweden, 178
Switzerland, 120, 129
Sylvester, Pope, 105-106
Syria, 92-93

T

Tantum Ergo, 172
Taoism (tou′ĭz'm), 270
telescope, Galileo's, 221

Ten Commandments, 37
Tetzel, John, 226-227
Teutons (tū′tŏns), 108
Thales, 65
Themistocles, 60-61
Thor (thōr), 108, 123, 178
Tiber River, 70, 71
Tigris River, 28, 29, *34*, 44, 127
    Valley of the, *15*
    See also Valley of the Two Rivers
time, measuring, 30-31
tournaments, feudal, 140
Tours, Battle of, 126-127
Tower of London, 184
Trent, Council of, 231-232
Troy, 51, 91
Truce of God, 141
Turkey, 33
Turks, 117, 145-152

U

United Nations, 267
universities, building of, 169
Ur, *29*, 37
Urban II, Pope, 146-147

V

Valley of the Two Rivers, 28-31
Vandals, III, 200
vassals, 134
Vatican Council, Second, 272
Vatican Library, 214
Venice, 154, 174
Vergil (vûr′jĭl), 91
Vespasius, Flavius, 100
Vesuvius, Mt., 7
Vinci, Leonardo da, 217, 219
Virginia, colony, 252

Visigoths (vĭz′ĭ·gŏths), 109, 111
volcanos (vŏl·kā′nō), 7, 17
Volga River, 205

W

Wars of the Roses, 230
Western civilization, 14
Western Empire, 105, 111-112
Westminster Abbey, 183
Wheel, development of the, 17, *18*
William the Conqueror, King, 182-184, 185
Wittenberg
    Cathedral, 226
    University, 225
Woden, 109
Wolsey, Cardinal, 231
Worms, Concordat of, 205, 227
writing
    Chinese character, 35, 47-48
    Chinese picture–, 45
    cuneiform, 29
    Egyptian hieroglyphics, 25
    Egptian picture–, 25
    See also alphabet, numerals

X

Xerxes, 60-61

Y

Yellow River, 44
Yugoslavia (yōō′gô·slä′vĭ·à), 66, 129

Z

Zeus, 54, 71, 93

Typography and design by William Nicoll of Edit, Inc.
Format by F. Sadlier Dinger
Set in 11/14 and 9/11 Times Roman Linotype by M & L Typesetting & Electrotyping Company
Body printed by Cadillac Printing and Lithographing Corporation
Cover printed by Reehl Litho., Inc.
Cover finished by G. H. McCauley Finishing Co.
Bound by John F. Cuneo Company
Published by William H. Sadlier, Inc., New York and Chicago